The Call for Women Bishops

The Call for Women Bishops

Edited by

Harriet Harris and Jane Shaw

First published in Great Britain in 2004 by
Society for Promoting Christian Knowledge
36 Causton Street
London SW1P 4AU

British Library Cataloguing-in-Publication Data
A catalogue record for this book is available from the British Library

ISBN 0–281–05621–8

10 9 8 7 6 5 4 3 2 1

Designed and typeset by Kenneth Burnley, Wirral, Cheshire
Printed in Great Britain by Ashford Colour Press

Contents

Contributors

Marilyn McCord Adams is Regius Professor of Divinity at the University of Oxford and Canon of Christ Church, Oxford. Formerly, she was Horace Tracy Pitkin Professor of Historical Theology at Yale University, and Professor of Philosophy at UCLA. Her publications range over medieval philosophy and theology, and philosophical theology, and include major books – *William Ockham* (2 vols; University of Notre Dame Press, 1987) and *Horrendous Evils and the Goodness of God* (Cornell University Press, 1999) – as well as many articles.

Rosy Ashley recently trained for ordination at Wycliffe Hall in Oxford and is completing graduate work at the London School of Theology before taking up her Orders.

John Barton is Oriel and Laing Professor of the Interpretation of Holy Scripture in the University of Oxford, and a Fellow of Oriel College. He is also the Proctor for the clergy of the University of Oxford in the General Synod. He is the author of numerous books on the Old Testament and biblical interpretation.

Tina Beattie is Senior Lecturer in Christian Studies at Roehampton University of Surrey. She is the author of several books including *God's Mother, Eve's Advocate: A Marian Narrative of Women's Salvation* (Continuum, 2002).

Myra Blyth is Moderator of the Churches' Commission on Racial Justice in Britain, and Lecturer in Liturgy and Ecumenics at Regent's Park College, Oxford. She was, until recently, Deputy General Secretary of the Baptist Union of Great Britain, the first woman to hold that post, and before that she was Executive Director of the World Council of Churches, for Relations.

Peter Carnley is Archbishop of Perth and, since 2000, has been Primate of the Anglican Church in Australia. He ordained the first women to the priesthood in Australia in 1992, in Perth Cathedral. He is the author of several books including, most recently, *Reflections in Glass: Trends and Tensions in the Contemporary Anglican Church* (HarperCollins, 2004).

Ruth B. Edwards is non-stipendiary Priest in the Scottish Episcopal Church and an Honorary Canon of St Andrew's Cathedral, Aberdeen. She was formerly Senior Lecturer in Divinity at the University of Aberdeen, and also served as New Testament Tutor and Chaplain at Ripon College Cuddesdon, Oxford. She is the author of several books of New Testament scholarship and of *The Case for Women's Ministry* (SPCK, 1989).

Robin Gibbons is a Greek Catholic Melkite Priest and liturgist. He is Director of Theology and Religious Studies Programmes in the Department of Continuing Education, Oxford, and Senior Lecturer in Theology, Saint Mary's College, Twickenham.

John Gladwin is the Bishop of Chelmsford, and prior to that was the Bishop of Guildford.

Barbara Clementine Harris was, in 1988, the first woman to be elected a bishop in the Anglican Communion and she was ordained and consecrated as the Suffragan Bishop of Massachusetts. She retired in 2002 and is now an assistant bishop in the Diocese of Washington, DC.

Harriet Harris is the Chaplain of Wadham College, Oxford and Chaplain of the University Church in Oxford. She is also an Honorary University Fellow of the University of Exeter. Her publications include *Fundamentalism and Evangelicals* (Oxford University Press, 1998) and *Faith Without Hostages* (SPCK, 2002).

Bill Ind is the Bishop of Truro, and prior to that was Suffragan Bishop of Grantham, Lincoln.

Carolyn Tanner Irish is the tenth Bishop of the Diocese of Utah in the USA, and was elected to that office in 1996. She was appointed archdeacon in the Diocese of Michigan in 1986, and later served on the staff of the Shalem Institute for Spiritual Formation, and the Washington National Cathedral. She is an honorary Fellow of Linacre College, Oxford.

Penny Jamieson was elected as the seventh Bishop of Dunedin, New Zealand, in 1989, the first woman in the Anglican Communion to be a Diocesan Bishop. She is the author of *Living at the Edge: Sacrament and Solidarity in Leadership* (Continuum, 1997).

Christina Le Moignan is a Methodist minister. She was President of the Methodist Conference from 2001 to 2002, and Chair of Birmingham District from 1996 to 2004. She has served as a minister in several churches, was a tutor at Queen's College, Birmingham and Principal of the West Midlands Ministerial Training Course.

Rebecca Lyman is the Samuel C. Garrett Professor of Church History at the Church Divinity School of the Pacific, Berkeley, California, and is a priest in the Episcopal Church. She is the author of *Christology and Cosmology: Models of Divine Activity in Origen, Eusebius and Athanasius* (Oxford University Press, 1993) and *Early Christian Traditions* (Cowley Press, 1999) as well as numerous articles on the early Church.

Walter Paul Khotso Makhulu is Archbishop Emeritus of Central Africa.

Esther Mombo is the Academic Dean of St Paul's United Theological College in Limuru, Kenya. She lectures throughout the Anglican Communion, and addressed the November 2003 Primates meeting at Lambeth.

Bridget Nichols is lay chaplain to the Bishop of Ely, and is a liturgist. Her publications include *Liturgical Hermeneutics* (Peter Lang, 1996) and *Literature in Christian Perspective* (Darton, Longman and Todd, 2000).

Carrie Pemberton is an Anglican priest and founding Executive Officer of CHASTE (Churches Alert to Sex Trafficking Across Europe). She has established a theological training college and centre for women's development in the Democratic Republic of the Congo. Her writings include *Circle Thinking: African Women Theologians in Conversation with the West* (Brill, 2003), and she co-authored *Anglicanism: a Global Communion* (Mowbray, 1998).

Jane Shaw is Dean of Divinity, Chaplain and Fellow of New College, Oxford. Her publications include *Miracles in Enlightenment England* (Yale University Press, forthcoming) and various articles on modern ecclesiastical history. She is also a Chaplain of Christ Church Cathedral, Oxford, and has been a theological consultant to the Church of England House of Bishops.

David Stancliffe is the Bishop of Salisbury and prior to that was Provost of Portsmouth Cathedral. Since 1993 he has served as Chair of the Liturgical Commission of the Church of England. He is the author of *God's Pattern* (SPCK, 2003) and *The Pilgrim Prayer Book* (Continuum, 2003). He is also an honorary Fellow of Trinity College, Oxford.

Vincent Strudwick is Fellow Emeritus and Chamberlain of Kellogg College, Oxford, and was formerly Principal of the St Albans and Oxford Ministry Course. He is an honorary canon of Christ Church Cathedral, Oxford.

Geralyn Wolf has been Bishop of Rhode Island, USA since 1996. Prior to that she was the Dean of Christ Church Cathedral in the Diocese of Kentucky, the first female Dean of a cathedral in the Episcopal Church in the USA.

Preface

THIS BOOK HAS GROWN out of a short booklet *Women and Episcopacy* which we produced and edited in the summer of 2002; we perceived the need for such a booklet, laying out the case for women bishops from various perspectives, at a time when the Church of England Working Party on Women Bishops was giving an interim report to General Synod in July of that year. It was published as a WATCH (Women and the Church) booklet and was sent out to all General Synod members by WATCH.

Soon after, we were approached by a number of publishers who believed that there was the need for a larger volume on the subject. This book is the result of those approaches. We quickly realized that this was an issue that went beyond the Church of England – although the ongoing call for and debate about the admission of women to the episcopate of the Church of England have created the immediate context for this book. The question affects the whole Anglican Communion and ecumenical relations. Furthermore, we have much to learn from each other: from those women who are already bishops; from those who have experienced the oversight of women, in Anglicanism and in other churches; and from those who are still deliberating upon the question. Hence, we commissioned articles for this volume from around the Anglican Communion, and from several other denominations.

We dedicate this book to the memory of two tireless and passionate workers for justice in the Church and society: Justus Markus and Monica Furlong. We had invited the Rt Revd Justus Markus, a suffragan bishop of Cape Town, to write from the South African perspective, and he had happily agreed to do so. He was diagnosed with cancer soon after accepting that invitation and died before this book was completed. Monica Furlong, well known to British readers, was a writer and spiritual leader in the Church of England. She too died of cancer while we were compiling this book. Both were enormously supportive of this project, and we remain grateful for their help and example.

HARRIET HARRIS AND JANE SHAW
Oxford

Acknowledgements

WE THANK RUTH McCURRY for her patient and skilful editing, and for her warm support of this project; and all the staff at SPCK who helped with the production of the book. We are also grateful to Deonna Neal for her invaluable editorial assistance in the last stages of this project.

The chapter on 'Authority' by Penny Jamieson has been taken and edited from her chapter on 'Authority' in *Living at the Edge* (Mowbray, 1997). We are grateful to Mowbray, a Continuum imprint, for permission to use this material.

We would also like to thank the Revd Ron Wood for permission to use his cartoon 'A woman's place is in the House of Bishops' on the front cover of this book.

Call for Change

1 The Calling of Women Bishops

Jane Shaw and Harriet Harris

CAROLYN TANNER IRISH tells the story of the morning of her ordination to the diaconate. Her young son wondered why she would soon be ordained for a second time. She carefully explained the threefold order of ministry to him. He went off and thought about it and came back a few minutes later and said, 'Hey, Mom, how come you decided not to be a bishop?' The punch line is that she did become a bishop, the Bishop of Utah. However, the point of the story is that no one just decides to be a deacon, priest or bishop; a person is called to each of these orders by the Holy Spirit working in that person's life and the church community. That calling occurs on the basis of inner stability, spiritual depth and gifts to be offered, and occurs regardless of gender. The Church's response to that call should be affirmed regardless of gender.

Here, the relationship between divine call and the reality of the earthly Church is an important one. The distinguished church historian Henry Chadwick puts it like this:

> All Christian ministry is a gift of the Spirit, a charism. It is neither an end in itself, nor an entity independent of a community, but rather a service for the building up of the Church (Ephesians 4.7–16). As a supernatural call, a charism belongs to the transcendent, divine order. As a service within the community, its action is seen in the visible historical order, in the society grounded in the discipleship of Jesus Christ and rooted in the continuing life of the Church.[1]

This raises the question of when the Church might fail to hear or respond to that 'supernatural call'. In discerning who has a call, the Church, in the visible historical order, is always vulnerable to mistakes and it is the contention of this book that in ignoring the call of women and their charism of oversight and the other tasks of a bishop, the Church has fallen prey to what Chadwick describes, in the same essay, as 'temptations and . . . secularising pressures'. While those wary of moves to ordain women as bishops worry that the Church might be bowing to secular pressures, in fact many of our contributors – including those writing on scripture (Ashley), liturgical practice (Nichols), and their experiences of ministry in Africa, North America and New Zealand (Mombo, Makhulu, Harris, Irish, Wolf, Jamieson) – perceive resistance to ordaining women as bishops as reflecting secular pressure or cultural misapprehensions.

By saying that the Church has ignored the call and gifts of women, we are not saying that women, simply because they are women, have distinctive 'feminine' gifts which are the particular or sole property of women because they are women. We are not advocating that sort of 'essentialist' argument, nor are we appealing to the oft-cited notion of 'complementarity' – the distinctly modern idea that men and women naturally have different and complementary gifts, a notion that our Christian foremothers and forefathers would not have recognized. Arguments that women are different from, and complementary to, men are used in Church and society to both conservative and progressive ends. They are used to excuse not giving women the same roles as men, and also as reasons precisely for having women fulfil the same roles as men, as complementary partners are seen to bring completeness to the role. Indeed, Bill Ind argues in this book, from his perspective as a bishop, that women should fulfil the role of bishop alongside men because of the dimensions they will bring to the episcopate, and he makes some suggestions of what this will contribute in completing the episcopate. We are not denying that people often do experience women's ministry differently from the ministry of men. Indeed, it may well be the case that women, because they have been excluded from the mainstream of leadership in the Church for the majority of the Church's history, have a particularly clear insight on the Church, especially in terms of what is or has been missing in the exercise of the three historic offices of deacon, priest and bishop. But our primary point is that women should not be excluded from the threefold order of ministry on the grounds of their gender: their calling should be tested, and they should be appointed, in terms of their gifts and 'fit' for the office, just as men should be.

We also want to say that the most significant thing that women bring to holy orders is simply the fact of being human, for wherever women cannot be ordained (and in the Church of England this is to the episcopate) the message is that men are closer to God, or more in the image of God, than women. While this view is not owned explicitly, and is clearly heretical, it is promoted in teachings about male headship, in which it is believed that men as ministers, husbands or fathers are called to exercise an authority analogous to the authority of God or Christ. It is also promoted wherever language about the fatherhood of God is taken analogically rather than metaphorically to mean that God really is somehow a 'Father'. Following this analogical use of 'Father', and Aquinas' view that analogy is a form of literal rather than figurative language, an Anglo-Catholic priest recently put an argument to the Deaneries of Cowley and Oxford stressing the mysterious 'importance' of male language about God, and proposing that 'God made the world, he did not give birth to it'.[2] Whether he realized it or not, he was endorsing a view that men are more like God than women; a danger that has dogged the Church down the centuries. In the early days of the Church there were even questions over whether women as women could be saved, and these apprehensions made their way into apocryphal writings such as the Gospel of Thomas. Such doubts about the salvation of women should have been quashed once for all by the time it was agreed that Jesus must have been fully human, because if he was not fully human be could not save us. All Christians would agree that the theologically significant point is not that Jesus became a man but that he became human. But closing certain orders to women strains the credibility of that conviction. This is why women have protested: if you will not ordain us, do not baptize us.

The importance, therefore, of 'seeing someone like you' (i.e. someone like one's own self) behind the altar or in a particular office in the Church, cannot be over-emphasized. If we believe that all human beings are made in the image and likeness of God – and the Bible does teach that! – then how do we enact that and make it real in the Church and in the world? The female bishops often speak to this in relating their experiences in the episcopate, and note that their being in that office often enables others to feel included in the Church. As Bishop Barbara Harris says of her presence as a bishop in the parishes of the Diocese of Massachusetts, 'Women and girls were encouraged to feel that they truly had a place in the Church and people of colour expressed their pride and their joy in God's doing a new thing.' This gets to the fundamental point of Christian theological anthropology: every child born is made in the image and likeness of God. But sometimes we need to see someone 'like us' in a sacred space to understand and *know* that. As Bishop Jane Holmes Dixon (Bishop of Washington, DC, *Pro tempore*, retired) said in her sermon at the tenth anniversary of the ordination of women to the priesthood, in the Diocese of Oxford, in April 2004: 'There is nothing – no thing – that speaks of God like seeing someone like you in that sacred space.'

The Church of England has ordained women as deacons since 1989, as priests since 1994. There are now about 2,500 female priests in the Church of England, out of a total of 10,000 priests. In Anglicanism, the historic threefold ministry has been seen as a whole, though in some cases, of course, people have felt called only to one of those offices (deacon), and in the majority of cases, only two (deacon and priest). The Church of England, in an act of innovation, opened the first two of these offices to women at different times – and it has yet to admit women to the episcopate. This has been a breach with tradition, at which even the conservative evangelical pressure group Reform balks. In an early submission to the Rochester Commission, the Council of Reform wrote:

> We agree with the report of the House of Bishops that the ordination of women as presbyters and their consecration as bishops are in principle the same thing. We cannot accept the thesis . . . that the apostles themselves instituted the episcopate and the presbyterate as two distinct offices.[3]

Moreover, while some worry about the consequences for our relations with Rome and the East of consecrating women as bishops, we are discredited in the eyes of Roman Catholicism and Eastern Orthodoxy for having compromised the integrity of orders, and made a muddle of our own theology, by introducing a sub-set of deacons and priests who cannot in principle become bishops. In this book, Robin Gibbons is able to argue from both a Roman Catholic and Greek Orthodox perspective that 'having already ordained women as deacons and priests, [the Church of England] cannot theologically deny the next step'. He is one among many who find compelling the argument that women should be admitted to the episcopate as soon as possible in order that the integrity of the threefold order of ordained ministry be maintained. John Gladwin, Bishop of Chelmsford, says here, as he has said elsewhere, that the Church of England's present position on women bishops is illogical and untenable, precisely because it is a principle of Anglican orders that they should not be divided. Indeed, if we go back to Richard Hooker, the great Anglican apologist of the sixteenth century, we see him arguing in his *Ecclesiastical Polity* (VII.ii.3) that bishops are merely presbyters (priests) with special authority given to them. In short, the two cannot be divided.

The Church of England is now seeing many calls for women to be admitted to the episcopate. In July 2000 the Venerable Judith Rose proposed a motion at General Synod which asked: 'That this Synod ask the House of Bishops to initiate further theological study on the episcopate, focusing on the issues that need to be addressed in preparation for the debate on women in the episcopate in the Church of England.' The result is the Rochester Report, published in the autumn of 2004, which does not make recommendations but offers suggestions, outlining the arguments both in favour and against ordaining and consecrating women as bishops. During the several years in which this working party has been meeting and this report has been written, pressure has come from other parts of the Church of England to admit women to the episcopate. This has occurred informally in debates, newspaper articles, lectures and so forth, but it has also occurred formally through the structures of the Church in diocesan synods. In June 2002 Guildford Diocesan Synod passed a motion as follows: 'Guildford Diocesan Synod asks that General Synod bring forward legislation to permit the consecration of women to the episcopate in the Provinces of Canterbury and York without delay.' The motion was carried by 83 votes to 18, with six abstentions. In March 2003, the Diocesan Synod of Ripon and Leeds voted with an overwhelming majority in favour of women bishops. The likelihood is that the Guildford Diocese motion will be debated in General Synod in February 2005. When such legislation is prepared, it will need to be passed by a two-thirds majority in all three houses of General Synod and then by Parliament. We hope that this will be a single clause motion with provisions for good practice, rather than a motion complicated by legislation for yet more extended episcopal oversight.

We are concerned about the mixed messages given by a Church which both ordains women and enables their authority not to be recognized. We are also troubled by the practical effects this double standard has in parishes and among congregations, where people are unwittingly brought under the extended oversight of bishops whose stance they would wish to reject. Yet, as Peter Carnley writes, from his experience of handling these questions in Australia, 'purist positions sometimes have to be accommodated to what will be of most pastoral benefit to people, particularly as they process and come to terms with new developments'. We do not wish to see people alienated from the Church. Indeed, that is our whole point! Our experience and interpretation of the Church of England's situation, however, is that a Church which compromises women both alienates and is alienated from more people than a Church which does not.

In some parts of the Anglican Communion, the three orders were not split when the decision was made to admit women to the ordained ministry of the Church. When women were admitted to the diaconate, they were admitted to the priesthood and therefore to the possibility of being called as a bishop. This has been the case in the church in Africa, as we hear from Esther Mombo and David Stancliffe, although women have yet actually to be appointed as bishops in Africa. It has also been the case in Canada, the United States of America, Aotearoa, Polynesia and New Zealand. Barbara Harris was the first female bishop in the Anglican Communion, called to be Suffragan Bishop of Massachusetts, in the Episcopal Church in the USA, in 1988. She relates how this calling and election took place in her chapter. There are currently 16 female bishops in the Anglican Communion, in the USA, Canada and New Zealand. Other countries have agreed in principle to call and consecrate women as bishops, having admitted women to the priesthood. Peter Carnley and Ruth Edwards bring us up to date on the situations in Australia and Scotland respectively. Australia is considering how to care for those who cannot accept the ordination of women to the episcopate; Scotland is waiting to see whether women will fill current vacancies.

This raises questions about diversity in the Anglican Communion. We have a variety of practices with regard to the admission of women to the episcopate. How are we to handle this? This question of diversity is also raised with regard to other issues too; at present, most obviously sexuality. It is therefore a pressing issue. The hallmark of Anglicanism has long been the acceptance of diversity in belief and practice. We hear from a number of contributors, including Strudwick, Pemberton, Barton and Gibbons, how the very origins of Anglican theology, particularly in the work of Richard Hooker, engage us in plurality – something especially appreciated by Gibbons from his Catholic and Orthodox vantage point. David Stancliffe, Bishop of Salisbury, in his chapter articulates the hope that we can live with diversity and mutual respect. He writes:

> My dream is twofold. First, that the Church of England will recognize the Episcopal ministry of both men and women. And second, that all the Churches will be so empowered by the pursuit of the truth which is Christ's that our different emphases and interpretations are seen for what they are: complementary insights rather than the reasons for one part of the Church to seek to exclude those with whom they disagree in the name of some notional purity.

The notion of reception is often invoked by those who are opposed to women bishops, or who are nervous about them for any one of a number of reasons (ranging from misogyny to a genuine concern about how a diversity of practice may exist in reality). The idea of reception derives from the Roman Catholic Church, where it refers primarily to the process of assimilation and acceptance of the teachings or decisions of the Magisterium. In an idealistic or ideological view of reception, the process is essentially passive, and acceptance is an act of obedience.[4] Roman Catholic theologians, notably Alois Grillmeier and Yves Congar, have discouraged so passive a view of reception and stressed the active spiritual discernment involved. We are more familiar with processes of reception within ecumenism where the processes are clearly active: different Churches receive or decide not to receive from one another's traditions, gradually and through active and responsible discernment. The Church of

England is in a different situation from the Roman Catholic and ecumenical contexts, in declaring 'an open process of reception' in relation to the formal decision of General Synod in 1992 to provide for the ordination of women to the priesthood. The anomaly stems from introducing an open process of reception (as we might expect in ecumenical relations) regarding a formal decision made by a Church, relating only to the life of that one Church (as we might expect in a Roman Catholic context). This open-endedness over a decision that is both formal and internal to the Church of England has bred much confusion. Some understand 'reception' here to mean allowing a period of time for those uncomfortable with women's ordination to come to accept the Church's decision. Others believe it means that the Church of England's decision could in fact 'be reappraised' and is 'hypothetically reversible';[5] although since Orders are indissoluble, no actual ordination can be reversed. So, if in this scenario it were decided that the decision to ordain women as priests were to be reversed, the Church would therefore have to wait for all its women priests to die, and in the meantime would be bound to recognize that they had been duly and canonically ordained!

This is the background against which the Church of England is debating ordaining women as bishops. The openness of the declared process of reception provides plenty of scope for prevarication and appears insidious to those who wish to see the Church press on towards its theological conclusion of ordaining women as bishops. One concern amongst those wary of taking this next step is that insufficient time has been given to the reception of women priests, and that there still remains opposition to women priests. The insidious nature of this objection arises because no indication is given of when enough time would be deemed to have passed, and because we do not know what would count even as substantial opposition to women priests when the indications are that the vast majority of clergy and laity – as well as the wider public – clearly supports women in the priesthood and hopes that women will be admitted to the episcopate. This is evidenced, for example, in Ian Jones' recent report, researched and written on behalf of the Lincoln Theological Institute, on women and priesthood in the Church of England from 1994 to 2004, for which he undertook case studies and interviewed many clergy and laity. His main findings indicated majority support for women priests among both clergy and laity:

> Eighty-one per cent of clergy supported the 1992 decision to ordain women as priests, with even higher levels of support in many case study congregations. A significant number of respondents had never been able to understand why women were not priests, but there are

> also strong indications that support for women's priesting has increased over the decade.

He also concluded that 'A majority of participants in the study made a positive assessment of the impact of women's inclusion in the priesthood over the past ten years' while 69 per cent of clergy supported the admission of women to the episcopate, with similar levels of support among lay respondents. On the idea of a period of reception, however, 'clergy respondents voiced considerable ambivalence' and '35 per cent felt the term had "no useful meaning whatsoever"'.[6]

There is a further concern among those wishing to wait before admitting women to the episcopate, and that is a concern that the reception process is for the whole Church, and not just for the Church of England. So some wish to see not only the whole Anglican Communion, but Rome and the East agree on the matter of ordaining women as priests, let alone bishops, before taking any further steps. This raises the question of whether it is ever right for a part of the Church to set a precedent, to do something because it believes it is right, even when other parts of the Church do not at that time endorse a decision. If no part of the Church ever did so, the concept of ecumenical reception would not have arisen.

Here it is worth making an additional comment about historical precedent. While the historians in this volume have unearthed precedents from the early Church for ordaining women to senior positions, and from the roots of Anglicanism for doing theology in a way that makes good sense of that practice, we are not ultimately bound by historical precedent. We know that there were women leaders in the early Church, but even had there not been, that would not be a reason for not having women bishops today. As Carolyn Tanner Irish says in her reflection for this book, it is not 'reasonable . . . that past practice rather than evident need should set the boundaries of leadership in the Church'.

Concerns over reception are a potential hindrance to the prophetic nature of the gospel. Most significant developments within the Church, from baptizing Gentiles to ordaining the first women, have happened prior to a process of reception (indeed prior even to discussion!) for the good and straightforward reason that God is seen to have called these people and to have given them particular gifts. Debate and reception have followed later and have been a matter of our understanding catching up with what God has already done. Peter baptized Cornelius and then Paul took the gospel to the Gentiles because it was clear to them that Gentiles were receiving the blessings of the Holy Spirit, even though Jews still held Gentiles to be defiled. If the Church had waited for Peter and Paul's actions to be 'received', Christianity might still be a minority Jewish sect today. As it was,

Gentiles continued to be admitted into the Church despite the difficulties this posed; they were not made to wait on the sidelines until internal disputes were resolved. Florence Li Tim Oi was ordained priest in 1944 by the Bishop of Hong Kong so that she could minister to Anglican communicants in occupied China, even though traditionally the Church had thought that women would defile the sanctuary. People saw in Tim Oi a gift for priesthood, and the Anglican Communion has been debating and catching up with that insight ever since.

The questions that continue to be asked over whether the Church has received the 1992 decision to ordain women to the priesthood seem to fly in the face Gamaliel's principle, which was to leave the apostles to do their work and see whether or not God was in it: 'if this plan or this undertaking is of human making, it will fail; but if it is of God, you will not be able to overthrow them. You might even be found opposing God!' (Acts 5.38–9). The unquantifiable nature of the Church of England's reception process is threatening to create a no-win situation for supporters of women priests and bishops. Its open-endedness begins to look like slipperiness. No matter how well the ministry of women is working (and it is clearly not failing), and no matter how many people receive it with joy and have been transformed by it as an outworking of the gospel, without some unspecified degree of consensus, reached by some unspecified time, the nebulous and vague use of the concept of reception suggests that the whole process may be reversed and in the meantime threatens to stall any attempt to see women ordained as bishops.

The matter of reception is intimately related to that of ecumenical relations. Opponents of women bishops often focus on relations with the Eastern Orthodox Churches and the Roman Catholic Church, but the reality is that the admission of women to the episcopate is merely one of many factors which impede closer relations between the Anglican Church and those Churches. The reality is that those Churches do not recognize the orders of any deacons, priests or bishops in the Anglican Communion – male or female. By contrast, many of the Churches with which we have genuine and close ecumenical ties and are in communion do admit women to the episcopate (or equivalent status), including the churches of the Porvoo Agreement,[7] and the Old Catholic Churches of the Union of Utrecht. Significantly, in the case of Porvoo and the Old Catholic Churches, we recognize these Churches' place in the Apostolic Succession, and so we are already in communion with Churches that are both in the Succession and ordain women as bishops. Our *not* admitting women to the episcopate is in fact an impediment to closer relations with these and other Churches. This is most obvious in the case of the recent Church of England–Methodist talks, as Christina Le Moignan indicates in this book.

Sometimes the Church has to act before it is able to carry everyone with it. The unfolding of tradition shows us that, as do the multiple instances in scripture where new ground is broken. Need we recount examples? Jesus' breaking of the Sabbath in numerous ways, his associating with sinners or outcasts, and breaking all manner of social and religious convention; the apostles taking the gospel to the Gentiles, and Paul overriding the practice of circumcision; the development of the office of bishop; many of the changes brought in at the Reformation; church support for the abolition of slavery even while it remained a contested issue amongst Christians. To go back to Peter's unilateral act of baptizing the Gentile Cornelius, what Peter realized as soon as he met Cornelius and perceived the Spirit at work in him, was that 'God shows no partiality' (Acts 10.34). The witness of women as well as men indicates that God shows no partiality in who is called to the diaconate, priesthood and episcopate. The Church must now show no partiality in recognizing and responding to those calls.

Notes

1 Henry Chadwick, 'Episcopacy in the New Testament and Early Church', in *Tradition and Exploration: Collected Papers on Theology and the Church* (Norwich: Canterbury Press, 1994), p. 1.

2 Revd Dr Jonathan Baker, Principal of Pusey House, speaking to the Deaneries of Cowley and Oxford, at Ripon College Cuddesdon, 25 March 2004.

3 'Desiring What is True or Defending Desire? Reform's Presentation to the Rochester Commission (concerning Women in the Episcopate)', appendix as posted on the Reform website at <http://www.reform.org.uk/bb/defendingdesire.html> (accessed 6 August 2004).

4 Paul Avis, 'Reception: Towards an Anglican Understanding', in *Seeking the Truth of Change in the Church: Reception, Communion and the Ordination of Women*, ed. Paul Avis (London: T&T Clark, 2004), p. 22.

5 Ibid., p. 30.

6 Ian Jones, *Women and Priesthood in the Church of England: Ten Years On* (London: Church House Publishing, 2004), pp. xi–xii).

7 These are the Churches of the Porvoo Agreement: the Evangelical-Lutheran Churches of Denmark, Finland, Iceland, Latvia and Lithuania; the Estonian Evangelical-Lutheran Church; the Church of Norway; and the Church of Sweden. The Church of Norway and the Church of Sweden already have women bishops. Other churches in communion with the Church of England and admitting women to the episcopate include the Philippine Independent Church and Mar Thoma Syrian Church of Malabar.

Bibliography

Avis, Paul, 'Reception: Towards an Anglican Understanding', in *Seeking the Truth of Change in the Church: Reception, Communion and the Ordination of Women*, ed. Paul Avis (London: T&T Clark, 2004).

Chadwick, Henry, 'Episcopacy in the New Testament and Early Church', in *Tradition and Exploration: Collected Papers on Theology and the Church*. (Norwich: Canterbury Press, 1994).

Jones, Ian, *Women and Priesthood in the Church of England: Ten Years On* (London: Church House Publishing, 2004).

2 Why Not Have Women Bishops? Meeting the Arguments Head-on

John Barton

PROPONENTS OF WOMEN BISHOPS have awkward questions they can pose to opponents, and vice versa. How often have we heard it asked: 'Are you sure you're not simply selling out to secular values?' (a question which is asked by people on both sides of the issue – see how Esther Mombo in this book puts this challenge to opponents of women bishops in Africa). A case is only well made when all the opposing arguments have been given their best hearing and been fully addressed. This is what I aim to do in this chapter: to consider and tease out the wider implications of each argument against ordaining women as bishops (which in many cases are arguments made against ordaining women at all). In doing so I shall suggest that the logic of the opponents' own case may land them in somewhat hotter water than they suppose. I shall try to demonstrate an understanding of the case to be met, and shall not simply (as it was once put to me) 'lob hand grenades' into the 'enemy' camp; the image of military confrontation is quite inappropriate to a debate between Christians on these subtle issues.

There are arguments against women bishops that tend to appeal characteristically to Anglo-Catholics and evangelicals respectively. Anglo-Catholics tend to argue from tradition, evangelicals from scripture. But both groups, where they are opposed to women bishops (of course by no means everyone in either group is opposed), generally dislike the suggestion that they have different reasons for their opposition. They suspect that the attempt to present them as appealing to different reasons is a bid to 'divide and rule', and so to win the argument more easily. Accordingly, I shall examine a range of arguments. I shall not assume that there are 'Anglo-Catholic' and 'evangelical' arguments, but rather that there is a cumulative case against what is being proposed, much of which both groups – and perhaps others who do not belong to either side in this alignment – would see as persuasive.

Arguments from human nature

The strongest form of opposition to women bishops argues ontologically from the nature of the two sexes, and tends to result in what I would call an 'impossibilist' position. It is not just that women ought not to be ordained, but that they cannot be: the thing is an impossibility. My impression is that the present pope believes this. In the debate about the ordination of women to the priesthood, it produced the 'pork pie' argument: a woman can no more be ordained than a pork pie can. This was felt to be offensive, and was probably meant to be, but it only states in an extreme form something that is truly part of the logic of the position. Men and women are so different that orders simply will not 'take' on a woman, and any sacraments an 'ordained' woman purports to celebrate will be radically flawed or invalid.

It is possible to argue along these lines that the 'gut' reaction many feel to the ordination of women is not mere prejudice, but is grounded in a (perhaps inchoate or semi-conscious) recognition of something that is true of the orders of reality. We may not know why women cannot be ordained, but our instinctive feeling that they should not be points to some real truth about the nature of men and women which we ignore at our peril. The Church may not have known why it has never ordained women, but there was some deeper wisdom at work that we ought not to overturn lightly.

For those who argue in this way there is scriptural backing for an ontological argument in the story of the creation of humankind in Genesis 2, where man and woman are complementary, not identical. It is not, such people would say, a question of inequality: women are not being regarded as inferior to men. But they do have different distinctive characteristics, and these may be aligned with differences of appropriate function in the Church. Sometimes a sideways glance may be cast at orthodox Judaism, where women (it is said) have a high and honoured place, and there are distinctive religious functions they alone can perform, yet they may not become rabbis or lead prayers in the synagogue: such is not their appointed role.

An ontological argument may be linked with the use of the word 'priestesses' (though I have heard this term bandied about less in recent years than it used to be). C. S. Lewis famously argued that ordaining women would mean admitting an *undesirable* 'feminine' element into Christianity: not that Christianity is inherently masculine, but that it, like its parent religion Judaism, has always set its face against the particular type of 'feminine' aspect that implies a fertility-cult – the 'Baalism' against which Old Testament prophets spoke out, which involved 'priestesses'. It can be noted that there are proponents of women's ordination who would agree that it does open the door for such aspects to come in, but who think that is a good thing. This is definitely a minority position, but opponents of female ordination believe it is a logical one, and that on those grounds such ordination should be opposed.

For some who oppose women bishops, male 'headship', which we shall come to in more detail when looking at scriptural arguments, is rooted in eternal reality: scripture teaches it, not as a positive law, but as a 'creation ordinance'. I have heard this argument advanced by Anglican clergy not simply against women bishops or priests, but against all promotion of women to positions of leadership: there should be no women judges, hospital consultants, police inspectors or CEOs. This is a difficult position to maintain in the modern world, but it can be argued that it is in touch with a deeper wisdom than currents of secular thought. Perhaps we cannot put the clock back, but that does not mean it might not have been better if it had not gone forward, and in the Church at least we should maintain and observe the orders God has implanted in the creation. If the non-ordination of women is to be the one area where the 'secular' assumption that equality means interchangeability is not to apply, then so be it.

A number of strands are interwoven in these arguments, and I should like to ask their proponents whether they are sure they want to accept what they logically imply.

First, we might agree that men and women are not interchangeable without necessarily thinking that that is relevant to the question of ordained ministry. What are the characteristics of ordination as priest or bishop that go against the complementarity of the sexes? It is possible to construct an intricate argument according to which there is something 'male' about celebrating the Eucharist, but it is not clear to me that many opponents of women's ordination would actually buy into it. Eucharistic theology generally highlights features such as receptivity and openness which are widely thought of as 'feminine' rather than 'masculine'. It is far easier to argue for complementarity within a marital and sexual partnership, and perhaps in other human relationships, than to work it out in terms of the exercise of ministry. What is it about women that makes them unable to receive the gift of orders? So far as I can see, the argument from the different natures of men and women merely asserts that this is relevant to the sphere of ministry, without showing how or why this is so. To say 'men and women are simply not the same', while true, is a mere smokescreen when it is treated as obvious that this means women cannot be ordained. So I would ask, 'Are you sure that the admitted differences between men and women are relevant when it comes to considering their suitability for ministry? If so, why?' We need more arguments than we have been given so far.

Second, the 'priestesses' point. This is a term which is felt to be offensive, perhaps deliberately so, by most ordained women. Sometimes I think it has been used as a mere insult. But if there is a serious point here, I do not, again, see how it bears on the ordination question. Granted that Christianity has no place for priestesses in the sense of officiants at some kind of fertility rite, what evidence is there that ordained women in fact function in such a capacity or would ever do so? It is true, as observed above, that there are some women (and some men) who would welcome a 'feminization' of Christianity, but hardly to the extent that the term 'priestess' would become appropriate. What the vast majority of women seek in ordination is to carry out the same tasks that ordained men have done, including celebration of the Eucharist according to its established forms. They argue, no doubt, that they will bring different insights and gifts to these tasks from some men, but the number who would like to convert Christianity into a fertility religion constitutes a tiny fringe. My own experience of women clergy does not suggest to me that ordaining some of them as bishops would lead us back to Baalism. By all means, believe that if you feel you have solid evidence; but do not use it as a debating point.

Third, something should be said about 'gut reactions'. It is never easy to know whether an instinctive revulsion is a reliable guide to underlying truth, or prejudice dressing itself up as rationality. This is notoriously the case in another currently debated area: homosexuality. Some argue that the revulsion many people feel for some homosexual practices points to a basic wrongness about them, while others say that it is simply the result of centuries of conditioned responses which we should now unlearn. In the case of women priests and, perhaps more so, bishops, there is undoubtedly an instinctive opposition on some people's part, and a similar question arises. I can only ask, 'Are you sure your revulsion is not mere prejudice?' What strengthens me in the belief that it often *is* mere prejudice is what may be called the male 'vestry culture' of many churches. In the Anglo-Catholic case this is sometimes rather macho and sometimes a bit camp, but in either case it makes vestries an uncomfortable place for many women. In evangelical circles, it often takes the form of a kind of muscular Christianity born of experiences such as Bash camps, from which women tend to feel excluded. How far these culturally determined atmospheres tend to make those who feel at home in them hostile to the ordination of women is hard to say, but surely there must be a question.

If opponents of women bishops feel justified in asking how far proponents are merely the victims of secular culture, it seems fair to ask how far opponents may be victims of a smaller-scale ecclesiastical culture, which has nothing particular to do with the gospel, but everything to do with sociological factors. A cartoon in a recent edition of *New Directions* seemed to me to give the game away. It showed two small boys in church while a woman ministered at the altar, with one saying to the other, 'That's not a priest, it's your mum!' The cartoon communicated at once, and without explanation, to a certain constituency. But it misunderstands the nature of holy orders. It would be just as appropriate to say of a male priest, 'That's not a priest, it's your dad!' 'We have this treasure in earthen vessels' (2 Corinthians 4.7): a priest does not cease to be merely 'someone's dad'. There is something ridiculous about ordination – not women's ordination, but ordination as such. A mere mortal becomes the minister of holy things to the people of God. If popes need someone to remind them that *sic transit gloria mundi*, priests and bishops need constantly reminding that, on one level, they are simply someone's dad (or mum). Women bishops, if we get them, will need reminding of this fact just as much as male ones; but just as little will they thereby be hindered in their ministry. The minister of the gospel who forgets that he or she is just someone's parent (brother, sister, son, daughter) is the one to fear.

I understand the instinctive feelings of some opponents of women's ordination, because for years I felt them myself. I *just knew*, in my bones, that there was something wrong with ordaining women, and argued, as above, that this instinctive feeling was the index to some valid reason, even though I couldn't tell what it was. Occasional feelings of incongruity persist, as when I hear the *sursum corda* sung in a soprano register. I know I shall feel similarly when I first see a woman in a mitre. But I become steadily more and more convinced that my objections were not principled, but merely cultural. I hope others with the same gut reactions may be persuaded that this is true of them, too.

Arguments from tradition

To my mind the most powerful argument against ordaining women as bishops is that from earliest times this has never been done. The Church has a persistent and universal tradition against it. To depart from this is to raise grave questions of ecumenicity and of loyalty to the Christian past. It makes the prospect of eventual reunion with the great Churches that do not ordain women recede into the ever-more-distant future.

When this argument is probed, however, it turns out to contain a certain amount of question-begging. It is not, empirically speaking, true that there are no Churches that ordain women bishops. Leaving aside fellow-Anglicans, there are all the Lutheran Churches of northern Europe, including our partners in the Porvoo Agreement, the Churches of Scandinavia and the Baltic. In these Churches there have been women bishops for some time, some of them rather distinguished. Further, these Churches are, like the Church of England, within the historic succession. Their leaders are not simply *called* 'bishops'; they *are* bishops in the sense believed in by Catholic-minded Anglicans, 'successors of the apostles' in the sense that they can trace their lineage back to the ancient Church.

Now on a view of the Church of England that claims it is in continuity with the medieval Catholic Church and yet reformed itself at the Reformation, though without losing the historic succession, the presence of women bishops in Churches with very much the same history and self-understanding seems like a clinching argument for the possibility and validity of having them in our own Church. Evidently this is one of the changes that a reformed Catholic Church is entitled to make.

But opponents of women bishops, particularly from the Anglo-Catholic side, generally deny this conclusion. They argue that, in ordaining women bishops (in fact, in ordaining women at all), the Lutheran Churches in question have broken the succession. They have done something illicit. And the basis for arguing this can only be that what makes a Church part of the Catholic succession is undermined if women are ordained. This in turn must mean that some criterion other than the preservation of the succession is what makes such a Church 'Catholic'. This cannot be doctrine, for Anglicans have a wider spread of doctrinal beliefs than Lutherans, and everyone knows that many members of the Church of England are doctrinally Calvinist (one reason why the Latvian Lutheran Church would not sign the Porvoo Agreement!). Since Anglo-Catholics previously regarded the Churches in question as in the succession, it must be the issue of women's ordination that determines the matter. And in that case, the appeal to tradition is not to the Churches in the succession, but to Churches in the succession that do not ordain women, i.e. to the Roman Catholic and Eastern Orthodox Churches. Otherwise the argument is purely circular.

The criterion being used for recognizing a Church as 'authentically Catholic' is not really its preservation of the historic succession. The criterion is whether it obeys, on issues of ordination, the rules in force in the Roman Catholic and Orthodox Churches. They, not Churches in the Apostolic Succession as such, are being treated as providing the norms for church order. It is reunion with them that matters. It does not matter how many episcopal Lutherans have preserved the succession: if they deviate from Roman and Orthodox practice, they cease to count. (I have even heard such Lutherans described as 'a sect'.) But where does this leave the Church of England? On many matters it, too, deviates from the practices of Rome or of the Orthodox. It has married bishops; it marries people who are unbaptized; it does not recognize the authority either of the pope or of the Ecumenical Patriarch. On that criterion, how is it a valid Church, whereas the other Porvoo Churches are not? The logic of the case being argued here is surely that Anglicans ought to give up their separate existence and become Roman Catholic or Orthodox. My question of those who argue against ordaining women bishops on the grounds that 'authentic Churches have no such practice' is therefore, 'Are you sure you ought to remain Anglican? Should you not convert to the Roman Catholic or Orthodox Church?' Surely it would be more consistent to do so.

There is a weaker form of the argument from tradition, and this is the argument that ordaining women bishops is not wrong or impossible but simply *inexpedient* in the present state of ecumenical relations. The doctrine here is not that women cannot or should not become bishops as such, but that the time is inopportune. With this position I feel some sympathy. I would have more, if I thought that the prospects for union with Rome or Orthodoxy were quite good, and only the ordination of women got in the way. On the contrary, the prospects seem to me very poor: the hostile Roman Catholic reception of the most recent ARCIC documents, which seem to me to bend over backwards in a Roman Catholic direction, offers very little hope that reunion could come in the foreseeable future. Consequently I cannot see why the Church of England should hold off from doing one more thing of which Rome disapproves. Abstaining from making women bishops is not the one gesture that will clear the path. If we think it right to proceed, we should do so. This, of course, presupposes that Anglicans do not recognize the right of Rome to lay down the law. But if they do recognize that, then why are they still Anglicans?

Thus most of the arguments from tradition seem to me to be really covert arguments for Anglicans converting to Roman Catholicism, or possibly Eastern Orthodoxy. Precedents for ordaining women as bishops are not allowed to count if they occur in Churches other than the Roman Catholic and Orthodox ones. This means that the real test of a 'true' or authentic Church is its conformity to Rome or Constantinople, and if this is so, then the Anglican Church is clearly defective, and one ought to leave it. If you believe these arguments, then are you sure you should really go on being an Anglican?

It seems to me, as an Anglican who values the Protestant as well as the Roman Catholic inheritance of Anglicanism, that there is a further question to be asked about tradition. Even if there is a tradition, universal in the Church, that women may not be bishops, are you sure that the tradition is a sound one? Had Anglicans not asked that kind of question at the time of the Reformation, there would be no discrete Church of England with practices differing from those of Rome (allowing bishops to marry, for example). Tradition is a great thing, but as St Cyprian put it, 'tradition without truth is simply error grown old'. Evangelicals in particular might be expected to question whether post-biblical tradition is to be given quite the exalted place that it has acquired in the case against women bishops.

Even if there have never been women bishops until recent times, that does not necessarily mean that the demands of secular ideas are being given an inappropriate weight against tradition. I am not the first to point out that rather similar things could be said about slavery. The Bible assumes slavery as an acceptable institution, and throughout many centuries there continued to be slaves in Christian countries. The opposition to slavery, which finally brought about its downfall in Britain, certainly derived partly from Enlightenment ideas about the rights of human beings, and was thus far 'secular'. But it also rested on an attempt to take seriously certain imperatives, which people came to see as inherent in the gospel, that had not until then been realized. Presumably no one in the Churches would now be found to argue in favour of slavery, yet the opposition to it is comparatively 'modern' and has secular as well as religious roots. If I suggest an analogy with the ordination of women, it is not because I want to propose that that is on a par with the abolition of slavery or a similar manifestation of human rights. Rather, it is alike simply in being a case of a centuries-old tradition being reversed through a combination of insights from the secular world and a newly realized gospel imperative. This is essentially the answer I would give to the hard question with which this chapter began. In seeking the ordination of women we are not meekly abandoning centuries-old tradition for the sake of a secular ideal. Rather, we are reflecting seriously on a tradition we now believe to be flawed in the light of a gospel insight into the equal dignity of men and women, prompted indeed by some 'secular' thinking but not exhausted by it. It is a matter of having come to believe that tradition is in this respect flawed. After all, according to the Thirty-Nine Articles, even church councils can err, and in excluding the ordination of women as priests and bishops we believe they have indeed erred, though in a way that is entirely comprehensible in the light of social conditions prevailing at the time. To argue that the ordination of women as bishops is an idea whose time has come is not to express a harsh judgement on all previous ages, but to affirm that there can be progress in understanding what the gospel implies, just as there was on the question of slavery.

Arguments from scripture

There are texts in the New Testament that forbid women to exercise 'headship' over men. So far as leadership among Christians assembled for worship is concerned, relevant passages are 1 Corinthians 14.33–6 and 1 Timothy 2.12, which actually say that women should not speak at all during worship; though there is at least an apparent conflict with 1 Corinthians 11.5, which prescribes the conditions under which women may indeed do so. These texts amount to a strong biblical basis for those who deny the legitimacy of ordaining women as bishops or even, indeed, as priests – or deacons, I would have thought, though that seems to have been conceded.

There are several ways of dealing with these texts that appeal to 'liberals' such as myself. One is to question their authorship. Most critical biblical scholars think that 1 Timothy is 'deutero-Pauline', not from the hand of the apostle himself; and there are certainly commentators who believe that 1 Corinthians 14.33–6 is an interpolation from a later hand than Paul's, seeking to bring the apostle's own rather radical view of women ('[in Christ] there is neither male nor female', Galatians 3.28) into line with the more conventional norms of the later Church. In that case, from a 'liberal' perspective, these passages have rather less authority than they would have if they were genuinely Pauline.

Second, one may argue that they are culturally conditioned anyway, and belong to those elements in early Christian teaching that are not for all time, but restricted to the immediate generation in which they were written. Most Christians (not absolutely all, but most) treat the injunctions about women covering their heads in worship (1 Corinthians 11.5–16) in this way, as something that was for some reason regarded as necessary in Paul's immediate circumstances but that should not be generalized and applied in all times and places.

Third, it can be observed that Christians have never observed all the injunctions in the Bible as if they were of equal importance. Indeed, on this very question of the place of women in worship, rather few Christians in fact forbid women even to *speak* in church, as presumably they ought to do if they are to be strict followers of Paul. Female voices are often heard even in strictly evangelical churches; and most Anglicans, even those who will not tolerate the sacramental ministry of women, are quite content to have them preach (as the Roman Catholic Church, strictly speaking, is not – women may give 'talks', but not formal eucharistic homilies).

Fourth, many would say that in any case the New Testament is not to be construed as a form of law, such that we must do exactly what St Paul tells us. That is to reverse the proper order of law and gospel and to treat the teachings of Paul in just the way he himself did not want us to treat the Old Testament law, as a set of binding obligations applying not just to 'ethical' matters, but to questions which at the Reformation were called 'ceremonial'.

I should like to think that opponents of women bishops would carefully weigh all these arguments. But, being realistic, I doubt whether most will be swayed by them. On the first point, injunctions in the epistles are felt to be binding because they are scriptural, not because critical scholars think they are from St Paul. Further, the category of 'deutero-Pauline' material is not recognized by most conservative evangelicals anyway, who mostly think that St Paul wrote everything the New Testament attributes to him. The argument that Paul's teaching is culturally conditioned cuts no ice at all, for it is felt to be the beginning of a very slippery slope that will lead us to ignore scripture altogether. While it may be conceded that there are biblical instructions we do not literally obey, it is generally felt to be pretty obvious which are the important ones, and these are taken to include the regulations about female leadership.

Finally, the argument that the New Testament is not legally binding is felt, especially by those of either Calvinist or Catholic leanings, to be part either of a wrong-headed and antinomian Lutheranism, or else of a liberal agenda that simply ignores anything it does not like in the teaching of the apostle. Opponents of women bishops are not going to be talked out of their beliefs along any of these lines. I think in this they are mistaken, but I am under no delusions that they will undergo a sudden conversion.

I prefer, therefore, to argue as follows. Suppose we grant all the points made by conservatives about the New Testament's opposition to the exercise of 'headship' by women, does the ordination of women as bishops in fact contravene them? Are you sure, in fact, that a bishop is a 'head' in the form ruled out by such texts as we are considering?

Surely relevant here is that the Church of England has received the ministry of bishops within the context of a Reformation understanding of ordained ministry. The bishop's authority derives from the gospel he preaches and under which he stands, not from his position within a hierarchically organized structure. The Church of England does not reject hierarchy in *practical* terms. Like many other Churches (Methodism offers clear parallels) it is pyramidal in structure, though (unlike Roman Catholicism) it does not see the pyramid as coming to a point in one man, but as having a flattened top – authority is diffused among many bishops, not concentrated in a pope. But it does reject hierarchy as a *principle*. Anglicans do not see bishops as a special kind of being, set over their fellow-believers. A bishop is still just 'someone's dad'. There is nothing ontologically different about a bishop, from this point of view. Bishops do not exercise authority in such a sense that they are an *ultimate* authority on any matter. Their headship is relative, limited by bodies such as synods and, in England, by the courts and the laws of the land. Obedience is owed to them only 'in all things lawful and honest'; they are not meant to 'lord it' over their fellow-believers. I do not myself see why episcopal authority *so conceived* might not, even on a purely 'scriptural' basis, be exercised by a woman. I would ask evangelical opponents of women bishops in particular: are you sure you are not exaggerating both the importance and the status of bishops in thinking that a woman ordained to the episcopate would be exercising 'headship' in the way the apostle Paul forbids? Have you not bought too much into a 'Catholic' way of thinking about bishops? (Catholic but perhaps not Anglo-Catholic: for Anglo-Catholics, while they believe that bishops are necessary, are in my experience rather disinclined to accord much authority to them in practice – especially if they seek to forbid Anglo-Catholic practices!)

At any rate, I cannot see that women bishops raise any questions not already raised by the ordination of women at all, even to the diaconate – especially if, as many evangelicals believe, bishops do not really constitute a third 'order' but are to be seen as simply senior presbyters. On that understanding the question becomes one of degree: just how much authority must you have to be a 'head'? Perhaps one might argue that a woman cannot be an *arch*bishop, or cannot be Archbishop of Canterbury: but then Anglicans do not ascribe a quasi-papal headship even to the latter. It can reasonably be said that there is *no* 'headship', in Pauline terms, within the Church of England. Or, it can reasonably be said, there is a lot of it, beginning perhaps with the authority of Sunday-school teachers and working upwards to the archbishops, but with no clear cut-off point at which it becomes objectionable for a woman to exercise it. What cannot reasonably be said is that there is a special line separating bishops from everyone else.

Arguments from the unity of the Church of England

As we saw above, there is an argument from ecumenical inexpediency. One may suggest that it is inherently right, or at least permissible, to ordain women bishops, but that such an untraditional move would have the effect of sundering the Church of England still further from the Roman and Orthodox Communions. Now there is of course also an argument that cuts closer to home than this: that to ordain women as bishops will fracture the fragile unity that Anglicans enjoy with each other, and will be in effect schismatic. That there are already women bishops in other parts of the Anglican Communion is true, but may be felt not to justify English Anglicans in doing something which, it is argued, will tear the Church of England apart.

Someone who thought that having women bishops was vital – for example, on the grounds that without them the wholeness of Christian ministry is hopelessly impaired – might say that this should not be a consideration at all. We must do the right thing, whatever the consequences. But most Anglicans in England probably do not think that having women bishops is such a first-order issue as this. They see it as desirable, but not as essential. Such people can fairly be asked by opponents to weigh the consequences of going down such a road. Robert Runcie, when Archbishop of Canterbury, judged that it was in principle right to ordain women as priests, but that the time was inopportune because of the impairment of communion that would result. One might legitimately hold this to be true of ordaining women bishops too. Not everything that ought to be, or that can legitimately be done, ought necessarily to be done *now*: courses of action may be good, but not expedient.

May be, but not always! Opponents of women bishops inevitably talk up the schismatic consequences of introducing them, as they did the consequences of ordaining women as priests, but a sceptical observer may well decide to reduce the threat by a certain percentage to allow for (perhaps pardonable) exaggeration. The 'doctrine of the unripe time' can be valid, but it can also be a most convenient ploy to prevent changes that most people are in favour of. This may be partly a bluff that should be called.

Nevertheless, there clearly is a threat of schism. Both parties will of course claim that it is the other that is acting schismatically, but there is little point in this kind of name-calling. What would schism actually amount to? It would mean that 'traditionalists' no longer accept as valid the sacraments celebrated by those who received women bishops as duly ordained – but not vice versa. This would certainly have consequences for the constitution of the Church of England, and it is clear that the desire for a 'third province' is growing. Would it be a disaster if this came about? I cannot see that it would. Both groups would still recognize each other as Christians; both would retain a common Anglican ethos. It would be deeply puzzling to the public at large and would be likely to cost the Church of England some credibility, but the present wrangles are already doing that – especially since the issue at stake appears to be the equality of men and women, an issue which in all other spheres is regarded as open and shut. The Church looks ridiculous already, and probably would not look more so if there were a formal split. It would be a (lucrative) headache for lawyers, and something of a nightmare for diocesan officials. Things would eventually settle down to an equilibrium, and congregations might well move from one communion to the other over time. Some Anglicans would join the Roman Catholic Church, and others might move into more hard-line Protestant Churches where the ministry of women is not accepted. The world would not end.

3

Living the Change: On Being the First Woman Bishop in the Anglican Communion

Barbara C. Harris

. . . with the Spirit's gifts empower us for the work of ministry,
(From hymn 528 – *The Hymnal*, 1982)

TO ADDRESS THE QUESTION of why we need women bishops in its simplest form would be to respond to the question of why we need women priests – to *complete* that order of ordained ministry. To look at the issue at a deeper level, we need to consider what women have brought to the office that enhances episcopacy and strengthens the Church. Where, of course, I know this best is in the Episcopal Church in the United States of America (ECUSA) and I will leave commentary on other Provinces of the Communion to those who live and work in them.

The vote at the 1976 General Convention of the Episcopal Church to apply the ordination canons equally to women and men should have alerted thinking people not only to the possibility but to the probability of the nomination and perhaps the election of female bishops. Ordination of women to priesthood certainly opened the episcopacy to women as well. The when and where might have been in question, but the inevitability was not.

Interestingly, at the time of my election as the first female bishop in the Episcopal Church (and in the Anglican Communion as a whole), a group of Episcopalians generally opposed to women's ordination declared: 'The final crisis has come upon the Episcopal Church.' The election took place in 1988, immediately following the Lambeth Conference of that year at which bishops of the Communion reaffirmed the autonomy of each Province and certainly the right of each to order its own life and ministry. No small factor here was the insistence of African bishops, for example, that cultural issues such as polygamy needed to be addressed in the milieu to which they were common – an aspect of our common life that seems all but forgotten in the ensuing controversy over the election and consecration of the Rt Revd V. Gene Robinson as Bishop of New Hampshire and the acknowledgement that the blessing of same-sex relationships had been taking place in the life of the Church for some time.

Pockets of resistance to women in the episcopate and, indeed, exercising ministry in all orders here in the USA still remain. However, because it is no longer fashionable to voice or blatantly display sexist bias, some have taken theological and scriptural refuge against homosexuals in Holy Orders. When pressed, a strong bias against women is revealed as the root of their disaffection and much of their politicized activity in the Church in this country. What we are seeing is a 'feminization of homosexuality', for if one can show a gay man to be 'less than a man', the whole notion of the unsuitability of women can be acted upon.

The process of electing bishops in the Episcopal Church

It is important to remember that the polity of the Episcopal Church in the USA is founded on democratic principles which are consistent with our constitutional form of government. While it is true, historically, that bishops were often elected by our General Convention, that process was replaced by nomination and election by each autonomous diocese. The notion, however, of the whole Province having the final say over the consecration of a bishop survived. The process normally was to seek consents from, first, a majority of the Standing Committees of the several dioceses; then, upon receipt of those, to seek the consent of a majority of the bishops having jurisdiction (diocesans).

This was the procedure followed in my election and consecration. However, to retain the integrity of the electoral process as a Province-wide participatory one, our canons do provide for General Convention to reclaim its original authority if an election occurs within 180 days of that triennial gathering. In this instance there is the opportunity for further examination of each person in open committee hearings and extensive debate on the floor of both the House of Deputies and the House of Bishops before a vote is taken. This was the case for Gene Robinson and nine others elected bishops in the year 2003. What each procedure has in common is the participation of all three orders and the democratic means by which this is accomplished. This is somewhat different from processes followed in other Provinces of the Church. It is therefore understandable why many Provinces in the Anglican Communion are perplexed by our method and procedure.

At the consecration of a bishop, the service calls for an orderly series of testimonials which in each instance affirms the aforementioned steps required for consent to be properly obtained. It was for this reason that Presiding Bishop Edmond Browning, in my case, and the present Presiding Bishop Frank Griswold, in the case of Gene Robinson, felt they were on sound constitutional and canonical grounds to proceed with the consecrations. In both instances, the objections that were raised to proceeding with the consecration had nothing to do with the legitimacy or the integrity of the process. The objections arose from questionable theological assertions, having to do with gender and sexual orientation, which if, in fact, were grounds for stopping the process, should have been raised at the point of ordination to the diaconate.

Another feature of the democratic process is one fail-safe measure. During the consent process or even after its successful conclusion, the entire procedure can be halted by the Standing Committee of the electing diocese withdrawing its own consent. The election then becomes null and void. In recent memory, this has occurred in the US Church where previously undisclosed information arose that questioned the character of the bishop-elect.

The objections to women bishops

In all honesty, my election as the first woman bishop in the history of the Communion did generate great controversy for several reasons. First, I was a divorced person and it was said, though not documented, that no person divorced prior to nomination had ever been elected bishop. Second, I had not prepared for Orders via the usual three-year seminary path, rather through a rigorous alternative programme of study, and thus was regarded as not theologically well trained. Third, I was labelled by some as a left-wing, radical liberal. Add to that mix the reality of being an African-American, which is no small consideration in a Church that is admittedly racist. And for some, the fact that I had never remarried raised speculation regarding my sexual orientation – a factor generally overlooked in electing single men or, at least, not openly discussed in the press.

Thus the process of obtaining the consents of a majority of Standing Committees in the several dioceses and subsequently the consents of a majority of the bishops with jurisdiction was long and arduous, and at times seemed in doubt. One senior bishop of the Church, however, voiced the strong opinion that if the requisite consents were not forthcoming, that too could split the Church. I cite all the foregoing simply to point up that there was great need on the part of some to discredit the first election and derail the consent process so that no consecration would take place. For indeed, if there was *one*, there surely would be *others*.

Again, the objections voiced at my consecration, while aimed at me personally, were couched in terms of the notion that a constitutional change was needed to allow for a woman in the episcopate, that Episcopal acts such as confirmations and ordinations would not be recognized elsewhere in the Communion and that relationships with Rome would be irrevocably damaged. Interestingly, there were two objections offered at my consecration, two raised at the ordination of the second US woman bishop – Jane Holmes Dixon of Washington DC, and only one at that of the third – Mary Adelia McLeod, the first US woman diocesan. Since then, none has been expressed.

The impact of women bishops

With all of that said, the Church not only has weathered the storm of my own consecration and 14-year episcopate, but has seen the number of women bishops grow to 12 in the United States, 1 in New Zealand and 3 in the Church of Canada, giving a total of 16. Of that number only three have retired from the office to which elected – the Bishop of Vermont and the Bishops Suffragan of Washington, DC and Massachusetts. As the latter, I continue to be active as part-time Assisting Bishop in the Diocese of Washington DC.

It would be fair to say that our presence has had some impact on parts of the Communion and the larger Christian community in a number of ways. Several of us have been invited to participate in local, regional, national and international gatherings and events of significance. I recall, for example, my own participation as preacher at a 1990 World Council of Churches convocation on Justice, Peace and the Integrity of Creation in Seoul, Korea and an extended visit to the Diocese of Tokyo as the Church in Japan undertook its exploration of women's ordination. Similarly, Bishop Mary Adelia McLeod and I represented ECUSA at the consecration of Christina Odenberg, the first woman bishop in the Church of Sweden.

The experience of episcopacy

But what of the actual experience of episcopacy? Early on, I found, as I suspect others did as well, wide acceptance and affirmation of my ministry among older persons, who had seen so much change in their life-span that their attitude was quite simply: 'Why not women bishops!' They welcomed my preaching – though still radical to others – and such things as the personalized touch I employed in administering communion and in confirming and receiving people into the church, and providing a pastoral presence many said they had not experienced for some time.

Women and girls were encouraged to feel that they truly had a place in the church and people of colour expressed their pride and their joy in God's doing 'a new thing'. And many people felt it was truly of God because, given all the earlier-mentioned odds against me, it never could have been politically orchestrated.

During the nominating processes in various dioceses, it has been reported that many of the women presented themselves as strong candidates who were forthcoming, offered vision and tended to be prophetic in their preaching. Several had previous rich experience in other fields prior to entering ordained ministry. This was certainly true in my own case, having spent some 30 years in business and industry before being ordained to the diaconate. Their gifts and skills have made for a fuller episcopacy, more representative of the humanity of God's creation.

My sister bishop, Gayle Elizabeth Harris – presently Suffragan in Massachusetts – reminds us of something central in the scriptures. She says: 'We know that women have not been simply passive witnesses, but active proclaimers of the Good News.' And, as a Church claiming apostolic succession in the historic episcopate, we would do well to remember to whom we believe Jesus first appeared at his resurrection. Mary Magdalene herself, as apostle (one sent) to the apostles, offers reason enough for the unconditional acceptance of women to this order. Many selective 'traditionalists', generally opposed to women in Holy Orders, conveniently manage to overlook this part of the resurrection story or reduce it to trivia.

My experience of the ministry of bishop continues to be rich and rewarding. While at times it has been difficult to be a symbol, if you will, as the first woman bishop in the Communion, the rightness of women in this role has been demonstrated again and again. If this were not the case, I seriously doubt that they would continue to be elected. No longer a novelty, women cannot be ignored in the US House of Bishops. As we no longer sit in order of consecration, it is impossible to scan a meeting of the House and not see women's faces or hear their voices raised in the deliberations. As I continue to receive persons into this Church, both men and women tell me: 'You are one of the reasons I came to the Episcopal Church.' I suspect my sister bishops have heard similar testimonies and I would hazard a guess that as more are chosen for this office, they too will be looked upon as beacons of hope that 'There can be neither Jew nor Greek, there can be neither slave nor free, there can be neither male nor female – for you are all one in Christ Jesus' (Galatians 3.28).

4 From Icon to Action

David Stancliffe

THE DECISION OF THE GENERAL SYNOD of the Church of England to ordain women to the priesthood was made on 11 November 1992, the Feast of St Martin of Tours; and on that day – at the eleventh hour of the eleventh day of the eleventh month – the armistice that marked the end of the slaughter of World War I was signed. The two events are linked in the iconography of Martin. That great priest and bishop of Tours is better known in the popular mind as an unwilling conscript into the imperial army, leaning down from his horse as his attention is caught by something in the roadside. He draws his sword, slices his military cloak in two and gives half to a shivering beggar before passing on his way. But what the stained glass windows or statuary do not reveal is that this act of mercy is the prelude to a dream. That night Martin dreamed of Christ robed in the cloak that he shared with the beggar. That cloak drew together divided and broken humanity, the rich and the poor, the victors and the vanquished, with the promise of peace and unity for all humanity by the crucified Christ. It was a dream of peace on earth under the folds of Christ's robe for those exhausted by the futility and waste of human life in war; and it is a dream for those who long to see the whole ministry of the Church drawn together under the seamless robe of Christ.

In her speech to the General Synod in 1992, Sue Hope used this image of the 'seamless robe' of Christ's priesthood. Just as Martin's military cloak shielded both the solider and the beggar, so the seamless robe of Christ, never divided by the squabbling soldiers at the foot of the cross, embraces the whole human race. It was the ability of the gospel of Christ to transcend the boundaries between the social orders, between Jew and Greek, between slave and free, between male and female, that was a significant factor in ensuring its remarkably swift spread around the Mediterranean world in the early years. Christians had a vision of humanity, reconciled and united, that offered hope for the future – a future in which there was a place for everyone. This was radical; and for the established world, dangerously revolutionary.

'The beginnings of the new order which is the Church', said Sue Hope, 'are not biological but Christological, and in baptism male and female become, through Jesus, partakers of divine life. It is the sharing of the divine life which enables the Church to be a royal priesthood and to fulfil its calling to worship and to witness.' She went on to explore the 'communalization' of the priesthood: 'The priesthood of Christ is ours in the sense that it is held by the whole Body. It is a corporate priesthood rather than an individual one.' And she continued:

> The priesthood of the individual ordained priest is of one piece with the communal priesthood, it is of the same fabric . . . The priest is one such as ourselves, called to represent and focus our common priesthood: the priest is an icon of our common priesthood. When the community of male and female, clothed in the seamless robe of Christ's priesthood, acts as the icon of Christ, taking bread, blessing and breaking it, it is the individual priest who images the action of Christ in his Body, a Body made up of both male and female.
>
> The debate, therefore, is not properly about whether women can become priestly or have authority, for the seamless robe of Christ's priesthood has been flung over the whole body. The debate is properly about whether the Church in our generation believes the social and cultural restraints, which have so far inhibited women from acting as a focus for our common priesthood to have been lifted. This is not the importation of secular feminism, it is the making explicit of what is implicit in the Pauline gospel of the Church . . .[1]

I have quoted Sue Hope at some length for two reasons: first, because of her striking use of the image of the robe of Christ which has stayed with me since that moment; and second, because it was her speech, more than any other, which finally captured my cautious catholic spirit, and convinced me that the priesthood of Christ could only be adequately represented by both male and female priests, sharing a common humanity. Furthermore, that a priesthood of only one sex was an inherently defective icon of the priesthood of Christ, and that to ordain both men and women as priests was not only admissible, but essential.

But I want to move from the icon to the action. What are we to do to turn the vision that icon presents into reality? What is the task?

There are those who believe that the preservation of the catholic order meant that we should not have moved to bring this radical challenge of the gospel to an all-male priesthood into effect until every Church was ready to step forward together. But we have to ask: what is the distinctive witness of the Anglican tradition in this matter? Might it not be our Anglican vocation to pioneer the way in which the truth about ministerial priesthood is revealed and presented? Ought we not to take responsibility for showing our sister Churches that guarding the tradition does not mean locking up the past and throwing away the key but safeguarding the process of handing on; that is, of discerning the divine will afresh in each generation under the guidance of the Holy Spirit?

Let me write briefly of my visit to the General Synod of the Episcopal Church of the Sudan, meeting in 2000 for the first time in more than ten years. Its members had been gathered there for two reasons: to elect a new archbishop and to consider the ordination of women. I was to conduct the retreat for them before the meeting, and then to act as a kind of monitor during it. Electing an archbishop was a protracted job, with every vote being scrutinized by a panel of three judges. The next day we finally got to the ordination of women. Each bishop reported briefly on where his diocese had reached with regard to this matter, and then the floor was thrown open. There were speeches for about an hour and then a call for a vote. The matter was put, and the Synod voted overwhelmingly 'Yes'.

They were about to move on to the next business, when I intervened, saying that as I had to report to the Archbishop of Canterbury I would just like to clarify what they had decided. They had agree to ordain women deacons? Yes. And priest? Of course. And bishop? Why not! The seamless robe of Christ's priesthood was undivided. In one evening they had accomplished what we have still not managed to complete in the Church of England over many years.

Here was a Church arguing from scripture and tradition in a missionary context, making a principled decision and not looking over its shoulder all the time to see what other Communions – or indeed Provinces – were saying. In the Sudan, the primary emphasis was a clarity about our baptismal unity in Christ, and that the representative nature of the Church's ministry must reflect this seamless robe. In a country where Islam appeared less than wholly generous to women, the Church had a duty to do better.

A year later, at the Archbishop of the Sudan's pressing invitation, I was honoured to ordain the first four women priests there (and gave them a goat which I happened to come by – as one does – for their feast afterwards). And although I suspect it will be a number of years before a woman is elected a bishop, the Church in the Province has voted yes, and when the right candidate emerges she will go forward.

In southern Sudan, 40 years of civil war, with many men away fighting, have thrust women into positions of leadership in the civil community that would have been unthinkable in an African society a generation ago.

The task in the Sudan is to enable women to receive the education they need, to build up their confidence, and to nurture a social climate where their leadership becomes not only acceptable but something that is longed for. The task in England, where I am a bishop, is the reverse. Our women priests are well informed and confident: what is lacking among our (male) leaders is the nerve and the theological clarity to pursue the ordination of women to the priesthood to its logical conclusion. How can we represent the seamless robe of Christ's Church to the world if its representative ministry remains so visibly divided? We need to pursue the theological arguments with firmness, grace and clarity.

And this leads me, like Martin of Tours, to my dream.

My dream is twofold. First, that the Church of England will recognize the Episcopal ministry of both men and women. Second, that all the Churches will be so empowered in their pursuit of the truth which is Christ's that our different emphases and interpretations are seen for what they are: complementary insights rather than the reasons for one part of the Church to seek to exclude those with whom they disagree in the name of some notional purity.

The Church of England, with its history of handling unity among diversity, and distinguishing unity from uniformity, is well placed to offer its experience to other churches worldwide. Is not the model of the unity of the Church on the day of Pentecost one of a rich harmony, rather than a flat unison?

And why is this my dream? Because the message of the gospel has never been needed so badly. And it is not only that we are failing to preach a gospel of reconciliation in a world that is falling apart; we should have something unique to say about the value, worth and dignity of each human being, which we are denying institutionally by failing to let the seamless robe of Christ's priesthood be visible in our ordered ministry. This is an urgent task, and if we fail to accomplish it, the credibility of our gospel will continue to be seriously undermined. Yet again we will be accused of failing to practise what we preach. We believe that we are made in the image of God and that he is starting his new creation, incredible as it may seem, with us. The beggar may turn out to be none other than Christ himself, and it is of such that the kingdom of God is made.

Note

1 Reported in General Synod November Group of Sessions 1992 Report of Proceedings, vol. 23, no. 3, pp. 759–60.

5 Resisting Intransigence

Walter Paul Khotso Makhulu

SADLY, PATRIARCHY REIGNS SUPREME and, in Central Africa, men in the Church have tended to use culture to maintain their attitude to women. Scripture in many instances has been used to support the view that women should be kept down.

Liberation surfaces in secular society, especially where the law rules out discrimination. In religious communities in Africa, it is visible in the indigenous (independent) churches where women assume leadership roles. In certain instances, women have been founders of these churches. The Anglican Church of the Province of Central Africa (which covers Zambia, Zimbabwe, Malawi and Botswana) has depended on the loyalty, witness and service of women, yet has remained intransigent in refusing to ordain women. This is not for lack of candidates. I know of women lay ministers facing difficulties where some men simply refuse to recognize their ministry and leadership.

In my experience and judgement, outright denunciation of such attitudes would have been counter-productive. I preached by example, appointing women to positions that could not be contested. At the provincial level, I appointed a woman to be Chancellor. She is a sitting judge and no one could have contested her competence. In the diocese, I followed the same principle, extending it to the licensing of women lay ministers. I have sought always to discern people's calling, which is irrespective of their gender.

Tradition

6 Women Bishops in Antiquity: Apostolicity and Ministry

Rebecca Lyman

ANGLICANS HAVE ALWAYS looked back, particularly to the patristic period, as they have renewed their Church. We are all heirs of the complexities of our past, and this is especially true of Anglicans. Consider the Reformation defence of vernacular liturgy, biblical preaching, and married clergy, or the evangelical adaptation of apostolic life into social witness and personal holiness, or the Oxford Movement's revitalization of apostolic continuity and sacramental liturgy. The breadth of Anglican spirituality, as well as our belief in historical scholarship, has given us a Church both reformed and catholic in structures of authority. Spiritual leaders, from Thomas Cranmer to John Keble, might echo Henry Chadwick's summary of Jeremy Taylor's insight about the patristic era: 'From the wisdom of the past, the living tradition draws guidance, but Fathers and councils do not present a unanimous witness with an authority before which reason can only bow in submission.'[1]

Present questions concerning the episcopal ministry of women in Anglicanism therefore take their place within the theological diversity of our living tradition, the limits of authority provided by history, and our commitment to the continuing mission of the Church. The evidence of women's ministry has been much discussed in the last 30 years, and I do not intend to repeat many of those arguments here. Rather, I will evaluate the evidence of the leadership of women in antiquity in light of recent ecumenical and scholarly work on the history of episcopacy in late antiquity. I will conclude with reflections on what we may learn from our past in light of contemporary Anglicanism's global catholicity and the retrieval of the ministry of women.

Apostolicity and authority in antiquity

If the critical humanistic studies of the Reformation helped shatter the Church into diverse pieces with different readings of a common past through the authority of scripture, the critical historical studies of the present hold promise in bringing the Church back together. In the sixteenth century William Tyndale was declared a heretic for daring to translate the New Testament literally by using 'elder' and 'community' rather than the traditional terms 'priest' and 'Church' as defended by Thomas More. Today scholars from various Christian denominations are increasingly agreed on the evolution of terminology and ministries in the ancient Church. Our scriptural translations as well as our histories are beginning to occupy common ground. The historical evidence of women's leadership and the question of appropriate hermeneutics fit within the same ecumenical work and the current understandings of early church history. Almost 100 years ago, Frederick Loofs described the fragments of evidence of ancient Christianity as pieces of a kaleidoscope whose patterns could be changed by the eye or will of the interpreter.[2] This is not a statement of historical agnosticism as much as a warning about the limits of evidence available from antiquity and the inevitable strength of our convictions in the retrieval of our tradition. There should be no question concerning the historic continuity of the Christian faith and ministry from the apostles to our day, but there are many questions as to how to read the evidence of this continuity.

During the first two centuries of Christian life and mission, scholars agree that various small communities and leaders developed in the cities around the Mediterranean as a result of the first evangelists of the gospel. The multiplicity of these communities as well as the intense history of scholarship to defend certain structures of authority within this early diversity must be acknowledged.[3] As we know from the evidence of New Testament letters, various titles were given to people who performed a variety of functions within the community.

Some titles that appear consistently, such as evangelist, apostle, deacon, bishop or presbyter, probably refer to an early form of 'office'. Yet the titles themselves are both functional and descriptive, i.e. the 'sender of the gospel' (apostle) or 'overseer' (bishop) or 'elder/senior' (presbyter). While later traditions of ministry have clarified these titles in our understanding, in fact there seems to be a range of interpretation concerning their function and place within the community. Other titles which do not persist in later orders of ministry, such as 'patron' or 'widow', may seem more problematic, yet like 'presbyter', the word itself may or may not reflect an office, but rather a description of the role or social status of a person.[4] Recent scholarship has focused on several models of 'apostle' which are extant in various Christian texts. Extending beyond the traditional Twelve and Paul, 'apostle' could refer to those who embodied a personal witness to the risen Jesus and conveyed authentic teaching.[5]

At this point in the growth of the Christian movement, no central organization or pattern of ministry was consistent throughout these small house churches. The gospel was carried successfully to a variety of communities and places, which developed separately, but in communication with one another. We base our history on the occasional letters they exchanged.[6] During the second century we begin to see the gradual emergence of a consistent pattern of the threefold ministry of bishops, presbyters and deacons.[7] If Ignatius of Antioch described this pattern as necessary to the Church at the beginning of the second century, it was not attested commonly in other texts or geographical areas until later in the second century. For the most part, scholars agree that these leaders, whether called 'bishops' or 'presbyters', exercised the sort of oversight which ensured the continuity of teaching from the apostles. One may understand the traditional idea of direct succession from the apostles to the bishops as symbolizing a continuity of leadership and a genealogy of authenticity, but not necessarily historically evidenced everywhere and always in these particular offices of bishop and apostle.

Women as leaders in ancient Christianity

The leadership of women in early Christianity therefore needs to be read against this varied historical pattern of the first two centuries. Biblical and historical evidence show that women were numerically significant and acknowledged workers in many communities of the first and second centuries. Whether or not these women should be understood as part of the continuity of the orders of ministry has been the perennial dispute from the first century to the present day.[8] These centuries of argument reveal that the leadership of women is hardly a product of modern Western feminism, but has been a tension within the charismatic ideals and institutional realities of Christian life since the apostles. Thus, in the gospel accounts themselves, the description of women's roles is different. Mark identifies women as 'disciples' whereas Luke portrays women as 'supporters'.[9] The authority of Mary Magdalene as the first witness to the risen Christ was also contested in ancient literature. Although her status as 'apostle' was recognized in the early centuries, her authority as a leader, especially with regard to Peter, was disputed in canonical and apocryphal works. However, early commentators such as Hippolytus of Rome emphasized the paradox of her gender as chosen by Christ to be an apostle:

'Lest the female apostles doubt the angels, Christ himself came to them so that women would be apostles of Christ . . . Christ showed himself to the male apostles and said to them . . . "It is I who appeared to these women and I wanted to send them to you as apostles."'[10]

The ambiguity of the titles of leaders and ministers generally in this developmental period is thus only compounded when one tries to retrieve the significance of these references for women in the New Testament epistles. In Romans 16, Paul greeted 28 persons, nine of whom were women. Recent scholarship has argued that the titles of Phoebe as 'patron' or 'deacon' or Junia as 'apostle' should not be discounted as honorific, but like other designations applied to men, these show a characteristic blend of function and office. The significance of the recovery of Junia as a woman called an 'apostle' by Paul is heightened by the later theological position that insisted no women had been apostles. Rather like the paleo-anthropological finding of the skull of 'Lucy', the rarity of Junia as 'apostle' gives us a startling glimpse into a past we find we do not fully know. As in the case of Mary Magdalene, her status as apostle was defended by ancient Christian theologians including Origen, Jerome and Chrysostom; the latter commented echoing Hippolytus on Mary Magdalene, 'Oh, how great is the devotion of this woman that she should be counted worthy of the appellation of apostle.'[11] The existence of women with these titles in the New Testament and the defence of these same titles and functions by later ancient theologians must argue against a historical hermeneutic that assumes women were not nor could not be ministers in mainstream Christianity.

This evidence of course does not deny the clear tension in the New Testament writings between the numbers of women cited in various roles and the teachings against women in leadership. Women such as Lydia, Chloe and Nympha were owners of houses in which Christians met. Missionary couples such as Prisca and Aquila were teachers. Prisca is mentioned first as a sign of her importance; she was the teacher of Paul and the corrector of Apollos. The tensions concerning gender in these small communities reflect the general volatile atmosphere of fluid leadership and inclusive membership together with traditional household codes.[12] Paul's warnings for order to the Corinthians have much to do with the general charismatic and utopian life of the communities that made space not only for women, but also for Hellenists, poor and enslaved to exhibit authority.[13] By the same token, the warnings of the pastoral epistles about order and leadership focus not only on women, but also on justifying the leadership of wealthy male property owners. Given the ancient importance of order and outward conformity regardless of inner motivation, the Christians who embraced traditional household codes inevitably tried to limit the role of women along with slaves.[14] The importance of the household as the place for the earliest Christian conversions, liturgy and organization therefore could cut both ways for women: private space could encourage leadership, but traditional codes of patriarchical order could also be evoked to limit it.[15] In the same way, the story of Eve could be turned in different ways to either justify women's authority as renewed human nature in Christ or to condemn it in violation of hierarchy and obedience.[16] This mixture of evidence concerning the role of women confirms that women were indeed functioning as leaders, and the warnings function to stop something which is already happening. Taking both the evidence of ministry titles and the warnings against women's leadership, we may say confidently that women were active in various ministries in some communities of the Church, and their leadership in some communities was controversial. Histories of ministry therefore must include the presence of women rather than assume their absence in congruence with the later exclusion of women from orders of ministry.[17]

Women's participation in the first two centuries therefore fit within the local and largely charismatic basis of ministry in the early Church. Their leadership as well as participation may have reflected the higher status of women within the community than in the culture surrounding them, yet recent studies emphasize the participation of late antique women in many social and economic spheres hitherto unnoticed.[18] The prominent place of women as martyrs, teachers, prophets and widows was interpreted theologically in various literary accounts to show the power of the gospel to subvert and defeat the dominant social and spiritual structures. Thus, Blandina in *The Martyrs of Lyons*, whose tortured body became the image of Christ to her community, bore the weight of both gender and social class: she was a disfigured servant who became a victor. Ironically, the follower of Paul and preacher of the gospel, Thecla, has been remembered more for the opposition of Tertullian to her authority than for the description of itinerant and continent female preachers that her story preserves. The strength of the oral tradition around her life and death was reflected in the enduring cult and devotion to her tomb in Asia Minor. Even Epiphanius, an opponent of heresy and women leaders, defended Thecla.[19] Prophets were important members of communities who presided at liturgy as well as offered guidance through visions.[20] 'Widow' was a title that designated not only marital status but also the first ascetics who appeared to teach, distribute alms and advise the community.[21] These active women reflected the new universal ideals of the early communities as well as the varieties of ministries in the ancient Church.

Leadership and controversy

The theological controversies among Christians in the second century led to the increasing definition of 'apostolic' in order to preserve and embrace the authentic teaching of Jesus. Irenaeus defined apostolicity as including the succession of bishops from the apostles, the selection of scriptural books as a canon, the rule of faith, and especially charity, which binds all together. Discerning apostolic teaching and practice therefore depended not only on the succession of bishops, but also on testing their teaching – and character – with scripture and belief. Notably, Irenaeus never referred to himself as bishop, but rather presbyter. He also recognized and defended the diversity of local practice in the communities spread around the Mediterranean: 'Our unity is revealed in our diversity.'[22] If a consistent division existed between 'heretical' leadership of women and orthodox denial of this, Irenaeus, who has every occasion to discuss and condemn women's leadership in his polemics, does not. In stark contrast to Tertullian, he does not associate women's leadership with heresy, and defends the prophetic authority of women.[23]

In the third century in the context of social crisis and increased persecution, ministry is increasingly centralized around the power of the bishop in many communities. The earlier functional varieties of office begin to be defined and ordered ritually. In Syria the role of the widow was curtailed, and deaconesses as a special order to minister to women was created.[24] At the same time in Egypt, Origen was criticized for preaching without ordination by his bishop, though other bishops declared that this was a traditional practice. Cyprian as Bishop in North Africa limited the traditional power of the confessors to forgive sins. Given these trends, evidence from this period that refers to women's leadership is often contested or deemed 'heretical'; that is, from a group not in the mainstream such as Montanism. An inscription from Phrygia that refers to a woman presbyter is therefore assumed to be 'Montanist' solely on the basis of the title as applied to a woman.[25]

Women and ecclesiastical centralization

Yet, the polemic against women in ordained leadership persisted into the fourth and fifth century. Church orders were emerging in various places, but these practices of distinguishing ministries, even for women, were not universal. Legislation was aimed not only against schismatic women such as Montanists, but ordained women internal to the mainstream community. This evidence strongly suggests that women in various local communities were continuing to receive ordination and exercise authority in the community. At Nicaea in 325 women as deacons were explicitly ranked with the laity; as Henry Chadwick comments, 'The need for such a canon implies that some churches held the opposite view.'[26] In Asia Minor a council forbade the ordination of women as presbyters, which implies that this practice is continuing.[27]

At about the same time, Epiphanius, the bishop of Cyprus who was utterly devoted to orthodoxy and order in the Church, mounted a furious distinction between women in Orders, who had received ordination through the laying on of hands, and charismatic ministries. He reflects the routinization of ministries and the separation of ascetics from clergy, and reflects problems with gender in his explicit encouragement of men to exclude women and denying any orthodox historical precedent.[28] Finally, in tandem with an inscription of a woman presbyter from southern Italy, we hear a pope complain about the priestly activities of women still continuing.[29] The evaluation of this evidence generally rests on whether one accepts the possibility of women in Orders in the fourth and fifth century. Given the slow growth of centralization of canon law during this inaugural period of councils, and the diversity of ministries of women, it is historically plausible that women in varied places were leading communities within the Church. They were clearly not schismatics. In each case the burden of argument seems to be on those who are condemning the practice, and attempting to impose consistent order over earlier charismatic or regional practices.

This sort of legislative centralization and focus on clerical consistency reflected the tremendous changes of the fourth and fifth centuries as Christianity became the official religion of the empire. Bishops therefore acquired public social roles as well as increasingly complex liturgical ones. These shifts challenged bishops to display leadership not only as Romans through masculine virtues of *gravitas* and power, but also as Christians with humility and simplicity. As patrons of the urban poor, many bishops embraced asceticism, avoided sophisticated vocabulary, and presented themselves as a new kind of Roman leader.[30] The golden age of patristic preaching mirrored these profound changes within episcopacy as bishops became visible community leaders as well as rhetors of orthodoxy. Not surprisingly, manuals on being a priest appear as Chrystostom or Ambrose reflected on the new political roles. Women as charismatic and ascetic teachers, including Macrina the elder sister of Basil and Gregory, or Olympia the friend of Chrysostom, were influential spiritual and political mentors in this transformation. Asceticism and clerical celibacy became an important mark of the bishop's autonomous spiritual authority within the state, balancing Christian ideals of feminine virginity with the public masculine power of the Roman patron.[31]

Women bishops in late antiquity

Were women explicitly titled 'bishops' in late antiquity? Several inscriptions exist that preserve the title of 'episcopa' for women, but these have been interpreted in light of the perceived plausibility of women actually exercising such an office. Given the significant number of women active in mainstream Christianity and the possibilities of leadership for exceptional educated or aristocratic women in late antiquity, one cannot rule out the possibility *tout court*. For example, the inscription from the tomb of the mother of a pope as 'episcopa' has been seen as an anomaly. The question is whether this title refers to her ecclesiastical office or is a honorific title referring to her role as mother. Since there are no contemporary parallels to her title extant to confirm either argument, i.e. that she was called this as a mother of a bishop or that she was indeed a bishop, we are again faced with a paucity of evidence which raises more questions than answers. Resolving it by saying that it is difficult or impossible to imagine a woman bishop in the fifth century is not a historical argument.[32] Given the persistence of women leaders into the fourth and fifth centuries, one can equally argue for reality of the ecclesiastical title.

Looking over this evidence of shifting models of ministry and continued controversy over the leadership of women, may we speak of women bishops in antiquity? The answer to this question relies on the same blend of local practice, changing function and diverse ministries that we must evaluate in the history of male bishops. We may certainly cite women who were remembered and praised for their apostolic roles, including Mary Magdalene and Junia. Their gender was explicitly seen as integral to the proclamation of the gospel as socially and personally transformative. Women such as Lydia who offered households in the first two centuries were participating in administrative kinds of activities including financial management and hospitality that were the critical context of early Christian expansion and underlay the emergence of the title and office of 'episcopos'. The central function of widows as teachers, administrators and advisers is also significant; based on her role in the community, Grapte of Rome has been argued to be an early bishop.[33] Women were clearly respected teachers of authentic truth, from Prisca, the teacher of Paul and Apollos, to Thecla, the revered teacher of Asia, to Macrina, the abbess and philosopher of the fourth century. All these women were leaders within mixed communities. If no woman explicitly has the title of bishop in the first two centuries, we may note that Irenaeus never referred to himself by this title nor did Clement of Rome, though both are cited as evidence of episcopal succession in late antiquity. Traditionally, their importance as leaders in the community and defence of tradition outweighs the necessity of an explicit title. Such a criteria should also be applied to the evidence concerning women in leadership in the mainstream community. In the evolution of the orders of ministry, women were active participants, valued advisers, and strong leaders in all aspects of Christian life. In spite of continual controversy, their persistent presence testified to the vitality and spiritual power of Christian reflection and practice.

Women and Anglican definitions of episcopacy

The evidence for women as 'overseers' in antiquity is present, if direct references to the office are few and contested. I have argued that to insist on a literal reading of titles and offices in antiquity begs the critical historical question of how we now interpret the history of ministry. Equally important, the recovery of the breadth of ministries and apostolicity in antiquity has begun to reshape Christian unity in our ecumenical age. Anglicans in particular have always defended both the necessary continuity and creative historical modification of episcopacy. In our tradition, the succession of bishops has been both a sign and a guarantee of apostolic continuity, but we have always placed this within the broader authority of scripture as well as the stream of prayer, practice and belief. Women as administrators, teachers and presbyters were part of this continuity of overseers who maintained apostolic continuity, even if their possession of the office was sometimes controversial. Indeed, the leadership of women persisted even as the role of the bishop itself changed over the course of the first four centuries reflecting the challenges of a controversial Church, a persecuted Church, and finally an imperial Church. Just as Polycarp, who presents himself as a humble teacher, is not the political and ascetic Ambrose, neither is the married evangelical Cranmer or the catholic Gore. In each one, the expression of episcopacy was adapted to express the transforming power of the gospel in reference to the needs of the contemporary world.

Given the development of later tradition, which consistently excluded women from clerical offices, can women today be traditional and universal representatives of the apostolic gospel? According to ancient definitions of apostolic authority and ministry, women already have been. The history of their varied service in fact represents and incarnates the breadth of Christian understanding of apostolicity as including scripture, tradition and ministerial succession. As recently noted by the House of Bishops, representatives of different traditions have come to recognize that:

> . . . on the one hand the apostolicity of the Church is wider than historical episcopal succession and on the other hand integral to the

> ministry of oversight is the sense of helping to maintain the Church in the faith of the apostles and that orderly continuity in the ministry of oversight (episcope) is one of the means given by God for maintaining the Church in the faith of the apostles.[34]

This statement reflects the continuing ecumenical and Anglican recovery of the breadth of apostolicity that has included various forms and theories of episcopacy. Anchored in tradition and scripture, Anglican bishops have adapted to minister in society as a means of renewing and preserving apostolic continuity. Reformation ideals of bishops included learning, holiness and especially preaching; to John Jewel, the bishop's fidelity to scripture was the defining mark of the true Church.[35] Rejecting equivalence between bishop and presbyter in the violent discussions of the seventeenth century, Anglicans revealed an acceptance of historical criticism as well as an affirmation of apostolic order necessarily ensured by bishops. Hooker treated episcopacy as both gradual and divinely directed.[36]

In the eighteenth and nineteenth centuries Anglicans ensured spiritual authority over against secular power by embracing the evidence of Ignatius of Antioch, and emphasized the bishop as the 'factor that grounds the identity of the Church'.[37] Bishops therefore as defined by historical scholarship and social context have been an important touchstone for how Anglicans wish to see change in the Church. From John Jewel's boast of the 'pastors, labourers and watchmen' who replace the 'oily shaven portly hypocrites' to the affirmation of a variety of cultural styles of leadership in global Anglicanism, the bishop represents both apostolic vitality and continuity.[38]

The ordination of women as bishops confirms and challenges these Anglican understandings of episcopacy. The broader definition of apostolicity which has always undergirded and renewed the sense of orders of ministry in Anglicanism is exactly what should be recalled for the evaluation of women bishops.[39] The recognition of this broad and rich tradition does not weaken the apostolic office of the bishop as much as ground it in the authentic working of the Spirit for the renewal of each generation and culture. To focus on the lively teaching and scriptural witness of apostolicity allows the bishop to be the agent of encouragement as much as of theological teacher. Women bishops therefore stand in continuity with the past as well as the future of Christianity. Wherever their heart may lie as evangelical or catholic, by their gender they represent a retrieval of ancient apostolicity of women as bearers of the gospel.

The ongoing development of the particular theological and ecclesiastical role of women bishops will reflect the specific cultural context of the branch of the Anglican Communion, as indeed bishops did in the ancient Church in Africa, Italy, Greece or Egypt. Each community must find for itself the proper images and reflection of women as apostolic representatives. Present conflicts within our Communion should not discourage us from pressing forward into a new global catholicity that echoes the unity and diversity of the ancient Church. Retrieving only the legality of orthodoxy, we miss the tolerance and local custom that early structures of catholicity and communion sought to protect, if not reconcile.[40] True global catholicity in our post-colonial world lies before us in the continuing reconciling work of Christ in all cultures. As Irenaeus defended his own Asian culture and practice in Rome, we may say, 'Our diversity is a sign of our unity.' The episcopacy of women is a piece of the restoration of that ancient catholic dream of all races and countries held together by the One who came to heal all.

Notes

1 Henry Chadwick, 'Traditions, Fathers, and Councils', in *The Study of Anglicanism*, ed. Stephen Sykes, John Booty and Jonathan Knight (London: SPCK, 1998), p. 113.

2 Jaroslav Pelikan cites this illustration in *The Vindication of Tradition* (New Haven: Yale University Press, 1984), p. 109.

3 See the brief but excellent summary of the history of scholarship on ministry in Harry O. Maier, *The Social Setting of the Ministry as Reflected in the Writings of Hermas, Clement and Ignatius* (Waterloo, On.: Wilfrid Laurier University Press, 1991), pp. 1–5.

4 On the ambiguities of titles and institutions of 'presbyter', see Maier, *The Social Setting of the Ministry*, pp. 117f.

5 Concise summaries of this scholarship are found in Ute E. Eisen, *Women Officeholders in Early Christianity: Epigraphical and Literary Studies*, trans. Linda Maloney (Collegeville, Minn.: Liturgical Press, 2000), pp. 47–62 and Ann Graham Brock, *Mary Magdalene, the First Apostle: The Struggle for Authority* (Cambridge, Mass.: Harvard Divinity School, 2003), pp. 1–71.

6 Rowan Williams, 'Does it Make Sense to Speak of Pre-Nicene Orthodoxy?', in *The Making of Orthodoxy: Essays in Honour of Henry Chadwick*, ed. Rowan Williams (Cambridge: Cambridge University Press, 1989), pp. 1–23.

7 For histories of the transition from the communities of the apostles to orders of ministry see Francis A. Sullivan, SJ, *From Apostles to Bishops: The Development of the Episcopate in the Early Church* (New York: Newman Press, 2001), pp. 217–30; see also Hans von Campenhausen, *Ecclesiastical Authority and Spiritual Power in the Church of the First Three Centuries* (London: Adam and Charles Black, 1969). Maier, in *The Social Setting of the Ministry*, cautions against too much scepticism concerning the succession of bishops from apostles, simply replacing generalizing agnosticism with the universal apostolic succession, when historically one must look at particular communities.

8 Ruth B. Edwards, *The Case for Women's Ministry* (London: SPCK, 1989); cf. John Wijngaards, *No Women in Holy Orders? The Women Deacons of the Early Church* (Norwich: Canterbury Press, 2002).

9 On the different portrayals of women as disciples in Mark and followers in Luke see Mary T. Malone, *Women and Christianity*, vol. 1 (Dublin: Columba Press, 2000), pp. 46–8.

10 Quoted in Brock, *Mary Magdalene*, pp. 1–2.
11 Quoted ibid., p. 146.
12 Maier, *The Social Setting of the Ministry*, p. 38.
13 Antoinette Clark Wire, *The Corinthian Women Prophets: A Reconstruction through Paul's Rhetoric* (Minneapolis: Fortress Press, 1990).
14 Philip A. Harland, *Associations, Synagogues, and Congregations* (Philadelphia: Fortress Press, 2003), pp. 194, 235; cf. Maier, *The Social Setting of the Ministry*, p. 45.
15 On the importance of the 'household' for the shaping of Christian life and ministry, see L. Michael White, *The Social Origins of Christian Architecture* (Valley Forge, Pa.: Trinity International Press, 1996), p. 143; cf. Maier, *The Social Setting of the Ministry*, pp. 15–28.
16 Women apostles rectify the disobedience of Eve in Hippolytus: Brock, *Mary Magdalene*, p. 1; the use of Eve for justifying gender hierarchy is in 1 Timothy 2.13–14.
17 The classic argument for this is Elizabeth Schüssler Fiorenza, *In Memory of Her: A Feminist Theological Reconstruction of Christian Origins* (New York: Crossroads, 1983).
18 See the interesting interpretation by Rodney Stark in *The Rise of Christianity: A Sociologist Reconsiders History* (Princeton: Princeton University Press, 1996), pp. 107–11. Cf. Eisen's summary of recent work on women in antiquity, *Women Officeholders in Early Christianity*, pp. 15–17.
19 Stephen J. Davis, *The Cult of Saint Thecla: A Tradition of Women's Piety in Late Antiquity* (Oxford: Oxford University Press, 2001).
20 See Eisen, *Women Officeholders in Early Christianity*, pp. 71–3. The *Didache* in fact warned congregations to give deacons and bishops equal respect; prophets could improvise prayers at the Eucharist.
21 Bonnie Bowman Thurston, *The Widows: A Women's Ministry in the Early Church* (Philadelphia: Fortress Press, 1989); cf. Eisen, *Women Officeholders in Early Christianity*, pp. 150f.
22 On the discussion of his titles, see Mary Ann Donovan, *One Right Reading? A Guide to Irenaeus* (Collegeville, Minn.: Liturgical Press, 1997), pp. 9–10. Irenaeus' comment is in Eusebius, *Church History* 5.4; he is recommended to the bishop of Rome in a letter as 'brother and confessor' and finally as a 'presbyter'.
23 See *Adversus Haereses* 1.13, where Marcus' corruption of women is criticized, not women's leadership.
24 Thurston, *The Widows*, pp. 96–105.
25 Compare the interpretation of William Tabbernee, who concludes on the basis of the title alone that the inscription is Montanist in *Montanist Inscriptions and Testamonia* (Macon, Ga.: Mercer University Press, 1997), pp. 66–72, to Eisen, *Women Officeholders in Early Christianity*, pp. 116–123.
26 'The Church in Ancient Society from Galilee to Gregory the Great' in *Oxford History of the Christian Church* (Oxford: Oxford University Press, 2003), p. 54.
27 Compare Tabbernee, *Montanist Inscriptions*, p. 70 with Eisen, *Women Officeholders in Early Christianity*, pp. 121–3. The question rests on the identification of the women as 'presbyters' or 'widows/deaconesses'.
28 Eisen, *Women Officeholders in Early Christianity*, pp. 118–21.
29 Ibid., pp. 128–32. Tabernee agrees: *Montanist Inscriptions*, p. 67.
30 On these shifts see Peter Brown's *Power and Persuasion in Late Antiquity: Towards a Christian Empire* (Madison: University of Wisconsin Press, 1988).
31 On imperial bishops and clerical celibacy, see especially the discussion of Ambrose in Peter Brown, *The Body and Society: Men, Women and Sexual Renunciation in Early Christianity* (New York: Columbia University Press, 1988), pp. 348–65.
32 See the discussion of evidence and interpretation in Eisen, *Women Officeholders in Early Christianity*, pp. 199–209.

33 Ibid., p. 208.
34 *Apostolicity and Succession: House of Bishops Occasional Paper* (London: Church House, 1994), para. 10.
35 Richard Norris, 'Episcopacy', in Sykes (ed.), *The Study of Anglicanism*, p. 334.
36 Ibid., p. 340; cf. J. Robert Wright, *On Being a Bishop: Papers on Episcopacy from the Moscow Consultation* (New York: Church Hymnal Corporation, 1993).
37 Norris, 'Episcopacy', p. 343.
38 John Jewel's comment is cited in Patrick Collinson, *The Religion of the Protestants: The Church in English Society 1559–1625* (Oxford: Clarendon Press, 1982), p. 23; on the discussion of different cultural models and 'increasing pluralism in what it means to exercise episcopal oversight' see Vinay Samuel and Christopher Sugden, *Lambeth: A View from the Two-Thirds World* (London: SPCK, 1989), pp. 34–8.
39 For a similar argument applied to women priests, see Paul Avis, *Anglican Orders and the Priesting of Women* (London: Darton, Longman and Todd, 1999), pp. 48–9.
40 Caroline Bammel, 'Peacemaking and Religious Tolerance in the Early Church', in *Tradition and Exegesis in the Early Christian Writers* (Aldershot: Variorum, 1995), pp. 1–13.

Bibliography

Apostolicity and Succession: House of Bishops Occasional Paper (London: Church House, 1994).

Avis, Paul, *Anglican Orders and the Priesting of Women* (London: Darton, Longman and Todd, 1999).

Bammel, Caroline P., *Tradition and Exegesis in the Early Christian Writers* (Aldershot: Variorum, 1995).

Brock, Ann Graham, *Mary Magdalene, the First Apostle: The Struggle for Authority* (Cambridge, Mass.: Harvard Divinity School, 2003).

Brown, Peter, *The Body and Society: Men, Women and Sexual Renunciation in Early Christianity* (New York: Columbia University Press, 1988).

—— *Power and Persuasion in Late Antiquity: Towards a Christian Empire* (Madison: University of Wisconsin Press, 1992).

Campenhausen, Hans Freiherr von, *Ecclesiastical Authority and Spiritual Power in the Church of the First Three Centuries* (London: Adam and Charles Black, 1969).

Chadwick, Henry, *The Church in Ancient Society: From Galilee to Gregory the Great* (Oxford: Oxford University Press, 2003).

Collinson, Patrick, *The Religion of the Protestants: The Church in English Society 1559–1625* (Oxford: Clarendon Press, 1982).

Davis, Stephen J., *The Cult of Saint Thecla: A Tradition of Women's Piety in Late Antiquity* (Oxford: Oxford University Press, 2001).

Donovan, Mary Ann, *One Right Reading? A Guide to Irenaeus* (Collegeville, Minn.: Liturgical Press, 1997).

Edwards, Ruth B., *The Case for Women's Ministry* (London: SPCK, 1989).

Eisen, Ute E., *Women Officeholders in Early Christianity: Epigraphical and Literary Studies*, trans. Linda Maloney (Collegeville, Minn.: Liturgical Press, 2000).

Fiorenza, Elizabeth Schüssler, *In Memory of Her: A Feminist Theological Reconstruction of Christian Origins* (New York: Crossroads, 1983).

Harland, Philip A., *Associations, Synagogues, and Congregations: Claiming a Place in Ancient Mediterranean Society* (Philadelphia: Fortress Press, 2003).

Maier, Harry O., *The Social Setting of the Ministry as Reflected in the Writings of Hermas, Clement and Ignatius* (Waterloo, On.: Wilfrid Laurier University Press, 1991).

Malone, Mary T., *Women and Christianity*, vol. 1 (Dublin: Columba Press, 2000).

Pelikan, Jaroslav, *The Vindication of Tradition* (New Haven: Yale University Press, 1984).
Samuel, Vinay and Sugden, Christopher, *Lambeth: A View from the Two-Thirds World* (London: SPCK, 1989).
Stark, Rodney, *The Rise of Christianity: A Sociologist Reconsiders History* (Princeton: Princeton University Press, 1996).
Sullivan, Francis A., SJ, *From Apostles to Bishops: The Development of the Episcopacy in the Early Church* (New York: Newman Press, 2001).
Sykes, Stephen, Booty, John and Knight, Jonathan (eds), *The Study of Anglicanism* (London: SPCK, 1998).
Tabbernee, William, *Montanist Inscriptions and Testamonia* (Macon, Ga.: Mercer University Press, 1997).
Thurston, Bonnie Bowman, *The Widows: A Women's Ministry in the Early Church* (Philadelphia: Fortress Press, 1989).
White, L. Michael, *The Social Origins of Christian Architecture* (Valley Forge, Pa.: Trinity International Press, 1996).
Wijngaards, John, *No Women in Holy Orders? The Women Deacons of the Early Church* (Norwich: Canterbury Press, 2002).
Williams, Rowan (ed.), *The Making of Orthodoxy: Essays in Honour of Henry Chadwick* (Cambridge: Cambridge University Press, 1989).
Wire, Antoinette Clark, *The Corinthian Women Prophets: A Reconstruction through Paul's Rhetoric* (Philadelphia: Fortress Press, 1990).
Wright, J. Robert, *On Being a Bishop: Papers on Episcopacy from the Moscow Consultation 1992* (New York: Church Hymnal Corporation, 1993).

7 Bishops and the Formation of Anglicanism

Vincent Strudwick

WHILE THE *THEOLOGICAL* CASE for ordaining women to the episcopate must surely be related to the debate and decision that approved the ordination of women as priests, with additional attention being given to the 'headship' issue in scripture in view of the role of episcopal oversight, there is clearly an issue related to the *tradition* that has to be clarified. My hunch is that there is a nervousness, in some quarters at least, about 'changing' the episcopate in a way that will make its members less recognizably identified with the historic episcopate. Since the break with Rome in 1534, there has been a desire among many members of the Church of England to proclaim the validity and orthodoxy of Church of England bishops, although it is only in the last century and a quarter that this desire has been expressed in terms that it has been hoped would prove acceptable to Eastern Orthodox and Roman Catholic authority – and acknowledgement of this has never come.

The Roman Catholic question is: what are you doing when you make a bishop? The Anglican response has been in terms of the Ordinal and the continuity of the laying on of hands in the Apostolic Succession. But the issue is much more complex than that and needs to be worked at quite apart from the question of ordaining women to the episcopate, though that is vitally pressing and now urgent.

Tradition and precedent

At the end of the nineteenth century, there was a disinclination to acknowledge the development of tradition (in spite of Newman). Moreover, as far as allowing differences in the tradition, influenced by differences in the culture, this was regarded as nothing less than condoning heresy as well as schism. So the 'picture' of a bishop, drawn from the high Middle Ages, becomes the 'norm' against which episcopacy is measured. Picture a bishop. We close our eyes and for many the picture that emerges is that of a middle-aged man (probably white) in a pointed hat; and although we know that neither age nor clothing nor gender is the essence of episcopacy, the impact of the unconscious/conscious image is powerful. The picture is formed by our cultural formation rather than through our theological insight, but it is none the less powerful for that.

Indeed, in the sixteenth century Bishop Jewel had to combat a similar picture and wrote, 'Bishops have at times had certain ornaments such as crosses and mitres . . . which pomp the ancient bishops, Chrysostom, Augustine and Ambrose, never had.'[1] He is making the point, among others, that the office of bishop is culturally conditioned and changes; something that his protégé Richard Hooker, the influential late sixteenth-century apologist for the newly formed Church of England, expanded in his work, noting that some early bishops had small episcopates, like large parishes. The system in which they operated was different, and that difference radically changes the expression of the office. This is to say that tradition is necessarily dynamic rather than static; the sixteenth-century reformers of the Church in England understood that.

The appeal to 'tradition' is nevertheless often confused with a search for precedent. In this chapter I hope to show that the two are different and that this was perceived as the Church of England, newly separated from papal authority, tried to discover its identity and renew its understanding of the gospel, in the sixteenth and seventeenth centuries. This 'renewal of understanding' was achieved in a 'long reformation'; not a single event with an agreed alternative theology and ecclesiology, but a process undertaken through four successive reigns by people with conflicting views and differing methodologies. Because of this, any appeal to precedent alone may find itself reaching conclusions that justify different theological positions and ecclesial 'shaping'. For, during the whole of the reign of Elizabeth I, a 'tradition' was in formation; and, as the Church of England seeks to renew itself as a Church in the twenty-first century, a conversation with those who were part of the original formation may lead us to a better understanding of what we are about.

The important questions we ask in the course of this conversation will not be simply ones concerning precedent. For example, the question 'Did the sixteenth-century English Reformers favour women bishops?' is not quite to the point. The answer is that some may have done, and some may have not, but most probably did not ask the question, and they certainly did not have the information concerning precedent that we have today. As Rebecca Lyman discusses in this book, we know that there are interesting and important pieces of evidence which point (in my view conclusively) to women's leadership roles in the Church in New Testament times. They appear to be of equal importance and of the same kind as those of men –

whatever those leadership roles were. As such roles developed and changed, we find evidence in both inscriptions and archaeological evidence for the existence of women as well as men called 'presbyters'. The change from the Apostolic era to that of the Graeco-Roman Church saw the development and transformation of leadership roles, and the issue of 'women' became a matter for debate; but there is evidence that in some places women continued to exercise leadership, using the new, accepted title of 'bishop'.[2]

However, these evidences of precedent (which were not available to the Church of England's founding fathers) can be evaluated only in the context of an understanding of 'the tradition' and how it developed through the centuries. It is from this wider understanding of how the tradition develops that the important questions will emerge.

The 'ages' of the Church

The events of the sixteenth century, when the Church of England emerged, represented a dramatic change to the whole of the Church in Europe; but such change does not stand isolated from the continuous process of change throughout the whole history of Christianity.

Writing in the 1940s, the Roman Catholic historian Christopher Dawson tells us of successive 'ages' of the Church from New Testament times to the present day and expresses the process in this way: 'In spite of the unity and continuity of the Christian tradition, each of the successive "ages" of the Church's history possesses its own distinctive character, and in each of them we can study a different facet of Christian life and culture.'[3] In each of the 'ages', the Church's concern is to live and express the 'everlasting gospel', but no one age can encompass the 'face-to-face' truth of God. The best it can do is to embody the Christian message of hope in a cultural form and structure that resonates in the society it seeks to serve. I have long been indebted to Dawson's thesis, which identifies 'six' such ages. Each of these, he says, begins and ends in crisis. The first is a crisis of growth when the Church is faced with a new historical situation and 'begins a new apostolate'; then there is a period of achievement with new forms of theological thinking reflected in art, architecture and ways of life; finally there is a phase of decay and the Church is attacked from within and without.

Dawson sees the 're-invention' of the Church in each age as expressions of successive campaigns in an unending war. In each campaign, the church authorities tend to stress the continuity of the campaign with previous ones, and with its original mission.

However, it seems to me that, in the transition from one age to another, the shift is so great that the forms of the Church and the institutions of its governance undergo a *mutation*. This is a biological process of change which can result in a new species, so radical is it. So throughout the 2,000 years of the Church's history, *episcopacy* (the concern of this chapter) has undergone many changes, some of them of the order of 'mutation'. There were, of course, elements of continuity – theological continuity – in terms of function. Bishops in each of the 'ages' have taught, preached, ordained, exercising 'oversight' and pastoral care. However, the social context in which they have done this means that there has been significant discontinuity between the way those functions were perceived and expressed in one age and another. The sociological cultural 'system' in which they operated was different, and that difference affected the expression of the office. Polycarp, the second-century bishop of Smyrna, might just have recognized his office in that exercised by the great Augustine, Bishop of Hippo in the fifth century; but he would be hard pushed to recognize that of Anselm of Canterbury in eleventh-century England, let alone that of Rowan Williams in the Anglican Communion of the twenty-first century.

In Dawson's thesis, the Church is not bound to conform to cultural norms; it is not subject to the limitations of human culture. Nevertheless it can take the forms and institutions it needs from any culture and organize them into a new unity. This new unity becomes the external expression of the Church's spirit and the organ of its mission to the world. In this sense, it reinvents herself and 'makes Church' anew.

Dawson's 'six ages' range from the Apostolic Church, the Graeco-Roman Church steeped in Hellenic culture, the age of Constantine, or 'the age of the Fathers'; the age of the transplanting of Christianity to Europe; the age of Christendom, from the eleventh to the sixteenth centuries; the age of Renaissance and Reformation; and the sixth age (the modern) which follows the age of Reason. My focus in this chapter will be the age of Renaissance and Reformation, the age in which Anglicanism (though it was not called that then) was born. In particular, I will look at the work of two figures who were important in the formation of Anglican identity: John Jewel and Richard Hooker. But there is an implicit question throughout my essay: are we now at the beginning of a seventh age?

The age of Renaissance and Reformation

The sixteenth-century mutation that led to a new Church in England was not isolated from events in Europe, but the interpretation of what happened is, of course, controversial. As I understand it, Luther was not the *cause* of 'the Reformation' but rather the catalyst for ecclesial change in Europe, which was undergoing one of its periodic mutations. The change in mindset that we associate with 'the Renaissance' signalled the cultural change that heralded a new 'age' for the Church, because society was changing. This was a volatile situation which provoked excitement as horizons opened up, bringing evidence of a new world; excitement as national groupings became more confident; excitement as neglected ideas were examined again when books from the East circulated in Europe – all these excitements helped to transform a monkish university debate in 1517 into an international event, and catapulted Luther into prominence. This created a situation in which, as a result of the 'Luther factor', a permanent theological gap between separated understandings of the gospel resulted in new ecclesial groupings.

The underlying issue in all these new groupings – and in this, England was no exception – was '*By what authority* do we understand, live and preach the gospel?' Humanists such as Erasmus and Thomas More – both later to oppose Luther – questioned the way the tradition had developed and the 'authority' for this development. Bible or Church? Which should be the ultimate authority? This question persisted throughout the Reformation 'age', and persists in various forms today.

In his well-known *Utopia*, More allowed his character Raphael to articulate a rather ambiguous position with regard to biblical and priestly authority in an interesting hypothetical example. In his response, William Tyndale presses the logic of Raphael's case, and argues,

> If a woman, learned in Christ, were driven unto an isle, where Christ were never preached, might she not there preach and teach and administer the sacraments, and make officers? . . . Nay, she may not consecrate. Why? If the Pope loved us as well as Christ, he would find no fault therewith, though a woman at need ministered the sacrament, if it be so necessary as ye make it.[4]

Here an illuminating argument is implied: does the conception of 'Church' serve the ministry, or is the ministry there to serve the Church? Should we not be reinventing the Church so that people's gospel needs are met, by a leadership and ministry based on service?

England experienced four legislative 'Reformations'. The first of these legislative 'Reformations' took place under Henry VIII between 1529 and 1547 and separated the Church of England from papal jurisdiction and made the king 'Head of the Church of England'. Important issues of authority were also raised in the establishing of an English text of the Bible in all churches in 1538. While the English text was made available, in accordance with reforming principles, it was chained in churches, in order that the common people should not be able to read it and discuss it at home, and come to possibly 'wrong' opinions about its meaning. As the (reforming) Archbishop Thomas Cranmer put it in the 1540 editions, if you want to know what the Bible means, 'Go to thy curate and preacher.'[5] A subsequent Act of 1543 restricted Bible reading on the grounds that it created discord among the uneducated. This was vital for subsequent developments as the 'formation century' for the Church of England unfolded: the Bible is foundational to the tradition, but its interpretation, rather than its words, are the important thing; and that is a function of the Church.

The second legislative Reformation took place under his young son, Edward and the faction around him. In this period, 1547 to 1553, two versions of the Prayer Book (1549 and 1552, the second less conservative than the first) were produced, and an Ordinal, all reflecting the beginnings of real change. The Ordinal, published in March 1550, signals such change but, in this instance, not radical change. First of all, there is unambiguous affirmation of a threefold ministry of leadership in the form of bishops, priests and deacons. The form of episcopal ordination is modelled on the medieval *Sarum Pontifical*, although lacking some of the customary ceremonies.[6] As the Church all over Europe experienced conflict and change, redefining its theology and ecclesiology in a massive transformation from one 'age' to another, the Church of England alone outside the Roman Catholic Church, presented a form of leadership that most resembled that of the immediate past, rather than that of the New Testament. However, it tried to present it as such! The preface to the Ordinal reads:

> It is evident unto all men, diligently reading Holy Scripture and ancient authors, that *from the apostles' time* there have been these orders of Ministry in Christ's Church: Bishops, Priests and Deacons. Which offices were evermore had in such Reverent Estimation that no man might presume to execute any of them except he were called, tried, and examined, and known to have such qualities as are required for the same; and also by Publick Prayer, with the imposition of hands were approved and admitted thereunto by lawful authority. And therefore, to this intent that orders may be continued and reverently used and esteemed in the Church of England, no man shall be taken or accounted to be a lawful Bishop, Priest or Deacon in the Church of England, or suffered to execute any of the said functions, except he be called, tried, examined and admitted thereunto, according to the Form hereafter following.

In the transition to a new Church, even in this most radical part of the process, the immediate past precedent in leadership forms was preserved (including a distinction between 'office' and 'function') on the Reformist principle of appealing to scripture. This was not convincing and was the source of continuing challenge as the debate on the nature of the Church of England continued in the reign of Elizabeth following the seven years interruption of a 'return to Rome' in the reign of Queen Mary.

So the third legislative Reformation began in 1559 as Elizabeth cautiously considered what she had inherited, and what sort of society she hoped to create, for it was the 'discovery of England' that was her main agenda.

The consolidation of the Church of England

The Queen's concern was the building of the nation – currently a nation of factions related to education, hierarchy, wealth and religious belief. As Supreme Governor of the Church of England, she had the power to appoint bishops, and through this leadership to attempt the creation of a Church that would point the nation towards 'unity, peace and concord'. It would have to do this on the basis of the formularies, and the Prayer Book that was part of its foundation – for these, with minor modifications, had been re-enacted after her accession; but in themselves they did not comprise a model. This had yet to be invented.

One of her early appointments to the Bench of Bishops was John Jewel. A former academic at Corpus Christi College, Oxford, he fled to Frankfurt in Mary's reign where he became conversant with both reformers and reformed theology. There was a renewed burst of excitement as the reign began and the hope that 'Utopia' might be born in England, if they could get the changes right. So Jewel became the first divine to justify the emerging ecclesial community in his *Apology of the Church of England*. This was published in Latin in 1560, for its intended audience was the Church overseas, Catholic and Protestant. But it was deemed so effective that it was translated from the Latin into English by Lady Ann Bacon (mother of the future Lord Chancellor) in 1562. The translation was designed to help the English know and understand the nature of their Church, for it is important to understand that they didn't! As I have tried to indicate, the Church of England had not come floating down the Thames, fully formed; it was a fledgling, still in formation.

Jewel's justification of the nature of the fledgling Church, and in particular the form of its leadership, is instructive. His justification is based not solely on the grounds of scripture, but is part of a much more complex case. Bishops, he writes, have their origin in scripture, are developed by precedent and in England gain their authority through the Crown and Parliament (a lay synod in Jewel's view). What is more, their leadership brings 'reasoned and reasonable benefit'. Jewel admits that – reluctantly – the Church of England has become separated from the Catholic Church but affirms and attempts to demonstrate that, as an institution which must change with the times, the Church of England is changing in order to preach the unchanging gospel effectively, to 'promote comeliness and good order'. He contrasts this change with what has happened in the Roman Catholic Church, where 'change' has spelt 'corruption' and where the authority carries no warrant (for the papacy has no basis in scripture) and where their attempt to provide an 'authoritative' General Council is revealed as ridiculous by the sixteenth-century Roman Catholic instrument of reform, the Council of Trent, which he describes as 'a silly convent' which at times has convened only 40 bishops or so – who have then reported back to the pope to ratify their decisions.

In all this, the authority question is uppermost in his mind. Scripture is always referred to in his writing, 'From the Primitive Church we have not departed', but it is never the 'sola scriptura' of John Calvin; it is always scripture interpreted by the Church and tested out in the same part of the tradition judged relevant for the times.

Jewel does not deny that the episcopate is both an 'office' and a 'work', but 'A bishop, as Augustine saith, is a name of labour, and not of honour', and that is Jewel's emphasis; we are making bishops work in this newly emerging Church. The reissue of the Articles of Religion in 1563 ratified episcopal ordinance and that, together with the use of the Ordinal, ensured a continuous government of the Church.

However, beneath the surface of the 'form', the reality was changing – all in the heat of continuing debate, for from 1570 (the year of Elizabeth's final excommunication by the pope) the attack on bishops increased in intensity. The Puritans rightly judged that they would not get the Church they desired while the leadership did not match up to the principles on which a Church should be based. This was not an unreasonable challenge, and one to which I shall return later in reflecting on women bishops in today's Church of England.

A provocative thesis about the fundamental principles on which such a renewed Church should be based were set forward by Thomas Cartwright (1535–1605), a fellow of Trinity College, Cambridge, and for one year, until he was deprived in 1570, Lady Margaret Professor of Divinity. Hailed as the most gifted and learned of the Puritan Divines, Cartwright believed that everything in the structure and life of a Church should be subjected to the positive adjudication of Scripture. He acknowledged that time brought change, but believed that this increased the necessity of constantly monitoring the established order to evaluate whether or not it was 'sound'. Scripture is omnicompetent in this evaluation. St Paul had taught Christians to gain their certainty from 'the Word of God' and Cartwright believed that it was this dependence on scriptural authority that set them apart from the heathen. 'Where they (the heathen) sent men for the difference off good and evill, to the light off reason, in such thinges the Apostle sendeth them, *to the scoole of Christ in his Worde*, which onely is hable thoroughe faith to give them assurance and resolution in *all* their doinges.'[7]

This goes further than the position expressed by the Bishop of London in the reign of Edward VI, that while scripture was the necessary foundation 'required of things to be believed and done of necessity unto Salvation', it was not required in all things that be 'of themselves indifferent'.[8]

As the controversy developed in Elizabeth's reign, the definition of 'things indifferent' (*adiaphora*) becomes crucial; and, in determining this, the debate moves from that of an 'opposition' between the authority of bishop and magistrate on the one hand and the Bible on the other, to that of a debate that has to consider the role of reason in providing 'sureness'.

As Whitgift put it, 'What it *is* to be agreeable to woorde of God.' In his view it was reasonable that there should be nothing that was explicitly forbidden by scripture in the form and life of the Church. Cartwright pressed him to acknowledge the authority of reason as one of his principles – a point Whitgift was reluctant to concede.[9]

It was to be Richard Hooker's role to provide a theological defence of reason as an ingredient in seeking authority for what was done in the slowly evolving Church of England. Richard Hooker (1554–1600) owed his entry to Corpus Christi College in Oxford to Bishop Jewel, and became a Fellow in 1577. Subsequently being appointed Master of the Temple in 1585 where he entered the controversy I have been describing, he crafted what Diarmaid MacCulloch has called 'a huge, enormous book' *Of the Laws of Ecclesiastical Polity* in the 1590s, though some volumes did not appear until half a century after his death.[10]

Historians argue about what were Hooker's aims in writing his treatise. In my view, within a broadly conceived philosophical theology, and against the background of the controversy that had raged the whole of his life, Hooker sought to understand the process of change in society and the Church, and to identify the authority for that change – which is why he is so pertinent to the subject of this chapter.

By the time Hooker was writing his 'huge, enormous book', there was a decline in Presbyterian activism, but Hooker knew it was only a pause, and both moderate Puritans and the ordinary confused churchgoer (there were as many then as now) needed guidance. 'What certainty or knowledge can the multitude have?' he asked. As the Church reshaped itself, a certainty was necessary to commend the reshaping, and it is this that Hooker seeks to offer.

As a basis for his methodology, Hooker argues (like Whitgift and Conformists generally) that, where scripture provides guidance on matters concerning salvation, that is authoritative; but because of what he calls 'the change of times', many church affairs can't be determined by scripture and have to be referred to other sources of authority, and he warns that these taken together provide a probable rather than certain degree of assurance.

What is the greatest of these 'authorities'? It is what we loosely call 'Reason'. Hooker explains:

> The greatest assurance generally with all men is that which we have by plaine aspect and intuitive beholding. When we cannot attayne unto this, there what appeareth to be true by strong and invincible demonstration, such as wherein it is not by any way possible to be deceived, thereunto the mind doth necessarily assent, neyther is it in the choyce thereof to do otherwise. And in case these both do fayle, then which may greatest probability leadeth, thether the mind doth evermore incline.[11]

For Hooker, this is when the guidance of the Holy Spirit is sought; indeed, it is through Reason, guided by the Holy Spirit, that Christians understand the scriptures to be the Word of God, and in interpreting them it is 'a necessary instrument, without which we could not reape by the scriptures perfection, that fruite and benefit which it yeeldeth'.[12]

Hooker bases this reliance on 'Reason' as an authority on his conception of Natural Law: God has endowed humanity with this inbuilt commitment to seek good, and grow according to the purposes of the creator – whether people recognize him or not. By the light of Reason we can determine much about the ordering of both society and Church. This is a theological principle.[13]

The 'Regiment of Bishops'

The major (but not sole) contribution of Hooker to the debate about bishops is in Book VII of his *Laws*. Unfortunately this volume remained unpublished until 1662. It seems that Archbishop Laud, in the early seventeenth century, had a copy but kept it private, possibly because the 'mutation' that Hooker was illustrating and describing was not one with which he was in sympathy.

Richard Hooker challenges Article 39 in the Articles of Religion passed by Convocation in 1563, which endorses the Ordinal of the Book of Common Prayer in stating that 'Bishops, priests and deacons have continued since the Apostles' times'. Hooker says we should 'leave' this generally received persuasion that 'the Apostles themselves left Bishops invested with power above other pastors'. The pattern of bishops, priests and deacons evolved and did so by what Hooker calls 'divine instinct' because the Church needed the 'Regiment of Bishops' for its governance and oversight. They evolve as part of 'positive law' erected by the Church.

However, Hooker insists that the Regiment, not ordained by God but approved by God, takes different forms in different ages: 'the whole body of the Church hath power to alter with general consent and upon necessary occasions even the positive laws of the Apostles, if there be no commandment to the contrary, and it manifestly appears to her that *change of times* have clearly taken away the very reason of God's first institution'.[14] The 'whole body of the Church'? Surely a General Council? Hooker, like Jewel, is sceptical of what purports to be a 'General' Council and writes, in a famous passage about the nature of the Church militant, 'the Catholic Church is divided into a number of distinct societies, every one of which is termed a Church within itself', and in this particular society 'the Parliament of England, together with Convocation, is that whereupon the very essence of all government doth depend'.

So for Hooker, here was that authority, founded on Natural Law, and not contrary to Divine Law, which gives effect to *human* law, having the power to regulate ecclesiastical polity. This was done in Hooker's England 'where there is not any man of the Church of England, but the same man is also a member of the Commonwealth, nor any man a member of the Commonwealth which is not also of the Church of England'. Hooker argues that, in this context, Bishops are right for England. They have, in his view, as much 'precedent' as the leadership of Mr Calvin's choice; for the Apostolic Church which was not yet established, *is not to be made a rule for the constant and continual ordering of the Church*. The Church has the authority to change, and make Canons, Laws and Decrees, 'Neither God being author of laws of government for his Church, nor his committing them unto Scripture, is any sufficient reason wherefore all Churches shall forever be bound to keep them without change.'[15]

Hooker has great regard for the Word of God as delivered in scripture, the great themes of salvation. But he distinguishes this from what in the Church today is called 'biblical Christianity', involving a slavish following of precedent from Apostolic days. Hooker believes that this could lead the Church into grave scandal. He cites the example of the 'Kiss of Peace' at the Eucharist, which was common practice in New Testament times, but he says would cause grave scandal if introduced into worship in contemporary (sixteenth-century) society. The 'change of times' must be taken into account and '*adiaphora*' are those things which may change with the times. They are not 'things that don't matter' but 'are matters not authoritatively offered in scripture as pertaining to *Salvation*'.

So for Hooker, the leadership of the Church may change according to his methodology of being based in Natural Law (Reason) not contrary to Divine Law, and properly authorized by the Church in the society it serves. For Hooker, a bishop in the Commonwealth of England is part of the 'glue and sodor of the public weal' in addition to being

> a minister of God, unto whom with permanent continuance, there is given not only power of administering the Word and Sacraments, which power other Presbyters have, but also further power to ordain ecclesiastical persons, and a power of chiefty in government over Presbyters as well as lay men, and power to be by way of jurisdiction a Pastor even to Pastor's themselves.[16]

In Hooker's time, women bishops were not on the cards because, in sixteenth-century England, the human law (expressing the theological mind of contemporary society) could not envisage them performing those leadership functions. This was not because they were forbidden by precedent or scripture, but because it was thought they wouldn't work in that society: they would not carry 'authority'. Already the 'authority' question – where does it lie? – was shifting, and continued to shift in a changing society over the subsequent 400 years.

Hooker has continually been manipulated to support different causes in this continuing debate. Diarmaid MacCulloch writes: 'Hooker entered the eighteenth century a moderate Whig, a Lockean Whig, a moderate Tory, a ceremonialist parson and a non-juring defender of the Church's apostolic government.'[17]

Hooker has been continually *used* by party. Is that what I am doing in this conversation? I don't believe it is, because Hooker's views on what constitutes certainty in religious matters are fundamental to our present debates and, while they do not carry the authority of having been subscribed to without dispute throughout the history of the Church of England and the Anglican Communion, they do represent a substantial voice in the forming of the Anglican tradition, and carry intellectual weight even in the changed circumstances of the world and the Communion in the twenty-first century. Indeed, what we may call Hooker's historical and cultural awareness sheds light on our current concerns and divisions. He takes seriously a 'mix' of resources which together 'give authority'.

To summarize, there are scriptural warrants in matters pertaining to salvation, but without the Church being tied to the 'biblical Christianity' of the apostolic age; a concern to take seriously the traditions of the 'ages' of the Church, especially the patristic traditions; and the authority of contemporary judgements that arises from being human in a particular age with the duty of offering the gospel for the benefit of that society. For among the 'conformists' of his time, it was Hooker who was insistent that human law has force in the Church and that rational authority should be a regulating influence in human affairs. These laws are 'derived from the law of reason which is written in all men's hearts; the Church hath for ever no less than now stood bound to observe them whether the Apostle has mentioned them or no'. The opposition between 'scripture' and 'reason' today, characterized as the secularization of the gospel and Church, is for Hooker united in a theological principle which informs the developing tradition.

Questions arising

The questions that arise from this conversation with some of our founding fathers are, in my view, not questions concerning precedent – 'How many references to women bishops can we find in the apostolic and patristic periods?' The answer to this question is interesting and important but, in Hooker's methodology, not one that will clinch the argument. The fundamental question that arises is: *what kind of leadership does the Church of the Anglican Communion require?* In this society, mindful of the 'change of times', it must surely be a gender-inclusive leadership, releasing gifts that will change the style of leadership in the Regiment of Bishops as it is already changing the exercise of pastoral ministry.

A second question is: where will this leave those who cannot accept such leadership? While Hooker makes a distinction between bishops 'at large' and bishops 'with restraints' (i.e. with territorial boundaries), it seems to me that, in the light of the tradition, so-called 'flying bishops' are a nonsense. When the Church of England regularizes the current situation and ordains women priests to the episcopal office, then is the time for those who cannot conform to depart. In the long run, this will be much healthier for all concerned than the 'disguised schism' of a third Province. By the Grace of God, it will be 'the parting of friends', but for the unity and mission of the Church of England, it is the best option.

An anecdote about my own change of heart may be of use here. In 1988, I was a consultant at the Lambeth Conference, to help the bishops 'take Lambeth back to their diocese'. During the conference there was much talk about the ordination of women to the priesthood. The Americans were of course at the forefront of this – both for and against. One evening, I found myself (through a long-standing friendship with one of them) at an evening meal in a Canterbury restaurant with a group of bishops opposed to women priests, who were joined by some anxious Church of England bishops. Inevitably, they realized, there would come a time when the issue would have to be faced in England, but there would be some time to prepare. The subject of a non-geographical 'third Province' came up.

The Archbishop of Canterbury at the time was Robert Runcie, and when I went to give some lectures in the USA the following year, he asked me to take some soundings on what people there were saying about the theological and pastoral implications of such a possibility. I did so, and wrote to him on my return, saying that my impressions were favourable and that this might be the pastoral way of holding the Church of England together. Runcie saw the force of this but was not convinced. His anxieties centred on the Anglican Communion as a whole, and he feared that the pragmatic structure and uncatholic nature of a third Province would fracture permanently the theological integrity of the Communion, and impede ecumenical relations with Rome as well as causing an insuperable breach with the Orthodox. (This was in the period when, at the 1988 Lambeth Conference, in his final address he set out the hope for a renewed vision of papal primacy and outlined how Anglicans might approach this as a further step towards unity.) In the last 15 years, I have revised my own views – not least in light of the theological issues raised in this chapter.[18]

The Anglican tradition, in its quest for authority in preaching the gospel message and ordering a Church which expresses the divine presence of Jesus in the Eucharistic community, has something important to say to the Church of God throughout the world. What happens in the Church of England, at the very heart of the Anglican tradition, sends a powerful signal. By allowing a third Province we would be legitimizing in the tradition (to use a simile from Rowan Williams) something like a choral work with one whole vocal part missing – a harmony without the sopranos. Painful and difficult though it may be, I suspect that for the integrity of the pastoral ministry we offer and for our theological cohesiveness in relation to our ecumenical partners, we should follow the logic of our tradition, abandon the idea of a third Province, and move towards the ordination of women to the episcopate with alacrity.

With such issues at stake, the final question concerning women bishops must be, *what certainty or knowledge can the multitude have?* For the decision will affect the future lives and ministry of many who have been nurtured in the Church of England's tradition. The Church of England's methodology, forged in the sixteenth and seventeenth centuries, has never been one that has offered 'certainty'. That 'mix' of resources which Hooker used to tease out a 'polity' does not ring out as clearly as a papal encyclical or a verse of scripture, but it is a way of discernment that offers every member of the Church an opportunity to contribute to the debate and decision-making; *that* is part of our tradition. It is part of Hooker's gift to us that, as we weigh the theological arguments, we include among them an understanding of the cultural shifts that have taken place during our lifetime and evaluate them as part of our theological reflection.

Those of us who were interviewed in bishops' studies, where the smoke of Three Nuns tobacco mingled with Prinknash incense (and who loved it), have to learn to include our sense of loss in a cultural perspective that takes account of Dawson's thesis on the 'ages' of the Church, and evaluates such change as part of the theological debate. Unlike the continental reformers, Anglican conformists tended to believe that church affairs were regulated by a probable rather than absolute degree of assurance. On the basis of these probabilities our forefathers effected change. So should we.

Notes

1 John Jewel, *The Apology of the Church of England*, trans. Anne Lady Bacon, ed. Richard W. Jelf (London: SPCK, 1900), p. 126.

2 For example, Theodora Episcopa in the Church of St Prassed in Rome. See Ute E. Eisen, *Women Officeholders in Early Christianity: Epigraphical and Literary Studies*, trans. Linda Maloney (Collegeville, Minn.: Liturgical Press, 2000).

3 Dawson, Christopher, 'The Six Ages of the Church', in *Christianity and European Culture: Selections from the Work of Christopher Dawson*, ed. Gerald J. Rusello (Washington, DC: Catholic University of America Press, 1998), p. 34.

4 Quoted in David Weil Baker, *Divulging Utopia* (Amherst: University of Massachusetts Press, 1999), p. 68. See also William Tyndale, 'An Answere to Sir Thomas More's Dialogue', ed. Revd Henry Walker (Cambridge: Cambridge University Press, 1850).

5 Cranmer's preface to the Great Bible, in *Documents of the English Reformation* (Cambridge: J. Clarke, 1994), pp. 233–43). For more on this, see my 'English Fears of Social Disintegration and Modes of Social Control 1533–1611', in *The Bible in the Renaissance* (Griffiths, 2001).

6 Namely anointing, putting on of gloves and delivery of the ring and mitre.

7 In Thomas Cartwright, *The Second Reply to an Answere Made of M. Doctor Whitgift agaiainst the Admonition to Parliament* (London, 1575).

8 *Reply of Bishop Ridley to Bishop Hooper on the Vestment Controversy* (London, 1550).

9 See M. E. C. Perrott, 'Richard Hooker and the Problem of Authority in the Elizabethan Church', *Journal of Ecclesiastical History* 49 (1998).

10 Richard Hooker, *Of the Laws of Ecclesiastical Polity*, Books I–IV published 1594, Book V in 1597, Books VI and VIII in 1648 and Book VII in 1662. The edition I have used is *The Works of that Learned and Judicious Divine Mr Richard Hooker*, 2 vols (Oxford: Oxford University Press, 1850). The basis for this edition is the text edited by John Keble (4 vols, 1836). An accessible modern edition is *The Folger Library Edition of the*

Works of Richard Hooker, gen. ed. W. Speed Hill (Canbridge, Mass. and London: Belknap Press, 1977–93).

11 Ibid., I.xv.4.

12 Ibid.

13 Hooker writes of 'theological reason, which, out of principles in Scripture that are plain, soundly deduces more doubtful inferences': 'Mr Hooker's Answer to the Supplication that Mr Travers Made to the Council', in *The Works of Mr Richard Hooker*, vol. 2, p. 693.

14 Hooker, *Laws*, VII.v.8; italics mine.

15 Ibid., III.x.2.

16 Ibid., VII.iii.1.

17 'Richard Hooker's Reputation', *English Historical Review* (2002), pp. 803–4.

18 The Eames Commission, set up by the Archbishop of Canterbury to report on 'The Communion and Women in the Episcopate' in 1989, did not recommend a parallel Province, but supported the idea of Episcopal Visitors, which had already been debated in the USA as a temporary way of holding the Communion together over a time of crisis. See *Episcopal Ministry: The Report of the Archbishops' Group on the Episcopate* (London: Church House Publishing, 1990), pp. 246–9.

Bibliography

Baker, David Weil, *Divulging Utopia* (Amherst: University of Massachusetts Press, 1999).

Bray, Gerald Lewis (ed.), *Documents of the English Reformation* (Cambridge: J. Clarke, 1994).

Cartwright, Thomas, *The Second Reply to an Answere Made of M. Doctor Whitgift against the Admonition to the Parliament* (London, 1575).

Dawson, Christopher, 'The Six Ages of the Church', in *Christianity and European Culture: Selections from the Work of Christopher Dawson*, ed. Gerald J. Rusello (Washington, DC: Catholic University of America Press, 1998).

Eisen, Ute E., *Women Officeholders in Early Christianity: Epigraphical and Literary Studies*, trans. Linda Maloney (Collegeville, Minn.: Liturgical Press, 2000).

Hooker, Richard, *The Folger Library Edition of the Works of Richard Hooker*, gen. ed. W. Speed Hill (Cambridge, Mass. and London: Belknap Press, 1977–93).

Jewel, John, *The Apology of the Church of England*, trans. Anne Lady Bacon, ed. R. W. Jelf (London: SPCK, 1900).

MacCulloch, Diarmid, 'Richard Hooker's Reputation', *English Historical Review* 107 (2002), pp. 773–812.

Perrott, M. E. C., 'Richard Hooker and the Problem of Authority in the Elizabethan Church', *Journal of Ecclesiastical History*, 49 (1998), pp. 29–60.

Strudwick, V., 'English Fears of Social Disintegration and Modes of Social Control 1533–1611', in *The Bible in the Renaissance*, ed. Richard Griffiths (Aldershot: Ashgate, 2001).

8 Women and the Integrity of Anglican Orders

John Gladwin

ONE OF THE KEY CHARACTERISTICS of Anglican orders is the bond that holds the threefold ministry of bishops, priests and deacons together in unity. Indeed, it is a principle of Anglican orders that these three offices should not be divided. This is given practical expression in the requirement of all who are ordained priest to have been made deacon, and in the necessity of all who are called to the episcopate to have been in priest's orders.

It is therefore a serious matter, with the potential for introducing a fissure into this unity, for barriers to be created between one order and another. Twice in recent history in the Church of England, we have allowed the sex of a person to prevent them from proceeding from one order to another. Women were ordained deacon and so brought into holy orders on the basis that they may not proceed to priesthood. Then when that barrier was removed in 1994, another was created to keep them from being called to the office of bishop in God's Church. There is no other incident in the history of the Church where such action has been pursued. The Church's present position on women bishops is illogical and untenable.

There may have been pragmatic and pastoral reasons, concerning the reception of the ordained ministry of women, which justified such action. To make these arrangements anything but transitional (that is, to retain the bar to women bishops) would be to change the character of our orders. To deny some of our priests the possibility that the Church might call them to the ministry of bishop would introduce disorder into the heart of the ordained ministry. To do so on the basis of the humanity God has given to the individuals concerned raises disturbing questions about our obedience.

Others in this book will stress the issues of justice, inclusivity and the credibility of our testimony to the gospel in our culture. I share all these concerns. However, I want to put alongside these arguments one which suggests that a decisive and disciplined move to remove the final barrier to women and the practice of ordained ministry is not innovation but an act of affirmation of something excellent in our tradition.

I believe it is time to act. The common life of the episcopate is impaired in the contemporary world by the absence of women whom God is calling to this office.

9 A Roman Catholic's View on the Apostolicity of Women

Tina Beattie

IN THE ROMAN CATHOLIC TRADITION, the question of women bishops might seem hypothetical in the extreme, given the apparent *impasse* on the issue of women's ordination. Nevertheless, it is interesting to consider the theology of women's ordination in the context of the sacrament of Holy Orders, which is threefold: bishop, priest and deacon. The sacrament of Holy Orders has come to be understood as a distinctive category, which constitutes a 'spiritual and indelible character imprinted on the soul of the recipient of ordination'.[1] The distinction between the order of deacons and the priesthood is more clearly defined than that between priests and bishops,[2] but the latter tends to be represented in terms of degrees of participation in the fullness of the apostolic ministry, so that the priesthood is hierarchically subordinate to and derivative of the episcopacy. The Vatican II document, 'Decree on the Ministry and Life of Priests', explains the relationship as follows:

> Christ sent the apostles as he himself had been sent by the Father, and then through the apostles made their successors, the bishops, sharers in his consecration and mission. The function of the bishops' ministry was handed over in a subordinate degree to priests so that they might be appointed in the order of the priesthood and be co-workers with the episcopal order for the proper fulfilment of the apostolic mission that had been entrusted to it by Christ.[3]

According to this definition, apostolic authority constitutes the basis of the episcopacy and therefore of the priesthood. Given that there is a single sacrament of holy orders whose legitimacy derives from apostolic authority, the question of whether or not Christ conferred apostolic authority upon women is central to the debate about women's ordination. If women were indeed included as apostles, then it is difficult to justify the continuing exclusion of women from the sacrament of holy orders.

The Vatican has issued a number of documents justifying the exclusion of women from the sacramental priesthood. The most significant of these was the 1976 Declaration on the Admission of Women to the Ministerial Priesthood, *Inter Insigniores*,[4] issued by the Congregation for the Doctrine of the Faith. The declaration appeals to the tradition of the Church, the attitude of Christ and the practice of the apostles to defend its argument against the ordination of women. It goes on to explore the significance of the ordained priesthood in the context of the mystery of Christ as revealed in the nuptial relationship between the male Christ as bridegroom and the feminine Church as bride. Scripture, tradition and sacramental symbolism together are therefore interpreted in such a way as to entail the preservation of a masculine priesthood.

In 1994, Pope John Paul II issued an apostolic letter, *Ordinatio Sacerdotalis*, in which he reaffirms the position of *Inter Insigniores*. His final paragraph seeks to silence further discussion of the question of women's ordination by declaring 'that the Church has no authority whatsoever to confer priestly ordination on women and that this judgment is to be definitively held by all the Church's faithful'.[5] This stops just short of a pronouncement of infallibility, but it gives considerable power to those who would silence any debate or discussion about women's ordination.

But within Catholic teaching there is potential for doctrinal development, informed by scripture and tradition, that would allow for the ordination of women both to the priesthood and the episcopate (for within Catholic thinking it makes no sense to ordain a person to one order while holding that they are ineligible in principle for ordination to another). Insofar as the Anglican Church regards itself as part of one Holy Catholic Church, and understands its bishops to stand in the line of Apostolic Succession, the position I outline here might include an Anglican as well as a Roman Catholic perspective. With this in mind we can explore what theological perspective might emerge from focusing on the complex figure of Mary Magdalene and her role as the apostle to the apostles, a title used in the early Church, late antiquity and the Middle Ages.

Who is Mary of Magdala?[6]

In Eastern Christianity, Mary Magdalene has always been known primarily in association with her witness to the resurrection. However, in the Western Church she has also traditionally been identified with Mary the sister of Martha (see Luke 10.38–42; John 11.1–44), and with the woman who anointed Jesus (Matthew 26.6–13; Mark 14.3–9; Luke 7.36–50; John 12.1–8). This woman is identified in John's Gospel as Martha's sister, Mary (John 11.2, 12.3), and in Luke's Gospel she is described as 'a woman in the city, who was a sinner' (Luke 7.36–50).[7] Some attribute this apparently mythical construct to the homilies of Pope Gregory the Great, who in 591 said of Mary Magdalene:

> She whom Luke calls the sinful woman, whom John calls Mary, we believe to be the Mary from whom seven devils were ejected, according to Mark. And what did these seven devils signify, if not all the vices? It is clear my brothers that the woman previously used the unguent to perfume her flesh in forbidden acts. What she therefore displayed more scandalously, she was now offering to God in a more praiseworthy manner. She turned the mass of her crimes to virtues, in order to serve God entirely in penance, for as much as she had wrongly held God in contempt.[8]

In the first Roman Missal to be adopted universally in the Catholic Church in 1570, Mary Magdalene was designated a 'penitent' in the liturgy. The readings for her feast day on 22 July were taken from the Song of Songs (3.2–5, 8.6–7) and Luke's story of the sinful woman who anointed Jesus' feet. However, the revised Roman Missal published in 1970 after the Second Vatican Council substitutes the resurrection appearance in John's Gospel for the reading from Luke's Gospel, and it makes no reference to Mary as a penitent sinner.

In the last two centuries, various ancient non-canonical texts have been discovered which provide evidence of Mary Magdalene's widespread influence within some early Christian groups, as one who was particularly loved by Christ and gifted with special insight and understanding. The most significant of these writings is the *Gospel of Mary*, which records a conflict between Peter and Mary Magdalene over the question of her teachings and leadership.[9]

In recent years, feminist interpreters have argued that the depiction of Mary Magdalene as a sexually fallen, reformed sinner diminishes her status as a woman who was known as the 'apostle to the apostles' in the early Church. In fact, the more positive image of Mary Magdalene as a preacher and disciple persisted well into the Middle Ages, as can be seen from a wide range of medieval art and devotions. This has been discussed by a number of scholars such as Susan Haskins and Katherine Ludwig Jansen. Dan Brown's popular novel *The Da Vinci Code* exploits and distorts serious recent scholarship and textual discoveries to portray her as a central character in an alternative, woman-centred Christian tradition, identifying her as the woman sitting next to Jesus in Leonardo's famous painting 'The Last Supper'.[10]

Bearing in mind the complex task of deciphering a narrative with so many themes and interpretations, let me turn to a closer examination of possible alternative reading of scripture and tradition. Mary Magdalene's enigmatic presence throughout the Christian story might indicate that she was a woman with a particular revelatory message that is only now being fully explored, through the timely combination of the discovery of ancient texts, the emergence of feminist scholarship, and the pressing question of women's ordination.

Scripture, tradition and priesthood

Prior to the publication of *Inter Insigniores* in 1976, Pope Paul VI asked the Pontifical Biblical Commission to investigate the question of women's ordination from the perspective of the scriptures. The Commission's report notes the extent to which Jesus went against the conventions of the Jewish world of his time by surrounding himself with female followers, and it points to the significance of women as disciples and witnesses to the resurrection.[11] In particular, referring to the fourth Gospel it notes that 'After the resurrection, the evangelist emphasizes the role of Mary Magdalene whom tradition will call "the apostle of the apostles".'[12] The report acknowledges that 'The masculine character of the hierarchical order which has structured the church since its beginning . . . seems attested to by scripture in an undeniable way', but it goes on to ask, 'Must we conclude that this rule must be valid for ever in the church?' It finishes with the observation that 'It does not seem that the New Testament by itself alone will permit us to settle in a clear way and once and for all the problem of the possible accession of women to the presbyterate.'

Thomas P. Rausch observes that the difference between the Pontifical Commission's report and *Inter Insigniores* lies in the significance they attach to the practice of the early Church.[13] While both interpret the historical evidence as pointing to an exclusively masculine priesthood, the Commissioners ask to what extent this should be binding on the future Church, while *Inter Insigniores* takes it as evidence of the will of the risen Christ regarding the nature of the ordained priesthood in perpetuity. In this respect, Rausch points out that discerning the will of Christ does not entail a straightforward appeal to the historical Jesus, but is concerned rather with the ways in which the practices of the primitive Church reflect the guidance of the Holy Spirit. Rausch quotes Raymond Brown, who explains that

> . . . in speaking of the will of *Christ* ecclesiologists are going beyond the ministry to the risen Lord who acts through the Spirit. Classical church statements attribute the institution of sacraments and church

> order to Jesus Christ the Lord and not simply to what a modern scholar would call the Jesus of the ministry.[14]

Such provisos are necessary for anyone attempting to justify the nature of the priesthood through an appeal to the will of Christ, because the New Testament never calls the apostles priests (*hierei*), although biblical scholars argue that some of the other language used to describe Jesus' appointment of the Twelve evokes the ritual functions of Israel's priesthood.[15] My concern here, however, is to apply this method of discerning the will of the risen Christ to the resurrection appearance to Mary of Magdala in John's Gospel. In other words, bearing in mind that John's Gospel is believed to be the latest and the most theologically developed of the Gospels, and working on the hypothesis that it therefore offers a reliable guide to the ways in which the will of the risen Christ was being discerned by at least one branch of the primitive Church, I ask what chapter 20 of John's Gospel tells us about women's ministry.

The fact that all four Gospel writers report that women were the first witnesses to the resurrection[16] would seem significant for anyone attempting to discern the will of the risen Christ according to the criteria described above. Before asking to what extent the apostles represent the 12 tribes of Israel, or how closely the Christian priesthood is modelled on the priesthood of ancient Israel, or whether or not Christ initiated an ordained priesthood at the Last Supper, is it not appropriate to ask what message is being communicated to the early Church in this privileging of women witnesses at the resurrection? Yet it is as if the first resurrection appearances have been written off as a mere footnote or as incidental to the real message of Christ. For example, in 1 Corinthians Paul confidently asserts that the risen Christ

> . . . appeared to Cephas, then to the twelve. Then he appeared to more than five hundred brothers and sisters at one time, most of whom are still alive, though some have died. Then he appeared to James, then to all the apostles. Last of all, as to one untimely born, he appeared also to me. (1 Corinthians 15.5–8)

Brown, explaining this passage in the context of Christ's appearance to Mary Magdalene in John 20.11–18, writes:

> Paul recalls the tradition of the appearances of Jesus to show that, even if he came out of time and last of all, he did see the risen Jesus, just as did the other well-known apostles. There is no reason why such a tradition should have included an appearance to a woman

> who could scarcely be presented as either an official witness to the resurrection or as an apostle . . . [T]he resurrection appearances were first reported to root Christian faith in the risen Jesus and to justify the apostolic preaching . . . [A]ppearances to women and to minor disciples would be put in the background and would not form part of the kerygma.[17]

This is a revealing commentary, especially given the earlier quotation from Brown, which refers to 'the risen Lord who acts through the Spirit'. In John's Gospel, Mary goes running to collect Simon Peter and the beloved disciple when she discovers the empty tomb. Returning with her, Peter goes into the tomb and finds the burial cloths, after which he and the other disciple leave. Mary is left alone weeping, and it is then that the risen Christ appears. This would seem to suggest something decisive and intentional about the resurrection appearance, given that had it happened a few minutes earlier, Peter ('Cephas') might indeed have been the first witness. So must we conclude that in this instance, the risen Christ did not really know his own mind? Did he miscalculate his appearance so that he turned up late and found, not the authenticating witness that Peter would have been, but only a woman, leaving his followers to set the record straight? In appearing to a woman, did he fail to take into account that this 'would not form part of the kerygma' and would therefore have to be ignored? Or must we rather conclude that, from the beginning, the men of the Church have been creating authoritative 'traditions' which, rather than acknowledging women as apostles and priests, have entailed considerable economies with the truth, starting with Paul himself?

Reclaiming tradition

The Catholic tradition encompasses a far more diverse spectrum of ideas and debates than is acknowledged by some modern interpreters. John Wijngaards uses the term 'cuckoo's egg traditions'[18] to describe the ways in which various false teachings have been nurtured that have threatened the integrity of the Christian vision. He points to slavery as an example of a practice which, for more than 1,500 years, was legitimated by church teaching and tradition even though it was 'spurious and contrary to the real tradition handed down from Christ',[19] and he likens this to the present position on women's ordination. Elisabeth Gössman demonstrates the extent to which the question of women's ordination has entailed considerably more subtlety and diversity in the theological tradition than recent Vatican documents acknowledge.[20]

One of the great strengths of the Catholic insistence on the shared authority of scripture and tradition lies in its recognition of the constantly unfolding relationship between history, culture and scriptural revelation, so that at its best, fidelity to tradition becomes not slavish conformity to the practices of the past, but a creative participation in the contexts as well as the contents of the Christian story. This means recognizing faithful feminist interpretation as part of a continuing struggle for authenticity and hope in which every generation must accept the challenge to tell the Christian story well, knowing that past and future generations might have different concepts of what that entails. In offering one particular reading, I am not saying that a feminist interpretation driven by a desire to legitimate the ordination of women necessarily offers a more original or essential meaning than an interpretation driven by a desire to argue against women's ordination, but it may offer a more ethical and revealing perspective in the context of the questions and challenges that confront the Church today. This is not to deny the claim in *Inter Insigniores* that 'Adaptation to civilizations and times . . . cannot abolish, on essential points, the sacramental reference to constitutive events of Christianity and to Christ himself.'[21] It is rather to say that, when the Roman Catholic hierarchy finds itself pitted against the spirit of the times in preserving a position that strikes many inside and outside the Church as unethical – a position that is undermined by a growing body of theological argument, and that cannot be clearly defended even by the Vatican's own biblical scholars – then that position must be challenged. So with these questions of method, interpretation and tradition in mind, let me turn now to the figure of Mary of Magdala, to ask what her story might look like from the perspective of contemporary concerns regarding women's ordination.

The apostle to the apostles

In the sixth century, Gregory of Antioch, in one of his sermons, imagined Jesus appearing to the women at the tomb and telling them, 'Be the first teachers to the teachers. So that Peter who denied me learns that I can also choose women as apostles.'[22] Ann Graham Brock analyses the New Testament and early non-canonical literature in the context of a struggle for apostolic authority between Peter and Mary Magdalene. Brock points to the many different factions in the early Church regarding the status of Mary Magdalene, suggesting that she was a figure of considerable controversy and political wrangling. Although Brock cautions that one cannot use the literary evidence to 'make the sociological leap that automatically pits a Petrine group against a Mary Magdalene group',[23] she argues that within the various factions and groupings of the early Church, there were

> . . . divergent authoritative traditions associated with these two figures [which] differed on at least one critical issue – whether Christ included women in the mandate to preach and proclaim the good news. The texts that call upon Mary Magdalene as the guarantor of their tradition consistently charge female leaders with significant words or visions to share with others. The texts for which Peter functions as the authority figure consistently do not.[24]

She observes that: 'Then, as now, the questions of authority, apostolic status, and women's ordination have proven to be not only highly relevant but also controversial for some.'[25]

In arguing for the apostleship of Mary Magdalene, Brock analyzes the different uses of the word 'apostle' (Greek *apostolos*) and the emergence of the Christian concept of apostleship. In particular, she cites Paul's claims to be an apostle based on the combination of a resurrection appearance and a divine commissioning. So, in Galatians 1.1, Paul introduces himself as 'Paul, an apostle, sent not from humans nor by a human, but by Jesus Christ and God the Father, who raised him from the dead.'[26] In seeking to identify a common theme in the attribution of apostleship by the New Testament authors, Brock argues that, despite different definitions, 'there remains nevertheless a fairly consistent portrayal with respect to two crucial elements: the resurrection appearance narrative and the element of divine intervention'.[27] This leads her to conclude, after a wide-ranging study of the literature, that 'if one takes into account the majority of the resurrection accounts, Mary Magdalene is certainly due apostolic authority'.[28]

Brock's work serves as an illustration of the extent to which new meanings are revealed and new possibilities present themselves if one sets aside claims to textual authority, in order to open up the multiple readings that emerge when texts are read side by side, in creative dialogue and conflict with one another. But to some extent, the practice of intra-textuality is embedded within the Catholic tradition, which has developed many of its symbolic meanings through a multi-faceted interweaving of the Hebrew scriptures with the story of Christ. With regard to Mary Magdalene, this includes references to the Genesis text and the Song of Songs. For example, Hippolytus identifies the women who witnessed the resurrection with the Bride in the Song of Songs:

> Those who were apostles before the apostles, sent by Christ, bear good testimony to us . . . Christ himself came to meet these women so that they should become apostles of Christ and through obedience accomplish what the old Eve failed to accomplish. From now on, in humble obedience, they were to make themselves known as perfected. O new consolation, Eve is called an apostle![29]

John's Gospel refers to Mary Magdalene going alone to the tomb 'Early on the first day of the week, while it was still dark' (John 20.1). The association of Mary of Magdala with the beloved of the Song of Songs evokes the disconsolate Shulamite who searches for her lover through the streets of the city. Mary, rising before dawn and weeping outside the tomb, becomes identified with the woman who says, 'I will rise now and go about the city, in the streets and in the squares; I will seek him whom my soul loves' (Song of Solomon 3.2).[30]

What happens if we read the farewell discourse of Jesus to his disciples in conjunction with the resurrection appearance to Mary Magdalene, incorporating into this the patristic association between Mary Magdalene and Eve, employing the traditional practice of intratextuality I have just described? This would not be an exercise in biblical scholarship as such, but a struggle for meaning whose method is authenticated by the practices of the past, and whose relevance must be formulated by the demands of the present.

The woman in the garden

Among feminist rereadings of the story of creation and the fall in the book of Genesis, Phyllis Trible's careful textual analysis liberates the text from its 'androcentric' and patriarchal interpretations, to offer a vision of a creation redolent with the promise but also the vulnerability of human love, sexuality and desire in a world of harmonious interdependence and care. She suggests that the relationship between the man and woman is 'a love story gone awry',[31] situating Eve's subordination to her husband and his claiming of authority over her within a post-lapsarian world in which 'imperfections become problems, distinctions become oppositions, hierarchies become oppressions, and joy dissipates into unrelieved tragedy. Life loses to Death.'[32]

In Mieke Bal's reading of Genesis, the hierarchical ordering of sexual relationships after the fall has been projected back onto the story of creation by Christian interpreters, lending divine authority to a patriarchal social order that finds no legitimation in the biblical story of creation.[33] In many ways, the story of the encounter between Mary Magdalene and Christ in the garden has suffered from a similar interpretative process. From the beginning, those readings that have been incorporated into the tradition as authoritative have sought ways to deny the most obvious meaning of the text, in order to render the woman subordinate to the other apostles. Other readings such as the *Gospel of Mary*, which might support a different interpretation, have, for a variety of reasons, been excluded from the tradition. The quest for an alternative tradition entails asking if the patristic insight that associates Mary of Magdala with Eve can help to inform a narrative of redemption and restoration which puts women at the centre.

The resurrection narrative in John's Gospel resonates with Christ's farewell discourse at the Last Supper. There, Christ seeks to reassure the disciples about the coming separation, emphasizing the fact that those who love him are incorporated into his relationship with God the Father. He tells them:

> In a little while the world will no longer see me, but you will see me; because I live, you also will live. On that day you will know that I am in my Father, and you in me, and I in you. They who have my commandments and keep them are those who love me; and those who love me will be loved by my Father, and I will love them and reveal myself to them. (John 14.18–21)

Later, the risen Christ reveals himself to Mary Magdalene, the only one who loves him enough to remain weeping outside the tomb, the one of whom the *Gospel of Philip* says, 'The Saviour loved Mary Magdalene more than all the disciples, and kissed her on her mouth often' (*Gospel of Philip* 63.34–5); a kiss which De Boer reminds us must not be understood 'in a sexual sense, but in a spiritual sense. The grace which those who kiss exchange makes them born again.'[34] In words that evoke his farewell to the disciples, Christ tells Mary to 'go to my brothers [*adelphous*] and say to them, "I am ascending to my Father and your Father, to my God and your God"' (John 20.17). It is at least feasible to suggest that the Gospel writer's description of the Last Supper is implicitly gesturing towards the resurrection appearance to Mary of Magdala, in crafting the story with its themes of weeping and joy, revelation and kinship. In the garden, Mary is the disciple who weeps and mourns, and who experiences the joy of the risen Christ. She receives the divine mandate to preach the Good News, and thus she becomes the first apostle. Brock writes that

> The Gospel of John . . . privileges the figure of Mary Magdalene over that of Peter. Rather than being one of two or several women at the tomb, in this gospel she, alone among the women, and indeed alone among all the disciples, is singled out to receive an individual resurrection appearance from Christ. Moreover, she also receives a commissioning from Christ to go tell the others what she has seen and heard.[35]

But there are other symbolic resonances too between the resurrection appearance and the farewell discourse. At the Last Supper, Jesus warns the disciples of the suffering that is to come, and he compares this to the pain of a woman in childbirth:

> Very truly, I tell you, you will weep and mourn, but the world will rejoice; you will have pain, but your pain will turn into joy. When a woman is in labour, she has pain, because her hour has come. But when her child is born, she no longer remembers the anguish because of the joy of having brought a human being into the world. So you have pain now; but I will see you again, and your hearts will rejoice, and no one will take your joy from you. (John 16.20–2)

This image of labour and childbirth seems an improbable choice if only men were present at the Last Supper. Perhaps there is an intended allusion to Eve's suffering, a suggestion that is strengthened if one attributes significance to Jesus' use of the word 'woman' (*gune*) in addressing Mary at the tomb: 'Woman, why are you weeping?' (John 20.15). Some interpreters suggest that when Jesus calls his mother 'woman' elsewhere in John's Gospel (see John 2.4, John 19.26), there is a possible reference to Eve.[36] Patristic writers made a connection between Mary of Magdala and Eve as mother of the living, sometimes pointing to a mystical association between the name Mary and Eve, as in the following quotation from St Peter Chrysologus:

> Mary [Magdalene] came. This is the name of Christ's Mother. Thus, in the *name* there came a Mother; there came a woman, to be the Mother of the living, who had become Mother of the dying, that it might be fulfilled what is written, *This is the Mother of the living.*[37]

This can be interpreted as meaning that the risen Christ liberates the woman from her captivity to a fallen social order, and from the position she finds herself in Genesis when God says, 'I will greatly increase your pangs in childbearing; in pain you shall bring forth children, yet your desire shall be for your husband, and he shall rule over you' (Genesis 3.16). Even as Mary recognizes Jesus as Lord, he refuses to exercise the kind of lordship that Adam exercised over Eve. '*Noli me tangere.*' Do not touch me, or do not 'cling' or 'hold on to' me. The word can be used to suggest sexual contact. In the renewed creation of the risen Christ, the woman is finally released from Eve's burden of misshapen desire: 'Your desire will be for your husband, yet he will lord it over you' (Genesis 1.16). Christ comes not as the man who lords it over women but as the incarnate God who heals, redeems and ordains the human creature, male and female, to be the priest of creation. The woman no longer clings to the man but is invited instead to become the apostle of the risen Christ, sent out from the garden not in shame and silence but in joyful acclamation: 'Mary Magdalene went out and announced to the disciples, "I have seen the Lord"' (John 20.18).

Conclusion

Mary is a ubiquitous and enigmatic presence who pervades the texts and devotions of the early and medieval Church. Hers is a story that reflects the capacity of tradition to develop and change in response to the deepest human needs and questions of every generation, but it is also a story that witnesses to the power of a dominant tradition to stifle competing voices and alternative visions. Reclaiming the place of Mary Magdalene as the apostle to the apostles urges the question: what stands in the way of women becoming bishops, given the role Christ entrusted to the episcopate of fulfilling the apostolic mission?

Notes

All biblical quotations are taken from the *HarperCollins Study Bible, New Revised Standard Version* (London: HarperCollins Publishers, 1993).

1 N. Halligan and eds., 'Holy Orders', in *New Catholic Encyclopedia*, 2nd edn, vol. 7, (Washington, DC: Catholic University of America Press, 2003), p. 41.

2 I want to set aside the issue of women deacons in this essay. While there is clear evidence of women deacons in the early Church, some claim that this was a different order from male deacons and therefore does not set a precedent for the diaconate of women in the Church today, while others argue that women deacons were ordained by the same ordination rite as men, and therefore participated in the same sacrament. See John Wijngaards, *The Ordination of Women in the Catholic Church: Unmasking a Cuckoo's Egg Tradition* (London: Darton, Longman & Todd, 2001), pp. 139–45.

3 'Decree on the Ministry and Life of Priests [*Presbyterorum Ordinis*]', in Austin Flannery (ed.), *Vatican Council II: Constitutions, Decrees, Declarations*, rev. trans. (New York: Costello Publishing, 1996), chap. 1, n. 2, p. 319.

4 References in this article to *Inter Insigniores* are to the numbered version found at <http://www.womenpriests.org/church/interlet.htm>. This website includes links to a range of excellent essays by biblical scholars and theologians questioning the arguments and claims of the Declaration.

5 *Ordinatio Sacerdotalis*, n. 4, at <http://www.womenpriests.org/church/ordinati.htm>.

6 Biblical scholars point out that 'Mary Magdalene' is a misnomer, since it refers to Mary's home town of Magdala and she should therefore be called either 'Mary of Magdala' or 'Mary the Magdalene'. See Carla Ricci, *Mary Magdalene and Many Others: Women Who Followed Jesus*, trans. Paul Burns (Tunbridge Wells: Burns & Oates, 1994), pp. 130–1; cf. Esther de Boer, *Mary Magdalene: Beyond the Myth*, trans. John Bowden (London: SCM Press, 1997), pp. 21–31.

7 For an analysis of these and other scriptures traditionally associated with Mary of Magdala, see de Boer, *Mary Magdalene*.

8 Gregory I, *Homiliarum in Evangelia*, quoted in Lucy Winkett, 'Go Tell! Thinking about Mary Magdalene', *Feminist Theology* 29 (2002), p. 21.
9 This is generally regarded as a Gnostic text, although de Boer disputes this interpretation: see *Mary Magdalene*, pp. 74–117.
10 See Susan Haskins, *Mary Magdalen* (London: HarperCollins, 1994); Katherine Ludwig Jansen, 'Maria Magdalena: *Apostolorum Apostola*', in *Women Preachers and Prophets through Two Millennia of Christianity*, ed. Beverly Mayne Kienzle and Pamela J. Walker (Berkeley: University of California Press, 1998), pp. 57–96; and Dan Brown, *The Da Vinci Code* (London: Transworld Publishers, 2004).
11 The report of the Commission can be found on <http://www.womenpriests.org/classic/appendix.htm>.
12 See part III of the report on the above website.
13 See Thomas P. Rausch, 'Ordination and the Ministry Willed by Jesus', in *Women Priests*, ed. Arlene Swidler and Leonard Swidler (New York: Paulist Press, 1977), pp. 123–31, reprinted with permission on <http://www.womenpriests.org/classic/rausch.htm>.
14 Raymond E. Brown, *Biblical Reflections on Crises Facing the Church* (New York: Paulist Press, 1975), p. 58, n. 45, quoted in Rausch, 'Ordination and the Ministry Willed by Jesus'.
15 See the discussion in Rausch's article.
16 In Mark's Gospel, the resurrection appearances are not included in the earliest and most reliable Greek manuscripts.
17 Raymond E. Brown, *The Gospel According to John (xiii–xxi)* (London: Geoffrey Chapman, 1966), p. 971.
18 Wijngaards, *The Ordination of Women*, p. 5.
19 Ibid, p. 15.
20 See Elisabeth Gössmann, 'Women's Ordination and the Vatican', *Feminist Theology* 18 (1998), 67–86.
21 *Inter Insigniores*, n. 21.
22 Gregory of Antioch, *Oratio in Mulieres Unguentiferas* 11, PG 88, 1863–4, quoted in Ann Graham Brock, *Mary Magdalene, The First Apostle: The Struggle for Authority* (Cambridge, Mass.: Harvard Divinity School, 2003), p. 15.
23 Brock, *Mary Magdalene*, p. 173.
24 Ibid.
25 Ibid., p. 174.
26 See ibid., pp. 6–8. Other passages cited include 1 Corinthians 1.1; 15.3, 5–8; 15.8–11; Galatians 1.11–16.
27 Brock, *Mary Magdalene*, p. 9.
28 Ibid., p. 159.
29 Hippolytus, *On the Song of Songs* XXV.7.6, quoted in de Boer, *Mary Magdalene*, p. 61.
30 See de Boer, *Mary Magdalene*, pp. 5–6.
31 Phyllis Trible, *God and the Rhetoric of Sexuality* (Philadelphia: Fortress Press, 1978), p. 72.
32 Ibid.
33 See Mieke Bal, 'Sexuality, Sin, and Sorrow: The Emergence of Female Character (A Reading of Genesis 1–3)', in *The Female Body in Western Culture: Contemporary Perspectives*, ed. Susan Rubin Suleiman (London and Cambridge, Mass.: Harvard University Press, 1986), pp. 317–38.
34 The quotation from the *Gospel of Philip* and these words from de Boer are taken from de Boer, *Mary Magdalene*, p. 71.
35 Brock, *Mary Magdalene*, p. 60.
36 See Raymond Brown, Karl P. Donfried, Joseph A. Fitzmyer and John Reumann (eds), *Mary in the New Testament* (Philadelphia: Fortress Press, 1978), pp. 188–90.

37 Peter Chrysologus, *Sermones* 64, quoted in Thomas Livius, *The Blessed Virgin in the Fathers of the First Six Centuries* (London: Burns & Oates, 1893), p. 191.

Bibliography

Bal, Mieke, 'Sexuality, Sin, and Sorrow: The Emergence of Female Character (A Reading of Genesis 1–3)', in *The Female Body in Western Culture: Contemporary Perspectives*, ed. Susan Rubin Suleiman (London and Cambridge, Mass.: Harvard University Press, 1986).

Brock, Ann Graham, *Mary Magdalene, the First Apostle: The Struggle for Authority* (Cambridge, Mass.: Harvard Divinity School, 2003).

Brown, Dan, *The Da Vinci Code* (London: Transworld Publishers, 2004).

Brown, Raymond E., *Biblical Reflections on Crises Facing the Church* (New York: Paulist Press, 1975).

—— *The Gospel According to John (xiii–xxi)* (London: Geoffrey Chapman, 1966).

—— *et al.* (eds), *Mary in the New Testament* (Philadelphia: Fortress Press, 1978).

de Boer, Esther, *Mary Magdalene: Beyond the Myth*, trans. John Bowden (London: SCM Press, 1997).

Flannery, Austin (ed.), *Vatican Council II: Constitutions, Decrees, Declarations* (New York: Costello Publishing, 1996).

Gössmann, Elisabeth, 'Women's Ordination and the Vatican', *Feminist Theology* 18 (1998), pp. 67–86.

Halligan, N., 'Holy Orders', in *New Catholic Encyclopedia*, 2nd edn, vol. 7 (Washington, DC: Catholic University of America Press, 2003).

Haskins, Susan, *Mary Magdalen* (London: HarperCollins, 1994).

Jansen, Katherine Ludwig, 'Maria Magdalena: *Apostolorum Apostola*', in *Women Preachers and Prophets through Two Millennia of Christianity*, ed. Beverly Mayne Kienzle and Pamela J. Walker (Berkeley: University of California Press, 1998).

Livius, Thomas, *The Blessed Virgin in the Fathers of the First Six Centuries* (London: Burns & Oates, 1893).

Rausch, Thomas P., 'Ordination and the Ministry Willed by Jesus', in *Women Priests*, ed. Arlene Swidler and Leonard Swidler (New York: Paulist Press, 1977).

Ricci, Carla, *Mary Magdalene and Many Others: Women Who Followed Jesus*, trans. Paul Burns (Tunbridge Wells: Burns & Oates, 1994).

Trible, Phyllis, *God and the Rhetoric of Sexuality* (Philadelphia: Fortress Press, 1978).

Wijngaards, John, *The Ordination of Women in the Catholic Church: Unmasking a Cuckoo's Egg Tradition* (London: Darton, Longman & Todd, 2001).

Winkett, Lucy, 'Go Tell! Thinking about Mary Magdalene', *Feminist Theology* 29 (2002), pp. 19–31.

10 Do We Need Women Bishops?

Christina Le Moignan

THIS IS A LIVE QUESTION, to put it mildly, for both parties to the Covenant of 2003 between the Church of England and the British Methodist Church. But it is not the same question for both parties. Anglicans take for granted the ministry of bishops and ask, 'Should any of them be women?' Methodists take for granted that ordained ministry includes women and ask, 'Should any of them be bishops?' But, though the questions are different, the Anglican debate needs to take into account the Methodist question, and the Methodist approach to answering it. For in a Covenant relationship the parties may not only learn from each other's experience; they need also to be aware of each other's sticking points. What follows, which should be stressed is a strictly personal Methodist view, is offered in that 'Covenant partner' spirit.

Methodists are currently exploring how episcopacy might be 'taken into our system'. This exploration began some years before the Covenant, in the context of developing relationships with the Church of England, but the Methodist Conference of 2000 decided that the question should be looked at independently of any particular existing or potential ecumenical relationships. A working party is accordingly due to report to Conference in 2005 on 'what kind of bishops' we might have (if any). Clearly Methodists will want to take their Covenant partner's understanding and experience of episcopacy with great seriousness, while remaining free to evolve that model of episcopacy which will most closely accord with the Methodist ethos.

In a similar way, while the Church of England will of course make its own decisions about women bishops, it will be wise to take with some seriousness Methodist understanding and experience of the ministry of women. A Methodist contribution to the debate might be as follows:

1 Methodists have an experience to share of the ministry of women as ordained presbyters where women and men are accepted as ministers

without distinction. (That is not, unhappily, to say that all Methodist women ministers have always felt, or been, fully accepted as ministers; but certainly the rules offer no sanction for discrimination against them.) It is not for Methodists to judge a sister Church that had a vastly more complicated situation to face when it decided to ordain women as presbyters. But Methodists would want to make the positive point that the unity of ordained ministers is important, and that the equal treatment of men and women within ministry is part of that unity. Thus an Anglican episcopate which continued to exclude women, or which accepted them with a degree of ambivalence, would be defective in Methodist eyes.

2 Methodists have some limited experience of women in the leadership positions that are most obviously parallel to the Anglican episcopate: Presidents of the Conference and Chairs of District. As the present writer has served in both these roles, it is difficult to be too glowing in the assessment of this experience, but it is her belief that the Methodist Church would want to own this ministry very much as it has the ministry of women presbyters as a whole.

Both these points have underlined experience, and unashamedly so, because Methodists have a belief to share in the validity of experience as a source for theology, alongside scripture, reason and tradition. Of course 'experience' needs careful testing, but we take it seriously as a guide in everyday life, and ignoring it in our theologizing risks that theologizing becoming totally unreal. Methodists are not afraid to say that they *know* from experience that in the ministry of women in episcopal roles they have a gift of God. To deny or give up this gift would be for us to dishonour the giver, and we shall not do it.

And we hope that it is a gift our Covenant partner will be ready to receive.

Authority

11 Can a Woman Have Authority Over a Man? Some Biblical Questions and an Evangelical Response

Rosy Ashley

CAN WOMEN EXERCISE AUTHORITY over men? For many evangelicals, this is the question at the heart of the debate over women bishops precisely because some consider it necessary to have a man in a position of 'spiritual authority', 'covering' women priests in the exercise of their duties. This is supported by an appeal to the doctrine of male headship, which emerges from the notion of a divinely instituted creation order of male authority and female submission. Recent 'role theology' has amplified this understanding of headship with a particular interpretation of biblical material defining certain gender roles.[1] The website of the conservative evangelical pressure group within the Church of England, Reform, provides an example of this way of thinking, stating that 'Men are to take the position of overall leadership and will demonstrate their authority through teaching the whole congregation, while women are to help them in that role and, specifically, are needed to teach and train the women.'[2]

It is not always clear in the teaching on headship whether the 'spiritual authority' possessed by men is envisaged as innate, part of their masculinity and rooted in an ontological suitability for leadership, or a function and responsibility that they are required to undertake. Certainly, much traditional teaching viewed men as inherently more spiritual and rational than women, who tended to symbolize the lower part of human nature, represented by the body and sexuality.[3] As this lower part of the self was seen as the source of sin, women were regarded as innately inferior, with a greater proneness to sin. It made sense in that world view, therefore, to entrust overall authority in spiritual matters to men.

This belief in female inferiority is no longer widely held. However, while men and women are generally now regarded as possessing the same capabilities and essential nature, some argue for a functional difference between men and women, established by a divinely instituted social order of male authority and female submission, rooted in creation itself.[4] Grudem and Piper, as well as Reform, are among the contemporary exponents of this position, which maintains that women cannot hold ultimate authority – not because of inferiority or lack of innate ability, but because of the need to maintain a social order which, having scriptural warrant, is inviolable.

The difficulties in the current debate on headship arise because 'the ethos of both coequal discipleship and the patriarchal pattern of submission can claim scriptural authority and canonicity', as the New Testament scholar Elisabeth Schüssler Fiorenza expresses it.[5] How do we interpret the coexistence and interaction of such seemingly diverse emphases in scripture?

Evangelical interpretations of scripture

Proponents of headship start with the assumption of a divinely instituted, permanent social order of male priority, sometimes supported by an appeal to the eternal subordination of the Son to the Father. Often, 'what is portrayed as the position or experience of women in biblical times is mis-apprehended as what scripture enjoins',[6] with descriptive or occasional practices being universalized into prescriptive norms. There is a paucity of textual material: there are only two passages which directly refer to the male as 'head' (1 Corinthians 11.3 and Ephesians 5.22) and one text which appears to forbid women from exercising authority over a man (1 Timothy 2.12). Nevertheless, these passages have provided a lens through which teaching on the relationship between the sexes has been understood.

Evangelical exegetes, however, are increasingly aware of the need to contextualize the biblical text. The Bible is God's Word 'as God's communication *in* history, not above it or apart from it'.[7] The issue becomes

> not whether a passage is normative but whether the normative principle is found at the surface level (that is, supracultural) or at the principal level underlying the passage (with the surface situation or command applying mainly to the ancient setting). All biblical statements are authoritative; some however, are so dependent upon the ancient cultural setting that they cannot apply directly today since there are no parallels.[8]

The task then becomes one of distinguishing between what is culturally relative and those texts that transcend their original setting, being normative for Christians of all times. To do this, we need to consider the 'headship texts' within the whole framework of scripture. Dick France writes that 'a truly biblical hermeneutic must not confine itself to the overt pronouncements of the apostolic writers, but must be open to the biblical evidence as a whole, including its narrative and incidental parts'.[9] I shall adopt the approach of a number of scholars[10] and prioritize those theological principles and motifs that are rooted in creation, Jesus' ministry and the Bible's own forward-looking eschatological perspective, understanding the particular teaching of the Epistles in this light. Being aware of the cultural conditioning of the text's author, the author's intention in writing and the specific situations addressed will also help discern whether there are genuinely comparable situations today to which the teaching can be applied. Before looking directly at the 'headship texts', therefore, I shall consider the wider context of scripture's teaching on men and women, starting with creation, and looking at Jesus' teaching and early Church practice.

I shall agree with Richard Bauckham that the witness of scripture contains 'a strongly egalitarian *direction* of thought, operating especially to critique relationships of privilege, which gives to one person or class privileges or rights at the expense of others who lack them'.[11] This egalitarianism is manifested both in direct opposition to hierarchical relationships and, less obviously, in accepting hierarchical structures while relativizing and transforming them. I shall attempt to show that, because of cultural and missionary constraints, the egalitarian vision of the new age ushered in by Jesus was unevenly applied in the early Church. However, these seeds of transformation have continued to make an impact on cultures down the ages, subverting slavery and racial and sexual oppression in the movement towards liberation for all.

Creation

Proponents of male headship argue that a creation order of male headship and female subordination was established *before* the Fall, contrary to those who see disharmony between men and women beginning when sin enters the world. The argument for male headship is based on five premises taken from the creation account in Genesis 2: Adam's prior creation; woman being created from part of man; woman being named by man; humankind being called 'man'; and woman's description as 'helper' for man.

Starting with Adam's prior creation, this does not signify superiority, as the remainder of the narrative of creation makes clear. God creates the world before humanity in Genesis 1 and animals before humans in Genesis 2. Equally, the argument of firstborn privilege does not apply to creation.[12] Primogeniture relates to birth, not creation, and only operates in the context of sons (making Adam's priority over a woman, Eve, irrelevant).[13] Another factor is that priority in the Bible does not signify a position of authority, but rather a double portion of inheritance (Deuteronomy 21.17) – nowhere indicated for Adam in contrast to Eve. While the idea that first is superior is certainly prevalent in human culture, it is not a God-given moral principle.[14]

Woman's creation from man (Genesis 2.22) has been seen by some to impute a derivative, non-autonomous existence to woman and therefore an inferior status. However, the argument that woman is inferior because she is derived from man cannot be relied upon unless it is also accepted that man is inferior to dust. The author's purpose is to emphasize the essential unity within humanity, as woman is created from the same nature and substance as man.

Neither does woman being named by man (Genesis 2.23) indicate male priority. Hebrew scholars explain that 'woman' is not a name, but rather a cry of recognition. The grammar of Genesis 2.23 is described as a chaotic expression of joy along the lines of 'one like me!' 'In calling the woman, the man is not establishing power over her but rejoicing in their mutuality.'[15] Naming was a convention in ancient society that denoted rule – Adam exercised dominion over the animals in naming them (Genesis 2.20). However, it is only *after* the Fall that Adam exercises his rule and gives woman a name in the traditional way, calling her Eve (Genesis 3.20).

Some have seen male headship in God naming the human race 'man'.[16] However, the Hebrew 'adam' in Genesis 1.26–8 is the collective noun for mankind, a general reference to human beings which includes women. This is confirmed by Genesis 5.2 which states that, at creation, both male and female were named 'adam'. Furthermore, if 'adam' referred to the male alone, woman would not be included in the expulsion from the garden (Genesis 3.24).[17] The collective noun adam is only used as a proper name for the male *after* the Fall, testifying to the fractured relationship between the sexes. 'No longer denoting undifferentiated humanity, it becomes, in 3.22–4, a generic term that keeps man visible but pushes woman into obscurity . . . Generic *adam* has subsumed *issa* (woman) in the androcentric, fallen world.'[18]

Finally, woman's creation as 'a helper as his partner' (Genesis 2.18) has been interpreted as indicating her suitability for supportive rather than leadership roles. However, this is a misunderstanding of the word 'helper'. The word used for helper (*ezer*) in the Old Testament refers to a person who rescues others in situations of need.[19] Of the 19 uses of the word *ezer*, 15 are about God bringing help to needy people.[20] 'Helper' could therefore suggest superiority (on the basis of its usage about God) yet in this passage it is modified by the phrase '*knegdo*', meaning 'fit for him'.[21] Rather than inferiority or superiority, this denotes supplementation, similarity and total equality.[22] The combination of 'helper' and 'fit for him' denotes partnership, not subordination. The idea here is of man and woman being counterparts.

The author of Genesis 2 details the diversity of humanity, with the creation of sexual difference, in terms of sexual relatedness, not sexual priority.[23] God creates woman because 'it is not good for man to be alone' (2.18). Without woman, man is incomplete, needing relationship not just with God and creation, but also with 'one like him'. Created of the same substance, male and female are ultimately to reunite into one flesh (2.24). 'So far as Genesis 2 is concerned, sexual hierarchy must be read into the text, it is not required by the text.'[24]

Fall

If we read creation in this way, then we can see that the subordination of women to men was not part of God's original design. Rather, it resulted from humanity's sin (Genesis 3.16). Some, however, have argued that the Fall took place because Adam failed to exercise his creation order headship; that Eve demonstrated her need for male authority as she was targeted by the serpent and the first to sin. On this reading, the Fall does not institute male authority, but merely turns its benevolent expression into an oppressive one, characterized by domination.

As we know, traditions developed in both Judaism and Christianity which blamed woman for the entrance of sin into the world.[25] In Genesis 3, however, God is seen to make no distinction in the way that he relates to Adam and Eve after the Fall. He calls them both to account for their sin, and holds them individually responsible.

Similarly, there is nothing in Genesis 3 to indicate that Eve usurped Adam's leadership in being the first to eat from the tree of good and evil. Some have argued that 'your desire shall be for your husband' indicates an innate female tendency to want to control or 'overthrow' a husband's innate authority, based on a similar use of the words 'desire' and 'rule' in Genesis 4.7.[26] However, Bilezikian argues that this interpretation of 'desire' (used only three times in the Old Testament) requires considerable tampering with the biblical text and that the more straightforward interpretation of desire as 'urge for union' makes better sense.[27]

The idea that Adam ruled over Eve prior to the Fall makes the declaration that 'he will rule over you' redundant. Rather, the curse that 'he will rule over you' *introduces* hierarchy; it does not transform an existing rule.[28] Despite the catastrophic consequences of their sin, Adam and Eve are never told that their sin is disobeying God's creation order. God does not hold Adam responsible for them both on the basis of male spiritual authority or leadership. Rather, their sin is disobeying God's command not to eat, Eve through deception and Adam through compliance with that deception.

The emphasis of Genesis 3 is on the mutual nature of sin. Banished from the garden, sin makes an impact on the lives of both men and women, though in different ways. Mutuality of relationship is replaced by a battle of the sexes in which both genders are implicated. The woman desires her husband, but God predicts that man will, in fact, rule over her (3.16). Communion has become conflict and domination replaces desire.

As Judy Brown argues, male rule has come into the world as a result of the Fall and needs to be resisted. It 'is no more God's design than that weeds should overtake the garden'. As we 'medicate as much of the pain out of birthing as possible . . . modernize as much of the toil out of farming as possible . . . use science to avoid physical death, and salvation to avoid spiritual death', a consistent interpretation of the consequences of the Fall requires that male hierarchy be resisted.[29]

It would seem, therefore, that there is nothing in the creation narratives of Genesis 2 and 3 to indicate that God intended men to exercise a headship role over women. In fact, the creation accounts of Genesis 1 and 2 can be read as evidencing a state of mutuality, equality and co-operation between male and female as God's ideal for humankind. Male and female are both made in the 'image of God' with a common calling to exercise joint authority over creation by God and joint responsibility for procreation (Genesis 1.26–8). The 'cultural mandate' is to be exercised together, the Genesis 2 account elaborating this point that 'it is not good for man to be alone' (Genesis 2.18) as humankind was made for community.

Indeed, contrary to the arguments of 'role theology',[30] it is interesting to note that it is only *as a consequence of the Fall* that gender comes to be associated in any way with role or function. God describes how the consequences of humanity's alienation from him will be the fragmentation of their joint responsibilities. Where God intended male and female to exercise authority and rear children together, male and female now become primarily associated with only part of the joint mandate, Adam with dominion over creation and Eve with procreation. Personhood narrows to a focus on just one aspect of being.[31] However, it is worth saying that these curses are descriptive, not prescriptive, and only introduce the *possibility* of sinful behaviour, men and women remaining bearers of the image of God (Genesis 5.1), however distorted that image has become by sin.

Therefore, structures where women are legally and socially subordinate to men[32] can be seen to result from the Fall, not God's creation plan. However, despite the male-oriented cultic legislation in the Old Testament, representing God's accommodation to ancient Near Eastern customs,[33] an 'intrusion ethic' can also be discerned. This 'intrusion into the present of the final order to be brought by Christ'[34] means that mothers are to be honoured as well as fathers (Exodus 20.8), both are included as full members of the covenant community[35] and women receive a measure of legal protection and justice (Exodus 22.16, 22–4). In contrast to other Near East cultures, there are no commands for wives to obey their husbands, or regulations to deal with disobedient wives, or rules to delineate their subordination.[36] The Old Testament contains no doctrinal law or theory that justifies patriarchal structures.[37]

Finally, in terms of role, nothing in the Old Testament indicates 'that the leadership of women over men is somehow alien to their created nature'.[38] Miriam is seen alongside Moses as a national leader (Micah 6.4),[39] Deborah exercises religious, military and political authority over a whole country (Judges 4.4) and Huldah advises the king on God's will for Judah (2 Kings 22.14). Although the number of women leaders is small, they are sufficient to demonstrate that, if God himself commissions women to exercise authority, the principle itself cannot be wrong.[40]

New creation

The teaching of Jesus

Nowhere in the Gospels does Jesus ever speak of the subordination of women or mention 'headship' in his teaching. Jesus' message of salvation is aimed at individuals and takes precedence over headship-led family units (Luke 14.25–7). Both sexes are called to follow him (Luke 9.23) and to do the works of the kingdom (Matthew 28.18; Luke 12.32). The allegiance to Jesus that is required by discipleship makes the same demands on women and men (Matthew 10.37).

Jesus challenged traditional roles ascribed to women throughout his ministry, portraying a totally different attitude from Greek or Jewish contemporaries. Despite being socially marginalized and viewed as religiously inferior and culturally unclean, women were included in the group of disciples travelling with Jesus and, moreover, supporting him financially (Luke 8.2–3).[41] He taught that motherhood was secondary to the call to discipleship (Matthew 12.46–50), that women were to be educated, not restricted to domestic roles (Luke 10.42) and given access to the public arena.[42] He chose women to testify about him and commissioned them to preach the gospel.[43] Having seen the risen Christ and shared with men in the outpouring of the Spirit, women were equally qualified for ministry.

Jesus' teaching urges a social transformation and institutes a new community of brothers and sisters who are all equal servants and Jesus' friends (John 15.15). No longer are there to be 'masters', 'fathers' or 'teachers' among God's people (Matthew 23.1–10).[44] Rather, relationships are to be characterized by mutual service. Allegiance to Christ is to be prioritized over all relationships, particularly family ones (Matthew 10.37–8) and temporal social ones such as marriage which, despite being initiated by God at creation, can be renounced for the sake of the kingdom of heaven (Matthew 19.12), anticipating the new age where there will be no marriage (Matthew 22.30). Jesus is the model for female disciples to follow, as well as male, suggesting that gender is secondary to calling, gifting and character.

Other New Testament teaching

Luke makes Acts 2.17–18 programmatic for the new age. Now that the Spirit is poured out on all, in the life of the Spirit-filled community, 'your sons and your daughters will prophesy . . . my slaves, both men and women . . . shall prophesy'. Similarly, Paul states that now 'in Christ Jesus you are all children of God through faith . . . There is no longer Jew or Greek, there is no longer slave or free, there is no longer male and female' (Galatians 3.26–8). Both indicate that something new has come into being in Christ, underlining that the old social identifiers of race, sex and class are gone, as all are 'one in Christ Jesus', joint heirs in one family. Women and slaves can now fully participate in the worship of the covenant community. All are children of God and heirs, with the same status and inheritance rights (also Romans 8.15; Galatians 4.5–7; Hebrews 12.6).

Some have argued that these texts, particularly Galatians 3.26–8, relate only to equality before God in terms of salvation status with no social implications.[45] However, Snodgrass points out that the text is not primarily referring to salvation status for women and slaves because, although their relation to the law was different from that of free men, they already belonged to the covenant in Israel.[46] Rather, these verses are thought to be early baptismal liturgy,[47] and the equality has social and ecclesial as well as spiritual implications, which were to be embodied in the new kinship relationships within the Church. For Paul, spiritual and social dimensions cannot be separated, as the community of the Church *is* the gospel, demonstrating God's work and character in communities entrusted with the ministry of reconciliation in the world (2 Corinthians 5.14–21).[48] Being one 'in Christ' was to change the way that people related to one another.

Addressing the Jew/Gentile question was Paul's primary concern throughout his ministry, from both a theological and social perspective.[49] Paul passionately opposes Peter and Barnabas' refusal to eat with Gentiles as he is concerned to maintain the unity of fellowship 'in Christ' against Jewish cultural imperialism (Galatians 2.11–14). Paul also addresses the master/slave distinction when highlighting the slave Onesimus' new kinship status 'in Christ' to his master Philemon, calling the slave 'a beloved brother . . . both in the flesh and in the Lord' (Philemon 16). It is interesting to note that, by early in the second century, freedom in Christ was being realized socially as well as spiritually, as churches commonly purchased freedom for slaves on the grounds of their baptism.[50]

Similarly, the phrase 'male *and* female' has social implications for gender relationships within the new community. An unusual term in the New Testament for man and woman,[51] it recalls Genesis 1.27, where male and female are created in God's image and given joint dominion over the earth, underlining their equal status 'in Christ' before one another as well as before God.[52] As this passage is understood primarily in Jewish exegesis to refer to marriage and the family, it is likely that Paul is suggesting that, irrespective of procreative capacities and the social roles attached to them, patriarchal (meaning, literally, rule of the fathers) marriage is no longer constitutive of the new community in Christ. Women 'in Christ' have greater freedom and new options available to them, apart from men.[53]

Paul is not obliterating sexual or racial distinctiveness (as his teaching in 1 Corinthians 11 and Romans 9.4 makes clear),[54] but indicating that all forms of religious, class or sexual privilege are invalid and that there is both soteriological and functional equality for those baptized into Christ. The theologian Miroslav Volf writes: 'What has been erased in Christ is not the sexed body, but some important culturally coded norms attached to sexed bodies (such as the obligation to marry and procreate and the prohibition of women from performing certain functions in the church).'[55]

This social and functional equality within the community of the Church is evidenced in Paul's teaching on ministry in the body of Christ. All are priests (1 Peter 2.5, 9; Revelation 1.6, 5.10) and indwelt by the Spirit (Philippians 4.6–7). Authority to minister is eschatological, being based on the gift of the Spirit, not gender. Ministry is also corporate for the building up of the body (Romans 12.3–8; 1 Corinthians 12—14; Ephesians 4.11–12) and belongs to the whole community of faith. All are called to teach, admonish, judge, comfort, instruct and exercise discernment for themselves (Colossians 3.16; 1 Corinthians 2.15).

The practice of the early Church witnesses to the impact of this teaching. Women prophesy, lead house churches, teach and act as apostolic messengers (Junia in Romans 16.7). Priscilla was Paul's co-worker, accompanying him to Ephesus, hosting two churches

(1 Corinthians 16.19; Romans 16.4–5), and explaining 'the way of God' to Apollos (Acts 18.26), who then taught the whole Corinthian Church. Priscilla's name is placed in the text before her husband's, indicating that her ministry role was probably the more significant within the marriage.[56] Phoebe is named as a deacon, the same term applied to Apollos and Paul, of the church at Cenchreae (Romans 16.1–3). Paul appeals to his 'fellow workers' Euodia and Syntyche in a general letter to the Church in Philippi (Philippians 4.2), indicating their prominence and influence.[57]

There is no indication that women leaders in the early Church were instructed to have a man in 'spiritual headship' over them, as in some churches today. Paul advocates singleness for women for the purposes of ministry (1 Corinthians 7.34) with no mention of the need for male headship, revolutionary in a culture where women were not highly regarded and were vulnerable through lack of education. When Paul lists the single women who accompanied him on his travels, he does not suggest that they differed from men in that they taught only under his authority, or that the messenger/apostle Junia's ministry was 'covered' by his authority. While arguments from silence are never conclusive, Paul's writings suggest that the criterion for ministry was the anointing of the Spirit and opportunity, not gender.

It is hard, therefore, to argue for any universal model of male authority against the background of these examples of church leadership in the New Testament. Authority to minister in the early Church was both eschatological and social, vested in groups of elders. It is likely that these elders were male, given Greco-Roman social customs. Certainly, this is Paul's assumption when he refers to elders as being 'the husband of one wife' (1 Timothy 3.2; Titus 1.6), expecting them to be married men, not polygamous or divorced and remarried. However, he does not insist that elders can *only* be male. Given the radically counter-cultural sociology of the Christian community, it is probable that some prominent women would have assumed leadership roles. Certainly, women such as Nympha and Lydia would have led the churches meeting in their houses as an extension of their role as master of the household (Colossians 4.15; Acts 16.13–15).[58] While it is unclear what level of authority the named women who ministered in the Church exercised, there is no teaching *prohibiting* women from holding either the office of deacon or bishop.

'Headship' passages

We must now look at the passages directly referring to male headship, 1 Corinthians 11.2–16 and Ephesians 5.21–33. The first passage has traditionally been interpreted as establishing a principle of male 'headship' and female submission in the Church, and the second, of establishing this in the home. Other texts, such as 1 Timothy 2.11–15 and 1 Corinthians 14.33–5 are then interpreted through this headship perspective.

What does 'head' mean?

Before looking at the passages themselves, it is worth considering the meaning of 'head' (*kephale*). The traditional assumption has been that 'head' denotes a relationship of authority between man and woman, husband and wife. However, recent exegetical studies have established that there is, in fact, no established theological connection between 'head' and 'authority over'.[59] When 'head' had an authoritative sense in Hebrew (e.g. the head of a tribe), the translators of the Old Testament into Greek avoided using *kephale*, choosing other words that unambiguously conveyed a sense of rule and leadership.[60] Despite the hundreds of references in the New Testament to religious, governmental, civic, familial and military authority figures, none of them is ever designated as 'head'.[61]

Non-biblical usage of 'head' also reflects this view. Sporadic references in ancient literature to the head as ruling part of the body do not necessarily indicate a relationship of 'authority over', but rather pre-eminence and representation.[62] In any case, there was no unanimous agreement among philosophers and writers that the head was the ruling part. Onians writes that 'Plato favoured the head, Aristotle the heart, and Epicurus the chest, while the Stoics were divided'.[63] In contrast to our rationalist age, Paul and first-century readers saw the heart, not the head, as the source of decision-making and reason,[64] regarding the head as the source of life.[65]

Egalitarians have tended to favour the Greek understanding of 'head' as 'origin of life' as Paul's meaning in 1 Corinthians 11.3,[66] particularly in light of its metaphorical usage in Ephesians 4.15 and Colossians 2.18.[67] Recent research, however, has suggested a broader range of meanings for 'head', incorporating ideas of 'origins' alongside the most natural metaphorical sense of 'prominent, foremost, firstborn, representative'.[68] The head was prominent, representative of the whole body[69] and the most honoured part of the body (see 1 Corinthians 12.21–4).[70] This prominence might have come from being the origins of another or have a leadership significance but 'the metaphorical use of *kephale* does not of itself introduce ideas of authority or sovereignty into the text'.[71]

It is interesting to note that outside of Paul's letters the metaphor 'head' is nowhere found to describe either the relationship between husband and wife, or relations between men and women generally. We have to try, therefore, to determine what Paul means from the content of the passages themselves.[72]

1 Corinthians 11.2–16

The traditional interpretation of this passage has hinged on an authoritative understanding of verse 3, 'the husband is the head of his wife'. It has often been assumed that this establishes a top-down hierarchy between Christ and man, husband and wife and God and Christ, indicating relationships of authority and subordination.[73] The rest of the passage is interpreted in the light of male headship, with head coverings symbolizing woman's submission to men and the use of the creation narrative being seen as legitimating an extension of male headship to the Church.[74]

This interpretation may have partly been influenced by translating the human pair in verse 3 as 'man and woman' (NIV, NEB, KJV) rather than 'husband and wife' (NRSV) – the same expression is used in Greek for these two English expressions. However, Paul's argument in the passage is about shame and honour, and makes most sense of his choice of the metaphor 'head' if the marriage relationship is in view.[75] Even if 'man and woman' is preferred on the basis of Paul's later reference to creation (8, 9), the man and woman in question is the first married couple, so the marriage relationship seems to be the context for Paul's remarks.

Alternative readings of the passage suggest that Paul's concern is not primarily with marriage or male–female relations but with ensuring that both sexes wear gender-appropriate head coverings or hairstyles during public worship. His aim is to show that gender difference, symbolized by head coverings and hairstyle, does not have to be denied for there to be full equality in Christ. Set in the context of chapters 8 to 10, the passage reflects Paul's ongoing concern that individual freedom be limited for the sake of unity within the Church,[76] effective witness outside it,[77] and concern for the glory of God (10.31—11.1).

It is not clear exactly what was going on in Corinth or what practices Paul's comments relate to. It is possible that some men were wearing their hair long (1 Corinthians 11.4)[78] and some women either loosing their hair, common in cultic activities (11.5)[79] or not covering their heads when prophesying.[80] Rather than the traditional view that women were flouting convention to claim an authority not rightfully theirs, Mary Evans suggests that Paul is responding to concerns raised by women that 'by following convention, women were denying the equality of status with men that was now theirs in Christ'.[81] Whatever the practice, head coverings had a religious, class and sexual significance and were important symbols of male and female gender identity, incurring shame when gender boundaries were disrespected.[82]

Paul uses three arguments to persuade the believers to maintain culturally appropriate practice in public worship. The first is located in the shame/honour culture of Corinth (11.4–7).[83] He uses the metaphor 'head' to illustrate the theme of relational dependence running through the passage. When Paul writes 'Christ is the head of every man, and the husband is the head of his wife, and God is the head of Christ' (11.3), his concern is not with hierarchy but with relationships that bring glory and honour or shame and disgrace.[84] Through respecting gender-distinctive customs, men and women can bring honour to themselves (their own heads) and also to their metaphorical 'heads'.

Paul's second argument (11.7–12) uses the theme of creation to reinforce his point that men and women are in a position to bring glory or dishonour to one another through their created differences. First, referring to the Genesis 2 creation account, Paul argues that both sexes were created to reflect the nature and attributes of another: man's creation giving God glory and woman's bringing glory to man. The motif of glory relates 'woman *to man* as his *glory,* since in the social order she owed honour to man'.[85] Indeed, her very creation honours man, who, while coming first in creation, was incomplete, needing one who was 'flesh of my flesh' to complete the creation of humanity.[86] Woman is not the glory of man in a derivative sense (woman is not created in man's image) but because she brings completion to the creation of humanity and honour to it. Consistent with this relatively high view of women, Paul argues in verse 10 that a woman should cover her head in worship 'not because she is in the presence of man, but because she is in the presence of God and his angels'.[87] Then, in a radical affirmation of equality, Paul declares that she has authority to decide for herself about covering her head (literally, she has power over her own head).[88] He uses language of obligation to reinforce his point that he wants women to exercise authority and decide for themselves how to behave.[89]

Nevertheless, Paul says in verse 11, despite women having authority to decide for themselves how to dress in public, he stresses relational interdependence once again. Women's authority is qualified by the recognition that 'in the Lord' neither sex is independent but rather mutually dependent upon one another. And while the Genesis 2 creation order might mirror a patriarchal social order as reflected in the Church in Corinth, new creation 'in the Lord' points to Genesis 1, where there is no gender priority but 'all things come from God' (11.12). Sexual difference no longer means hierarchy, but interdependence and mutuality, for 'just as woman came from man, so man comes through woman' (11.12). 'This comparison cancels out the exclusive privilege of man: just as in the beginning Eve was made from Adam's rib, in all subsequent history man is born through woman.'[90] Women can prophesy as *women,* both maintaining their gender distinctiveness with head covering and exercising their gifts with freedom.

Paul's third argument (11.14–15) is that 'nature itself' (the fact that women's hair grows longer than men's) should help church members decide what to do. This underlines that these are social, not doctrinal matters, in Paul's eyes. While he is keen to urge them to recognize the impact of their behaviour on one another and to honour cultural practices when prophesying in public, he gives the Corinthians the freedom to 'judge for yourselves' what is socially acceptable practice (11.13).

Is Paul establishing a principle of male headship?

Paul uses the metaphor 'head' in this passage to relate wives to husbands and the Church to Christ, not to establish a principle of male headship. As we have seen, 'head' has no established meaning of 'authority over' and Paul uses the metaphor to convey a relational understanding, underlining positions of prominence and representation, and the existence of another upon whom the 'head' depends (a 'body', although not specified here until 1 Corinthians 12.12–27). He is not legitimating this relational inequality, instituting first-century relationships as a model for all time, but showing Christians how to live within a patriarchal shame–honour culture.[91]

Attempts to support male headship have been made by arguing that an eternal subordination of roles exists between Christ and the Father within the Trinity.[92] However, subordinationist or hierarchical interpretations of the Trinity were condemned in the fourth century as heretical, and continue to be rejected today.[93]

Paul's use of the creation narratives has nothing to do with legitimating a creation order reflecting male headship (which, as we have seen, is hard to argue from Genesis 1 or 2 creation accounts). Rather, he uses the creation narratives selectively to make two points. First, gender difference is God-ordained and can be honoured without a loss of freedom, as difference does not mean hierarchy 'in the Lord'. Secondly, men and women were made by God for mutual dependence, so should consider the impact of their behaviour on one another.

Finally, while Paul is addressing the whole Church and their conduct in public worship, his reference to headship relates to husbands and wives, not men and women in the Church. He does not extend the application of the metaphor of husband as 'head' of his wife to the Church. Christ alone is head of the Church, his body – man is only head of his wife. Men are not required to exercise 'headship' authority over the women in the Church. Indeed, Paul's only reference to authority in the passage is that possessed by women, who are free to exercise their prophetic gifting publicly in ways they deem culturally appropriate.

Ephesians 5.21–33

This text has been particularly influential in the argument for male headship as it is the only one that brings together the idea of male 'headship' and female submission. It also refers to the husband as 'head' of his wife in the context of the 'household codes'. Similar teaching can be found in 1 Peter 2.11—3.7, Colossians 3.18—4.1 and Titus 2.1—3.2, calling husbands to love and wives to submit, although there is no mention in these of the husband as 'head'.

To understand Paul's teaching, we need to consider his use of the household codes. The social order of his day was rooted in the hierarchically structured household of Aristotelian political philosophy.[94] The household was the basic unit of Greco-Roman society, and, while there were cultural variations among Jewish, Greek and Roman families, generally speaking households were run by a male *pater familias.* He had absolute power over his family in everything, including religion and moral conduct. Marriage was regarded as a secular, private affair, a practical necessity, contracted between families for financial and property reasons.[95] It was essentially unequal, wives generally being much younger than their husbands, and their role being to procreate. Failure to produce children often resulted in divorce. The patriarchal order of the household was considered a paradigm for the state.[96] Conversions to Christianity were regarded as politically subversive[97] as 'the Christian missionary movement conflicted with the existing order of the patriarchal household because it converted *individuals* independently of their social status and function in the patriarchal household'.[98] The small, non-influential New Testament churches therefore existed in uneasy relationship with suspicious and oppressive Roman governors.

Social conformity, therefore, had an apologetic purpose, to protect the Church from hostile criticism (1 Peter 2.15; Titus 2.3f.) while presenting a cultural defence of Christianity which gains it a better hearing in Roman society and makes the gospel attractive to unbelievers (1 Peter 3.1f.).[99] Authority structures were to be seen as 'God's servant for your good' (Romans 13.4), taxes were to be paid and respect shown to the Emperor (1 Timothy 2.2; 1 Peter 2.13).[100] In terms of household behaviour, Balch writes that its 'primary purpose . . . was to reduce the social–political tension between society and the churches'.[101] Fee comments that it was already shameful to convert to Christianity. It would never have occurred to Paul 'to add shame to shame by dismantling the *structure* of the household. That was simply in place. What he *did* do was in some ways far more radical: he applied the gospel to this context.'[102]

Paul then uses the household codes to show the Ephesians how to put away their former life (4.22) and adopt a new way of living within the existing structures of society. They are to 'live in love' (5.1), as 'members of one another' (4.25), being filled with the Spirit (5.18) which enables them to sing, give thanks (5.19–20) and 'be subject to one another out of reverence for Christ' (5.21).[103] The principle of mutual submission was to guide relationships between *all* believers. Radically departing from convention, Paul addresses every household member, starting with those with least power, showing them how to submit.

Once again, the metaphor 'head' acknowledges that the husband is the head of his wife, referring to the husband's position of prominence in the social order. As Perriman puts it, this is 'an observation about how things *are* rather than a prescription of how they *ought to be* on the basis of some theological or scriptural principle'.[104] However, the husband's headship is to be exercised like that of Christ.[105] It is not Christ's lordship that is analogous to the husband's headship, but Christ's self-giving. The allusion is to Christ as Saviour.[106] Being 'head' is to be seen, not in terms of rule, but of service.

Christ's headship is *for* the Church (Ephesians 1.22)[107] and he nourishes and equips his body as Saviour (Colossians 2.19; Ephesians 4.15).[108] So the husband is to use his position of influence as 'head' to benefit his wife. Rather than expecting to be served, he is to love his wife *for her good.* As Christ put the Church first in all things, so the husband is to put his wife's interests before his own, living to please and benefit her, as she does him (1 Corinthians 7.34).

Our contemporary expectation of love in marriage obscures the impact of Paul's teaching to husbands. Contrary to traditional codes that called husbands to lead or rule,[109] he three times calls them to love (*agapao*) their wives (5.25, 28, 33).[110] Paul interprets love very practically. Husbands are to care for[111] and feed (and possibly clothe) their wives (5.29a).[112] Her physical needs are to be regarded as of *equal* importance to her husband's needs (5.28a, 29, 33), thus raising her to the same level as him. The social reality was that husbands were in a position to abuse or neglect their wives and needed to be instructed how to love by Paul.[113]

Klein comments that these commands to the men would have been radical. 'A few partial parallels . . . exist in the ancient world, but none enjoins as sacrificial an abandonment of men's own rights and privileges as Paul's statement.'[114] Rooted in the teaching of Jesus, husbands are to learn from him and use their power as he did.[115] Christ as head lives to serve the body – so must the husband. This sacrifice of self in the service of another is directed towards the communion of love, as two become one flesh in the mutuality God intended at the heart of marriage (Ephesians 5.31).

Paul spends much less space calling on wives to submit. Perriman points out that the omission of the verb 'submit' in verse 22 indicates 'that subordination within the household is more of an accepted fact than a deliberate objective and that it is . . . the manner of subordination ('as to the Lord') that are of primary concern to Paul'.[116] The wife's submission is to her *own* husband[117] and his social *position*, not his masculinity. The 'authority to which the woman bows in her subordination to man is not the latter's but that of the *taxis* (order) to which both are subject'.[118]

Indeed, while submission is, in theory, always voluntary,[119] there is a close correlation in this and similar passages between the language of submission and obedience.[120] Although wives, unlike slaves, are not required to obey but only to submit, the example of submission given in 1 Peter 3.6 is Sarah's obedience to Abraham, indicating that submission can involve obedience.[121] In Titus, slaves are told to submit to their masters. 1 Peter calls wives to 'accept the authority of their husbands' (1 Peter 3.1). Paul explains wives' submission to their husbands with the word 'respect' (Ephesians 5.33), which literally means 'to fear' them.[122] It is likely that the freedom for wives to choose whether or not to submit to their husbands was strictly limited.

The need to submit to the social order does not seem to denote the equality that some have seen in Paul's call for mutual submission (Ephesians 5.21) but more reciprocity of response. Each household member had a responsibility towards another in the social order, but those responsibilities had different expression. However, the emphasis on the husband loving does not preclude the wife from loving – it is part of her call as a Christian (e.g. Ephesians 5.1; John 13.34; Romans 13.8). Similarly, husbands are not excluded from the general command to Christians to 'become slaves to one another'. (Galatians 5.13)

Is Paul establishing a principle of headship?

It is sometimes argued that, because of the allusion to Christ, Paul is teaching a universal principal of spiritual headship in marriage. However, Paul's concerns here are practical – the husband's headship and the wife's submission are socially and historically located, not spiritual or universal, and are set in the context of the authority structures of the day. Paul's equation of the husband's role with that of Christ as saviour (Ephesians 5.25) is based on the husband's *social* role as the provider for his wife (5.28, 29). There is no spiritual responsibility for the cleansing and holiness of his wife – this task belongs to God.

The wider witness of scripture confirms this view. Wives are also called to submit to non-Christian husbands (1 Peter 3.1), indicating the submission is a social not a spiritual requirement. The story of Ananias and Sapphira (Acts 5.1–11) also illustrates the absence of a principle of spiritual headship in marriage.[123] Peter questions both Ananias and

Sapphira separately about the deception perpetrated by Ananias with which Sapphira colludes. There was no headship defence for Sapphira. She is expected by Peter and the Holy Spirit to have made her own spiritual judgement and rejected the scheme as sinful. Both are held individually accountable for their sin (as were Adam and Eve) and both die.[124]

There are six instances in the New Testament where women are called to submit. As with the parallel instructions to slaves to submit, three of the six different instructions to women relate to expediency or appropriateness,[125] one relates to submitting to the husband's position of 'head' in the social order (Ephesians 5.22), one is an obscure reference to 'the law' (1 Corinthians 14.34), which probably relates to Jewish oral law,[126] and one relates to submitting to the Church's teaching (1 Timothy 2.11). Christ's voluntary submission in the incarnation is the most common example for all exhortations to wives and slaves to submit, encouraging free people to choose, within the limits of social structures, to follow Christ's example of assuming the role of servant (Mark 10.45; Luke 22.25–6).

By contrast, the doctrine of headship teaches that female submission is not voluntary, but part of the creation order replaces a voluntary action with an obligation and duty. This is a distortion of Christian relationships, which are not to be characterized by duty, obligation or obedience, but love. In linking submission and authority in ways that Paul does not, headship precludes the very expression of relational love that Paul is keen to promote.

The argument that God institutes particular social orders has been used historically to legitimate the divine right of kings, slavery and apartheid among other things.[127] It is human beings, not God, who are responsible for social ordering, reflecting the values of those holding power in the community.[128] The male headship that Paul recognizes in 1 Corinthians 11.3 and Ephesians 5.23 refers to a social arrangement, not an ontological endowment of male authority. This is further attested by Paul's encouragement of female celibacy (1 Corinthians 7.34, 40), indicating that women neither need a husband as a 'head' nor are designed for a particular supportive role.

1 Timothy 2.11–15 and 1 Corinthians 14.34, 35

These texts are also important in the case for male headship as they appear to support the idea of male and female roles. In both, women are restricted in the exercise of certain ministries in the Church. Paul's reference to creation order in the former text and 'the law' in the latter are deemed to give this teaching universal application.

Before briefly considering this argument, it is important to note that there is no mention of male headship in the pastoral Epistles. Despite the strong emphasis on good government within the Church in the face of heretical teaching by women, there is no command to husbands to rule their wives well, keep them under control or even to teach them.

At first sight, Paul's first letter to Timothy appears to forbid the exercise of female authority in the Church. It gives significance to Adam being created first and appears to legitimate male priority on the basis of the intrinsic moral weakness in woman. However, this text is not about church order but false teaching, which is being spread by local elders[129] Many men and women are being led astray (1 Timothy 1.3, 4.1, 5.15; 2 Timothy 3.6; Titus 1.11) and so Paul is writing to reverse existing policy. Women, who have been teaching in the churches in Ephesus, are now forbidden from doing so. Spreading heresy seems to have been a particular problem among women, perhaps because they were less well educated and therefore more open to being deceived. Alternatively, the likely Gnostic content of the teaching might have been attractive, with its claims to female priority.[130]

Whatever the reason, Paul's emphasis in this passage is that women should learn (1 Timothy 2.11)[131] so that they will not be deceived and lead others astray as Eve did.[132] Despite the prevalent view in Jewish and Hellenistic literature that women were inherently more gullible and prone to deception than men,[133] Paul stresses that the woman 'became a sinner' through deception – it was not part of her nature (2.14).[134] Paul stresses Adam's created priority (2.13) to counter claims that women were created first and to point to men's social and educational advantage in society. However, Paul does not legitimate this advantage, but seeks to address it in calling for women to learn.

Furthermore, the prohibition on women exercising authority does not relate to the ordinary exercise of authority.[135] Rather, it has the sense of dominating or exerting negative influence over another, and even has an association with murder.[136] The King James Version translates it 'to usurp authority over'. The Kroegers have suggested that the verb can also mean the 'ultimate creative source' or 'origin of', suggesting a translation 'I do not allow a woman to teach nor to proclaim herself author of man.'[137] Again, Paul might have used this particular word to address Gnostic heresies that taught that Eve was the creator of Adam. His comment that woman is saved through childbearing (1 Timothy 2.15) can also be explained as countering Gnostic views that marriage and childbirth were evil (also in 5.14).[138]

Paul's prohibition in 1 Timothy 2.12 therefore relates to uneducated women teaching heresy and seeking to dominate men in first-century Ephesus. There is no indication that his reference to creation order establishes universal male and female 'roles', as proponents of role theology have recently argued.[139] Neither does his reference to Eve's deception indicate that women have 'different inclinations' making them more prone to relationships than analysis, as some proponents of headship have read into this text.[140] Rather, Paul is using what Giles describes as '*ad hominem* arguments' to relate to specific problems found in the Church at that time, countering the arrogance of some women and their opportunities to give false teaching.[141] As Paul's reference to creation order does not legitimate universal female head covering (1 Corinthians 11.8, 9) neither does it legitimize the universal exclusion of women from teaching or exercising authority in the Church.

It is with this in mind, and in the light of Paul's encouragement of women to publicly prophesy in 1 Corinthians 11.5 that the passage in 1 Corinthians 14.34, 35 calling for women to be silent in church must be understood. A straightforward explanation of this text is that Paul is prohibiting questions during worship, a common way of learning in the Greco-Roman world. However, Perriman points out that in society at large, women did not speak publicly in either synagogue or public *ekklesia*, but only in the ecstatic cults. Paul therefore appeals to Jewish customs ('the law') to reinforce the prohibition on speech, concerned to avoid offending Jewish converts or visitors from the synagogue next door.[142] He is once again concerned about shame and public acceptability, calling women to submit to church order (1 Corinthians 14.40)[143] and to learn from their better educated husbands at home.[144]

Summary of Paul's teaching as it relates to gender

While the equal status of all believers is clearly taught in the New Testament, the teaching of the Epistles, which relate to specific situations, indicates that the outworking of this freedom was constrained by missionary and cultural concerns and also the expectation of the imminent return of Christ.[145] Paul's missionary imperative colours all that he does, accommodating himself to people and customs 'for the sake of the gospel' (1 Corinthians 9.19–23). He deals with gender in the same way as other marks of social status, maintaining a tension between conforming to societal norms and inward motivation. He both castigates circumcision (Galatians 5.2) and has Timothy circumcised (Acts 16.1–3), encourages slaves to gain their freedom where possible (1 Corinthians 7.21), and regulates the practice of slavery (Ephesians 6.5–9), encourages women to remain single for ministry (1 Corinthians 7.34) whilst telling them to submit to their husbands (Ephesians 5.22) and wear head coverings when prophesying in public (1 Corinthians 11.5).[146]

Paul's teaching maintains the tension between creation, culture and eschatological life in Christ, addressing the 'complex life setting of his readers with its multiple, overlapping, and mutually contradictory contexts'.[147] It is important that we, too, hold all these elements in tension when approaching these texts to distinguish between teaching relevant only to first-century culture and that which has universal application.

Conclusion

The current Supreme Governor of the Church of England with authority over male bishops, is, of course, a woman. At the same time, Christ is the head of the Church, not any monarch or bishop. No believer is head over another. As John Barton has written: a woman who is made bishop 'will not be claiming to be the "head" of anything . . . [but] only to be exercising a necessary but limited ministry for and on behalf of the whole church'.[148] To imply that bishops have headship is at odds with the dictates of the gospel and is anyway not borne out in experience. Again, to quote Barton: 'I have seldom heard any Evangelical ascribe to his or her bishop the kind or range of authority that would really constitute 'headship' in a sense incompatible with its being exercised by a woman.'[149]

The general witness of scripture gives no reason why women should not exercise similar authority in the Church to men. To suggest that they cannot exercise episcopal authority because of a divinely ordained difference in function, is simply unbiblical. The dominion given to both sexes at creation, the ministry of Jesus and much of the teaching and practice of the New Testament testify to this. Biblical passages which imply restrictions on women occur in the context of specific situations arising in the early Church as it interacted with its culture. To universalize this teaching distorts its meaning and sanctifies first-century cultural practices. In scripture, God commissions women to rule, judge, command, proclaim his will, correct, reprove, teach and train.[150] Taking an evangelical perspective, there is nothing either in the nature of woman or in God's will as revealed in scripture to exclude women from exercising authority when and where God calls them.

Notes

1 'A man, just by virtue of his manhood, is called to lead for God. A woman, just by virtue of her womanhood, is called to help for God': R. C. Ortlund, 'Male–Female Equality and Male Headship', in *Recovering Biblical Manhood and Womanhood: A Response to Evangelical Feminism*, ed. Wayne Grudem and John Piper (Wheaton, Il.: Crossway, 1991), p. 102.

2 Carrie Saudom, 'The Biblical Pattern for Women's Ministry – Limiting or Liberating?', at <http://www.reform.org.uk/tabloid/2000/womens-ministry.html>.

3 See Rosemary Radford Ruether, *Sexism and God-talk* (London: SCM Press, 1983), p. 79. This traditional position is reflected in the writings of most of the Patristic and

medieval theologians. Aquinas, for example, argues that the 'exclusively reproductive purpose of female existence makes women creationally subjected to men, who have stronger rational equipment': Kari Borreson, 'God's Image. Is Woman Excluded? Medieval Interpretation of Gen. 1,27 and 1 Cor. 11,7', in K. Borresen (ed.), *The Image of God: Gender Models in Judeo-Christian Tradition* (Oslo: Solum Forag, 1991), p. 225.

4 This was Calvin's position, summarized by Ruether: 'The hierarchical order is not a reflection of differences of human nature, but rather of differences of appointed *social office*. The man rules not because he is superior but because God has commanded him to do so. The woman obeys not because she is inferior but because that is the role God has assigned her': *Sexism and God-talk*, p. 83; italics here and in all other quotations in this article are in the original.

5 Elisabeth Schüssler Fiorenza, *Bread Not Stone* (Boston: Beacon Press, 1983), p. 92.

6 Roger Nicole, 'Biblical Authority and Feminist Aspirations', in *Women, Authority and the Bible*, ed. Alvera Mickelson (Leicester: InterVarsity Press, 1986), p. 43.

7 David Scholer, '1 Timothy 2.9–15 and the Place of Women in the Church's Ministry', in Mickelson, *Women, Authority and the Bible,* p. 215.

8 Grant Osbourne, *The Hermeneutical Spiral* (Leicester: InterVarsity Press), p. 327.

9 R. T. A. France, *A Slippery Slope? The Ordination of Women and Homosexual Practice: A Case Study in Biblical Interpretation* (Cambridge: Grove Books, 2000), p. 23.

10 For example, Willard Swartley argues for prioritizing 'theological principles and basic moral imperatives rather than . . . specific counsel on particular topics when these two contradict': *Slavery, Sabbath, War and Women: Case Issues in Biblical Interpretation* (Waterloo, Ont.: Herald Press, 1983), p. 230. See also Richard Longenecker, 'Authority, Hierarchy and Leadership Patterns in the Bible', in Mickelson, *Women, Authority and the Bible,* p. 81, and Kevin Giles, *The Trinity and Subordinationism* (Downers Grove, Il.: InterVarsity Press, 2002), pp. 247–50.

11 Richard Bauckham, *God and the Crisis of Freedom: Biblical and Contemporary Perspectives* (London: Westminster/John Knox Press, 2002), p. 118.

12 In the ancient world, primogeniture granted special privileges (primarily inheritance rights) to the firstborn male of the family. It was a culturally driven practice, bound up with family survival issues. It was often overturned in the Old Testament for more important considerations – e.g. with respect to Jacob and Esau.

13 Andrew Perriman, *Speaking of Women* (Leicester: Apollos, 1998), p. 178.

14 Rebecca Groothuis, 'Leading Him Up the Garden Path', *Priscilla Papers*, 16(2) (Spring 2002), p. 11.

15 Phyllis Trible argues that the Hebrew verb for 'to call' only indicates the establishment of power over something when linked with the noun 'sem' (e.g. when naming a child). This noun is absent in Genesis 2.23b but is present after the Fall when Adam names the woman Eve. See *God and the Rhetoric of Sexuality* (Philadelphia: Fortress Press, 1978), p. 99.

16 Raymond Ortlund, 'Male–Female Equality and Male Headship: Genesis 1–3', in Grudem and Piper (eds), *Recovering Biblical Manhood and Womanhood,* p. 98.

17 Mary Hayter, *New Eve in Christ: The Use and Abuse of the Bible in the Debate about Women in the Church* (London: SPCK, 1987), pp. 107–8.

18 Ibid., p. 108.

19 See e.g. Exodus 18.4; Deuteronomy 33.26, 29; Psalm 33.20; 70.5.

20 Clarence J. Vos, *Women in Old Testament Worship* (Delft: Judles & Brinkman, 1968), p. 15. Perriman writes that the use of *boethos* in the Septuagint (to translate *ezer*) is regularly applied to God and has the sense of an independent person who makes up another's lack. He points out that the word does not comment on the status of the helper, but rather on the one in need of help: *Speaking of Women*, p. 179.

21 Mary Evans, *Woman in the Bible*, 2nd edn (Exeter: Paternoster Press, 1998), p. 16.

22 Perriman, *Speaking of Women*, p. 179.

23 Evans, *Woman in the Bible*, p. 17.
24 Paul K. Jewett, *Man as Male and Female* (Grand Rapids: Eerdmans, 1975), p. 126.
25 To give just two examples: Ecclesiasticus 25.24, 'From a woman sin had its beginning, and because of her we all die'; Chrysostom writes that the whole female sex is 'weak and fickle' because Eve 'nagged' her husband to follow her into sin: *Homilies on Timothy* IX, in *A Select Library of the Nicene and Post-Nicene Fathers*, ed. Phillip Schaff, series 1, vol. 13 (Grand Rapids: Eerdmans, 1979), pp. 435f.
26 Susan Foh argues that 'desire' in Genesis 3 has the same meaning as in Genesis 4.7, where sin desires to master Cain, in the sense of possess or rule him: 'What is the Woman's Desire?', *Westminster Theological Journal* 37 (1974), pp. 376–85.
27 The former interpretation of 'desire' requires the insertion of the idea of 'overthrow' into Genesis 4.7: 'sin is lying at your door; its desire is to overthrow you, but you must master it'. Bilezikian argues that this interpretation requires treating the noun 'desire' as if it were a verb (desiring to overthrow), which does not make sense of the third use of 'desire' in the Old Testament (Song of Solomon 7.10). Rather, 'desire' should be seen as indicating 'an urge for associative union', resulting in the translation favoured by the NIV, 'sin is crouching at your door; it desires to have you, but you must master it': Gilbert Bilezikian, *Beyond Sex Roles: What the Bible Says about Woman's Place in the Church and Family* (Grand Rapids: Zondervan, 1997), pp. 264–6, n. 12.
28 William Webb has reviewed other blessing/curse formulas in Genesis. He concludes that, as all curse formulas initiate change in status and introduce conflict and hierarchy, this is a further indication that woman was not subordinate to man before the Fall: *Slaves, Women and Homosexuals* (Downers Grove, Il.: InterVarsity Press, 2001), p. 119.
29 Judy Brown, 'I Now Pronounce You Adam and Eve', *Priscilla Papers*, 13(4) (Fall 1999), p. 1.
30 A relatively recent doctrine of the essential equality but functional or role difference of male and female has been propounded by writers such as Wayne Grudem. Unlike the traditional position, which assumed female inferiority and therefore role difference, this doctrine separates nature from role and owes more to Hellenistic thinking and the nineteenth-century doctrine of separate spheres than to the witness of Scripture. For an in-depth look at this teaching, see Kevin Giles, *The Trinity and Subordinationism*.
31 Iain Provan, 'Why Bother with the Old Testament regarding Gender and Sexuality?', in *Christian Perspectives on Gender, Sexuality and Community*, ed. Maxine Hancock (Vancouver: Regent Publishing, 2003), p. 36.
32 For example, a Hebrew daughter sold into slavery could not go free as male slaves could (Exodus 21.7) and men could divorce their wives if they did not please them (Deuteronomy 24.1–4).
33 God tolerates practices such as polygamy (Deuteronomy 21.15–17) and slavery (Leviticus 25.44–6) which contradict his teaching as he 'reveals his covenant, redemptive purposes to men and women in divine accommodation to the cultural patterns in existence at the time when he gives his word': Harvie M. Conn, 'Feminist Theology', in *New Dictionary of Theology*, ed. S. B. Ferguson (Leicester: Inter-Varsity Press, 1988), p. 257.
34 Ibid., p. 257.
35 Women were, however, excluded from the priesthood, perhaps because of ritual uncleanness: Evans, *Woman in the Bible*, p. 30.
36 Vos, *Woman in Old Testament Worship*, p. 46.
37 Evans, *Woman in the Bible*, p. 25.
38 Ibid., p. 31.
39 Ruth B. Edwards, *The Case for Women's Ministry* (London: SPCK, 1989), p. 32.
40 Anne D. Atkins, *Split Image: Discovering God's True Intention for Male and Female* (London: Hodder and Stoughton, 1987), p. 135.

41 His choice of only male apostles was symbolic of the twelve tribes of Israel, which he had come to reach (Matthew 15.24), excluding both women and Gentiles. However, this has not disbarred male Gentiles from assuming all levels of church leadership and equally cannot disbar women.

42 John 4.4–26. The responsibility for male lust, one of the primary reasons for women's social exclusion and covering, is firmly placed on men (Matthew 5.28–30).

43 The male-dominated legal system, in which women's testimony was invalid, is contrasted to Jesus' choice of women to witness to his Messiahship (John 4.26) and his resurrection (Luke 24.6, 7; John 20.17).

44 Cf. Bauckham, *God and the Crisis of Freedom*, p. 125.

45 See, for example, James Hurley, who maintains that Paul was not speaking about relations within the body of Christ: *Man and Woman in Biblical Perspective* (Grand Rapids: Zondervan, 1981), p. 127.

46 Klyne Snodgrass, 'Galatians 3:28: Conundrum or Solution?', in Mickelson (ed.), *Women, Authority and the Bible*, p. 178. However, in Jewish law, the religious status of slaves and women was significantly inferior to that of men. They could be members of Israel under the law but could not fulfil their membership in the same way as a man or inherit the same blessings. See Perriman, *Speaking of Women*, p. 187

47 Social, sexual and ethnic differences are now irrelevant for salvation 'in Christ'. See Ben Witherington, 'Rites and Rights for Women – Galatians 3.28', *New Testament Studies* 27 (1981), pp. 593–604.

48 Richard Hays, 'Ecclesiology and Ethics and 1 Corinthians', *Ex Auditu* 10 (1994), pp. 31f.

49 Stephen Lowe argues from Romans and Ephesians that the paradigm of the Jew–Gentile relationship indicates that the theological status obtained in Christ has an impact on functional and social dimensions of existence for Gentiles within the body of Christ: 'Rethinking the Female Status/Function Question: The Jew/Gentile Relationship as Paradigm', *Journal of the Evangelical Theological Society* 34(1) (March 1991), p. 71.

50 At the beginning of the second century, Ignatius wrote to the Bishop of Smyrna telling him not to set free either male or female slaves at the Church's expense, presupposing that slaves who joined a Christian community anticipated their freedom being bought by the Church: Elisabeth Schüssler Fiorenza, *In Memory of Her: A Feminist Theological Reconstruction of Christian Origins* (London: SCM Press, 1983), p. 209.

51 Often mistranslated as 'male nor female', it broke the previous parallel structure.

52 Edwards, *The Case for Women's Ministry*, p. 55.

53 See Fiorenza, *In Memory of Her*, p. 211, and Witherington, 'Rites and Rights for Women', p. 599. This alternative for women to the traditional patriarchal marriage role is underlined in Paul's teaching on singleness in 1 Corinthians 7 and the understanding that marriage is a temporary social relationship which does not continue in heaven (Matthew 22.30).

54 Some have interpreted Galatians 3.28 as Gnostic, calling for an androgynous obliteration of sexual distinctiveness – see Robert Jewett, 'The Sexual Liberation of the Apostle Paul', *Journal of the American Academy of Religion* 47, supp. 1 (1979), pp. 65–9; Wayne A. Meeks, 'Image of the Androgyne: Some Uses of a Symbol in Earliest Christianity', *History of Religions* 13 (1973/4), pp. 185–6. However, Fiorenza points out that in early Christian theology 'male and female' was understood to refer to the first couple, as in Mark 10.6: *In Memory of Her*, p. 211.

55 Miroslav Volf, *Exclusion and Embrace* (Nashville: Abingdon Press, 1996), p. 184.

56 Indications of priority in leadership by the ordering of names can be seen in the early descriptions of Barnabas and Saul's relationship (Acts 11.26, 30; 12.25; 13.1–2, 7), which subsequently comes to be written as 'Paul and Barnabas' (Acts 13.42–3, 46, 50; 14.1, 23; 15.2, 12, 22, 35). See Webb, *Slaves, Women and Homosexuals*, p. 99.

57 Jewett, *Man as Male and Female*, p. 146.

58 Gordon Fee, 'Gender Issues: Reflections on the Perspective of the Apostle Paul', in Hancock (ed.), *Christian Perspectives on Gender, Sexuality and Community*, p. 75.

59 Anthony Thiselton, *The First Epistle to the Corinthians* (Carlisle: Paternoster Press, 2000), pp. 816–22, and Perriman, *Speaking of Women*, pp. 15–33.

60 The word *archon* ('ruler', 'commander', 'chief'), for example, appears at least 100 times as a translation for *ros* (Hebrew for 'head'): Perriman, *Speaking of Women*, p. 14.

61 Gilbert Bilezikian, 'A Challenge for Proponents of Female Subordination To Prove Their Case from The Bible', at <http://www.cbeinternational.org/new/free_articles/challenge.shtml>.

62 Grudem's methodological approach and analysis of 2,336 examples of the use of 'kephale' in Greek literature has been strongly challenged, as most of these uses are not metaphorical. Only 19 examples exist with any sense of 'authority over'. See Richard S. Cervin, 'Does 'kephale' Mean 'Source' or 'Authority Over' in Greek Literature? A rebuttal', *Trinity Journal* 10(1) (Spring 1989), p. 85–112.

63 R. B. Onians, *The Origins of European Thought about the Body, the Mind, the Soul, the World, Time and Fate* (Cambridge: Cambridge University Press, 1951), quoted in Gretchen G. Hull, *Equal to Serve: Women and Men in the Church and Home* (Old Tappan, NJ: Fleming Revell, 1987), p. 269.

64 e.g. Luke 6.45; Philippians 4.7; 1 Corinthians 2.9: 'no eye has seen, nor ear heard, nor the human heart conceived, what God has prepared for those who love him.'

65 The head was seen by many, including Aristotle, as the source of human sperm and therefore life. For example, Athena, the patron goddess of the Athenians, was supposed to have sprung directly from the head of her father Zeus. In ancient Rome, sexual intercourse was sometimes referred to as 'diminishing one's head'. Artemidorus of Ephesus, writing in the second century AD, maintained that 'The head is the source of life and light for the whole body' and that 'The head [*kephale*] is like one's parents because it is the source or cause [*aitia*] of one's having life'. *Oneirocritica* 2.7, 35.43; quoted in Hull, *Equal to Serve*, p. 271.

66 e.g. head of a river, as in Genesis 2.10 'headwater'. See particularly Stephen Bedale, 'Meaning of Kephale in the Pauline Epistles', *Journal of Theological Studies* 5 (1954), pp. 211–15, and Fee, *The First Epistle of the Corinthians*. However, there is limited evidence in the Septuagint for 'head' as 'source' or 'origin of life'.

67 They argue that this meaning fits with the context of the passage where God is referred to as the source of humanity (1 Corinthians 11.12) and man as the original source of woman (v. 8). On this interpretation, v. 3 would have to be translated 'the head of the woman is man'. See Gilbert Bilezikian, *Community 101: Reclaiming the Local Church as Community of Oneness* (Grand Rapids: Baker Books, 1985), p. 193, and Fee, *The First Epistle of the Corinthians*, p. 503. However, this understanding of 'head' does not seem to relate to the immediate context of vv. 4–7, which is emphasizing relationships that bring shame or honour to another.

68 The range of meanings that can be mapped are: 1. Physical top or extremity of an object (such as a mountain or river); 2. That which is first, extreme in either time or spatial terms; 3. That which is prominent; 4. That which is determinative or representative by virtue of its prominence: Perriman, *Speaking of Women* p. 32.

69 The most common metaphorical use of 'head' in Greek and Hebrew texts relates to a part denoting the whole (e.g. a head of cattle), the 'head' representing the whole person by virtue of its prominence. Therefore, 'to be head of a group of people simply means *to occupy the position at the top or front*': ibid., p. 31

70 Walter Liefeld, 'Women, Submission and Ministry in 1 Corinthians' in Mickelson (ed.), *Women, Authority and the Bible*, p. 139.

71 Perriman, *Speaking of Women*, p. 31.

72 Markus Barth, *Ephesians: Translations and Commentary 4–6* (Garden City, NJ:

Doubleday, 1974), p. 618.

73 Werner Neuer, *Man and Woman in Christian Perspective*, p. 111. However, had Paul meant to establish a hierarchy, he would have used the order God/Christ/man/woman, instead of Christ/man/woman/God ('Christ is the head of every man, and the husband is the head of his wife, and God is the head of Christ': 1 Corinthians 11.3). Paul's subsequent argument is about the interrelationships between the pairs, not about a hierarchical structure.

74 Thomas Schreiner, 'Head Coverings, Prophecies and the Trinity: 1 Corinthians 11:2–16', in Grudem and Piper (eds), *Recovering Biblical Manhood and Womanhood,* p. 124–39.

75 Even in the patriarchal culture of the day, there was no idea of women generally shaming or bringing honour to men.

76 See 1 Corinthians 8.9: 'take care that this liberty of yours does not somehow become a stumbling block to the weak'. Practice needs to be both permissible and beneficial to all (1 Corinthians 10.23–30).

77 Paul's missionary imperative allows for accommodation to culture as he becomes 'all things to all people that by all means I may win some' (1 Corinthians 9.22).

78 1 Corinthians 11.4 translates as 'down from the head', so Paul might have been speaking of long hair on men, which had effeminate or homosexual associations in wider culture, particularly as in 11.14 he calls short hair on men natural: Jerome Murphy-O'Connor, 'The Non-Pauline Character of 1 Corinthians 11.2–16', *Journal of Biblical Literature*, 95 D (1976), p. 625.

79 Jewish women had to bind their hair in public as loose, flowing hair was seen as a mark of sensuality and sexual availability. The Mishnah records the following: 'How does a man differ from a woman? He may go with hair unbound and with garments rent, but she may not go with hair unbound and with garments rent': Mishnah, Sotah 3.8, quoted in J. Bristow, *What Paul Really Said About Women* (New York: HarperCollins, 1991), p. 79.

80 Evans, *Woman in the Bible*, p. 87, points out that Paul addresses hairstyles in worship in 1 Timothy 2.9 (as in 1 Peter 3.3), suggesting that heads were not necessarily customarily covered in worship.

81 Ibid., p. 92.

82 Judith M. Gundry-Volf, 'Gender and Creation in 1 Corinthians 11.2–16: A Study of Paul's Theological Method', in *Evangelium-Schriftauslegung-Kirche: Festschrift für Peter Stuhlmacher zum 65. Geburtstag*, ed. Otfried Hofius *et al.* (Göttingen: Vandenhoeck & Ruprecht, 1997), p. 153.

83 Shame/honour, or 'agonistic', cultures, were organized around conflicts between men over issues of honour associated with male dominance and agency, while shame was associated with weakness and passivity. Shame was caused by seducing or offending the women belonging to a man's household; to avert this, women were restricted to the domestic sphere: Don Browning, 'The Problem of Men', in *Does Christianity Teach Male Headship?*, ed. David Blankenhorn, Don Browning and Mary Stewart Van Leeuwen (Grand Rapids: Eerdmans, 2004), pp. 5–6.

84 It was widely held that wives could shame their husbands by inappropriate behaviour, and that a group (or church) could be similarly shamed by the activity of an individual: Gundry-Volf, 'Gender and Creation in 1 Corinthians 11:2–16', p. 154. In the honour/shame culture of Corinth, husbands are dishonoured if their wives obscure their female sexual distinctiveness. Equally, Christ can be dishonoured by inappropriate behaviour by men (1 Corinthians 11.4).

85 Gundry-Volf, 'Gender and Creation in 1 Corinthians 11:2–16', p. 156.

86 Paul points out that man and woman are made of the same substance (v. 8), contrary to the widely accepted Greek view that woman was created from material inferior to man. 'For the sake of' (v. 9) is frequently used by Paul to describe the focus of his

ministry (1 Corinthians 4.10; 9.10; 2 Corinthians 4.15). It does not imply inferiority, as woman was created to meet a need in man.

87 Morna Hooker, 'Authority On Her Head: An Examination of I Corinthians XI.10', *New Testament Studies* 10 (1964), pp. 415–16.

88 Fee, *The First Epistle of the Corinthians,* p. 520.

89 The traditional interpretation of v. 10 takes 'exousia' in the passive sense, meaning a woman needs someone else to function as authority over her. However, Fee points out that, despite 103 occurrences in the New Testament, there is no known use of 'exousia' in the passive sense. Furthermore, the traditional interpretation relies on the insertion of 'a sign of authority on' after 'a woman ought to have' (see NIV translation) despite the total lack of textual warrant: ibid., p. 519.

90 Gundry-Volf, 'Gender and Creation in 1 Corinthians 11.2–16', p. 162.

91 Paul frequently uses theological language or Old Testament allusions to address specific cultural issues or to make particular points: for example, 1 Timothy 2.14; Romans 5.12; 1 Corinthians 15.21, 22.

92 For example, George W. Knight III, *The New Testament Teaching on the Role Relationship of Men and Women* (Grand Rapids: Baker Books, 1997), pp. 55–6, cf. Hurley, *Man and Woman in Biblical Perspective,* p. 167.

93 See Giles, *Trinity and Subordinationism,* chap. 5; Bilezikian, *Community 101,* pp. 192–202. Jewett argues that the subordination of the Son to the Father is not an ontological subordination in the eternal Godhead but a voluntary act of humility on the part of the Son for the purpose of redemption: *Man as Male and Female,* p.133.

94 Aristotle wrote, 'household management falls into departments . . . the primary and smallest parts of the household are master and slave, husband and wife, father and children'. Household relationships consist 'by nature [of] various classes of rulers and ruled. For the free rules the slave, the male the female, and the man the child in a different way': *Politics* 1260a9–14.

95 Patricia Gundry and Fee point out the stark differences between first-century marriage and current expectations of intimacy, partnership and mutual growth: Patricia Gundry, *Heirs Together* (Grand Rapids: Zondervan, 1980), p. 76; Gordon Fee, 'The Cultural Context of Ephesians 5.18–6.9', *Priscilla Papers* 16(1) (Winter 2002), p. 3–8.

96 David Balch writes that Greco-Roman political science often drew an analogy between the house and the city: 'the rejection of the husband's authority by the wife, or of the master's authority by the slave, or of the father's authority by the sons led to anarchy in both home and city, to the rejection of the king's authority and to the degeneration of the constitution from monarchy to democracy': *Let Wives Be Submissive: The Domestic Code in 1 Peter* (Chico, Calif.: Scholars Press, 1981), p. 76.

97 Ibid., p. 118. The Roman aristocracy viewed Christianity as being a threat to the social fabric. Criticisms levelled at believers included the charge of immoral rites, corruption of women, murder and treason against the state. The conversion of wives was seen as being particularly subversive.

98 Fiorenza, *Bread not Stone*, p. 74. She writes that accusations that Christianity subverted and destroyed patriarchal household structures through admitting wives and slaves were still being made in the second century.

99 Other religious groups produced religious codes for apologetic purposes. For example, the Jewish historian Josephus, writing at the end of the first century AD (contemporaneously with Paul), defended Jewish household management, saying that women were properly submissive and the Jewish house in a Roman city properly ruled: *Against Apion* II.199, 206, 216, quoted in Balch, *Let Wives be Submissive*, p. 118.

100 Obviously, this submission is limited to social matters and does not include anything which might compromise obedience to Christ; see e.g. Acts 4.18, 19; 5.28, 29.

101 Balch, *Let Wives be Submissive*, p. 81.

102 Fee, 'The Cultural Context of Ephesians 5.18–6.9', p. 7.

103 Gordon Fee points out that 'be [keep] filled with the Spirit' is the only imperative in the passage until v. 25, 'Husbands, love your wives': 'Gender Issues: Reflections on the Perspective of the Apostle Paul', in Hancock (ed.), *Christian Perspectives on Gender, Sexuality and Community*, p. 73.

104 Perriman, *Speaking of Woman*, pp. 50–7.

105 Evans points out that v. 24 starts with a strong 'But' (*alla*), which suggests a conflict between the husband's headship and the wife's submission: *Woman in the Bible*, p. 67. The way in which the husband is to be 'head' is not self-evident. He is to use his prominent social position as Christ does and sacrifice himself to love another.

106 The husband is not compared with Christ – the comparison is the submission of both Church and wife. Christ is to be the example for his behaviour in exercising his position as head.

107 Perriman, *Speaking of Women*, p. 44, points out that the subordination of all things under Jesus' feet (Ephesians 1.22) is an idea distinct from that of Christ as head – it is not explanatory of Christ's headship. Psalm 8.5–6 distinguishes the themes of glory and exaltation from those of subordination. Subjugation relates to enemies and is inappropriate as an understanding of Christ's headship of the Church, or, for that matter, of a marriage relationship.

108 The reference to Christ as Saviour refers to the Old Testament understanding of 'saviour' as provider and protector: Fee 'The Cultural Context of Ephesians 5.18–6.9', p. 8.

109 Craig S. Keener, *Paul, Women and Wives: Marriage and women's Ministry in the Letters of Paul* (Peabody, Mass.: Hendrickson Publishers, 1992), pp. 166–70.

110 Fee, 'Gender Issues', p. 73, suggests that this eliminates courtesans. Perriman also highlights references to sexual immorality earlier in the letter (Ephesians 4.17–19; 5.3–12), suggesting the marriage relationship was under threat: *Speaking of Woman*, p. 54.

111 The word for 'cares' in v. 29 is the same as that used in 1 Thessalonians 2.7 for the care of a child by a parent. It does not describe an equal relationship between adults.

112 John R. W. Stott, *God's New Society: The Message of Ephesians* (Leicester: InterVarsity Press, 1979), p. 230.

113 Peter also calls for husbands to treat wives considerately (1 Peter 3.7). Peter might have been thinking of the socially vulnerable position of wives, as well as their physical vulnerability, when he refers to them as the 'weaker vessel'.

114 William Klein, in William Klein, Craig Bloomberg and Robert Hubbard, *Introduction to Biblical Interpretation* (Dallas: Word Books, 1993), p. 418.

115 Husbands are not to be like the Gentiles and rule (Mark 10.42–5) but are to use their position to love, serve and lay down their lives for their wives. There are no longer to be 'masters, fathers or teachers' among them, symbolizing unequal relationships of mastery and servitude (Matthew 23.1–10).

116 Perriman, *Speaking of Women*, p. 53.

117 Not to anyone else's husband. Perriman, *Speaking of Women*, p. 54, also quotes Margaret MacDonald, who argues that early pagan anti-Christian polemic accused Christian women of neglecting their responsibilities to their husbands.

118 Evans, *Woman in the Bible*, quoting Karl Barth, p. 68.

119 Evans writes, 'As far as humans are concerned, submission is always voluntary. Only God is ever seen as subjecting others . . . to himself, to another or to futility (e.g. 1 Corinthians 15.24–28; Romans 8.20; Philippians 3.21; Ephesians 1.21–22)': ibid. No ruler or authority of any kind in the New Testament is told to subject others or ensure their submission.

120 Colossians 3.18, Titus 2.5 and 1 Peter 3.1 all have the same theme of wifely submission and husbandly love, although the motivation in 1 Peter is specifically missionary, relating to non-Christian husbands.

121 In Jewish tradition Sarah was the mother of women proselytes. She becomes the model for wives' missionary conduct, winning converts through submission (1 Peter 3.1): *Let Wives be Submissive*, p. 36.

122 Jewett, *Man as Male and Female,* p. 58.

123 S. Dixon, 'Men, Women and God', unpub. paper (1995), p. 4.

124 While proponents of spiritual headship would argue that it is of course necessary for a wife to resist sinful behaviour by her husband in practice (e.g. John Piper and Wayne Grudem, 'Overview of Central Concerns: Questions and Answers', in *Recovering Biblical Manhood and Womanhood,* p. 61), spiritual headship is taught as a male responsibility for the spiritual well-being of the couple, and it remains to be demonstrated how a wife is to learn to exercise spiritual judgement if she believes God has given that responsibility to her husband.

125 'as is fitting in the Lord' (Colossians 3.18); 'so that the word of God may not be discredited' (Titus 2.5); so that unbelieving husbands may be won for Christ (1 Peter 3.1): Giles, *Trinity and Subordinationism,* p. 254.

126 Some have argued that this relates to Genesis 3.16, where God describes man's rule over woman as a result of the Fall. However, this rule is not prescribed by God but is a result of sin, not the original created order.

127 Giles notes that a 'biblical theology' of slavery was developed in the mid-nineteenth century in response to social change and the ascendancy of abolition and that the 'biblical theology' for the permanent subordination of women developed in the 1970s as a reaction to the challenges of women's liberation. Both reflect a profoundly conservative social ideology, deemed to be ordained by God. For further parallels, see Giles, *Trinity and Subordinationism* chs 11–13.

128 For example, Giles points out that the nation of Israel moved from a twelve-tribe alliance to a monarchy and later to high-priestly rule as they adapted to changing circumstances: ibid., p. 209.

129 Cf. Acts 20 and 1 and 2 Timoth: 'Gender Issues', p. 76.

130 It is likely that the heresy in Ephesus had Gnostic aspects. Gnosticism taught that matter was evil and spirit good. There was no resurrection of the body as bodies were evil and physical pleasure must be denied (or some taught, gratified, as having no bearing on spirit). Gnostic writings often taught that Eve was created first or was the spiritual force that awakened Adam.

131 The chapter divides into three exhortations – to prayer (vv. 1–7), to propriety in worship (vv. 8–9) and to instruct women (v. 11). Only in this latter exhortation to 'let learn' is the imperative tense used, emphasizing v. 11 over v. 12 and thereby qualifying the radical command. The submission required of women is to the teaching of the Church: W. Fahrer, 'Questioning the Traditional Interpretation of 1 Timothy 2.11–15', unpub. paper (1990), p. 2.

132 Paul uses the creation narrative illustratively, paralleling with the problem in Eden the danger facing Ephesus of being led astray by women.

133 Philo thought that the snake spoke to woman because 'she is more accustomed to being deceived than the man . . . she easily gives way and is taken in by plausible falsehoods which resemble the truth': quoted in Perriman, *Speaking of Women,* p. 183.

134 Elsewhere in this letter, Paul names two male false teachers (1 Timothy 1.20), aware that men too are capable of being deceived. He warns both men and women to avoid deception in 2 Corinthians 11.3.

135 The word Paul uses here is *authentien* and this is its only appearance in the New Testament. It definitely does not mean 'to hold a position of authority over a man' – see Perriman, *Speaking of Women,* p. 171. The normal word for authority is 'exousia', used for example in 1 Corinthians 11.10.

136 Scholer, '1 Timothy 2.9–15', p. 205.

137 Richard Kroeger and Catherine Kroeger, *I Suffer Not a Woman: Rethinking 1 Tim. 2:11*

in Light of Ancient Evidence (Grand Rapids: Baker Books, 1991), pp. 101–3. They suggest that the Pastorals are opposing a Gnostic doctrine which pronounced motherhood as the ultimate reality. Eve was created first and was Adam's spiritual instructor, with superior knowledge gained through the wisdom of the snake. Therefore Paul, in order to underline the orthodox biblical account, stresses how completely deceived Eve has been.

138 Fee, 'Gender Issues', p. 77, suggests that Paul is concerned that young widows get married and have children and so be 'saved' by no longer adhering to and spreading false teaching, seeing 1 Timothy 5.14 as elaborating 2.15.

139 For example, Douglas Moo, in 'What Does It Mean Not to Teach or Have Authority Over Men? 1 Timothy 2.11–15', in Grudem and Piper (eds), *Recovering Biblical Manhood and Womanhood,* p. 182.

140 Daniel Doriani, 'History of the Interpretation of 1 Timothy 2', in *Women in the Church: A Fresh Analysis of 1 Timothy 2:9–15*, ed. Andreas J. Kostenberger, Thomas R. Schreiner and H. Scott Baldwin (Grand Rapids: Baker Books, 1995), p. 266.

141 Giles, *Trinity and Subordinationism*, p. 207.

142 Perriman, *Speaking of Women,* p. 119.

143 There is no indirect object for 'let them be submissive': ibid., p. 122.

144 Keener, *Paul, Women and Wives*, p. 82.

145 Paul expresses an urgency about mission, expecting the imminent consummation of all things, telling believers to 'stay as you are' (1 Corinthians 7.24, 26, 29, 31; Romans 13.11).

146 M. Powley, 'A Woman's Work', unpub. paper (2002), p. 9.

147 Gundry-Volf, 'Gender and Creation in 1 Corinthians 11:2–16', p. 171.

148 John Barton, 'Can Women Be Bishops?', in *Women and Episcopacy*, ed. Harriet Harris and Jane Shaw (WATCH, 2002), p. 12.

149 Ibid., p. 11.

150 Atkins, *Split Image*, p. 135.

Bibliography

Atkins, Anne D., *Split Image: Discovering God's True Intention for Male and Female* (London: Hodder and Stoughton, 1987).

Balch, David, *Let Wives Be Submissive: The Domestic Code in 1 Peter* (Chico, Calif.: Scholars Press, 1981).

Barth, Markus, *Ephesians: Translation and Commentary 4–6* (Garden City, NJ: Doubleday, 1974).

Barton, John, 'Can Women Be Bishops?', in *Women and Episcopacy*, ed. Harriet Harris and Jane Shaw (WATCH, 2002).

Bauckham, Richard, *God and the Crisis of Freedom: Biblical and Contemporary Perspectves* (London: Westminster/John KnoxPress, 2002).

Bedale, Stephen, 'Meaning of Kephale in the Pauline Epistles', *Journal of Theological Studies* 5 (1954), pp. 211–15.

Bilezikian, Gilbert, *Beyond Sex Roles: What the Bible Says about Woman's Place in the Church and Family* (Grand Rapids: Baker Book House, 1985).

—— 'A Challenge for Proponents of Female Subordination to Prove Their Case from the Bible', at <http://www.cbeinternational1.org/new/free_articles/challenge.shtml> (accessed 10 August 2004).

—— *Community 101: Reclaiming the Local Church as Community of Oneness* (Grand Rapids: Zondervan, 1997).

Borresen, Kari E. (ed.), *The Image of God: Gender Models in Judeo-Christian Tradition* (Oslo: Solum Forlag, 1991).

Bristow, John T., *What Paul Really Said about Women* (New York: HarperCollins, 1991).

Brown, Judy, 'I Now Pronounce You Adam and Eve: View of Marriage Based on Creation and Re-creation', *Priscilla Papers* 13(4), pp. 1–6.

Browning, Don, 'The Problem of Men', in *Does Christianity Teach Male Headship?*, David-Blankenhorn, Don Browning and Mary Stewart Van Leeuwen (Grand Rapids, Michigan: Eerdmans, 2004).

Cervin, Richard S., 'Does "kephale" Mean "Source" or "Authority Over" in Greek Literature?: A Rebuttal', *Trinity Journal* 10(1) (Spring 1989), pp. 85–112.

Chrysostom, St John, *Homilies on Timothy* IX, in *A Select Library of the Nicene and Post-Nicene Fathers*, series 1, vol. 13, ed. Philip Schaff (Grand Rapids: Eerdmans, 1979).

Conn, Harvie M., 'Feminist Theology', in *New Dictionary of Theology*, ed. S. B Ferguson (Leicester: InterVarsity Press, 1988).

Dixon, S., 'Men, Women and God: A Discussion of Headship and its Effects on the Church Today', unpub. paper, 1995.

Doriani, Daniel, 'History of the Interpretation of 1 Timothy 2', in *Women in the Church: A Fresh Analysis of 1 Timothy 2.9–15*, ed. Andreas Köstenberger, Thomas R. Schreiner and H. Scott Baldwin (Grand Rapids, Mich.: Baker Books, 1985).

Edwards, Ruth B., *The Case for Women's Ministry* (London: SPCK, 1989).

Evans, Mary J., *Woman in the Bible*, 2nd edn (Exeter: Paternoster Press, 1998).

Fahrer, W., Questioning the Traditional Interpretation of 1 Timothy 2.11–15, unpub. paper, 1990.

Fee, Gordon, 'The Cultural Context of Ephesians 5.18—6.9', *Priscilla Papers*, 16(1) (Winter 2002), pp. 3–8.

—— *The First Epistle to the Corinthians* (Grand Rapids: Wm B. Eerdmans, 1987).

—— 'Gender Issues: Reflections on the Perspective of the Apostle Paul', in Hancock (ed.), *Christian Perspectives on Gender, Sexuality and Community.*

—— and Stuart, Douglas, *How to Read the Bible for all its Worth* (Grand Rapids: Zondervan, 1982).

Fiorenza, Elisabeth Schüssler, *Bread Not Stone: The Challenge of Feminist Biblical Interpretation* (Boston: Beacon Press, 1985).

—— *In Memory of Her: A Feminist Theological Reconstruction of Christian Origins* (London: SCM Press, 1983).

Foh, S., 'What is the Woman's Desire?' *Westminster Theological Journal* 37 (1974), pp. 374–83.

France, R. T., *A Slippery Slope? The Ordination of Women and Homosexual Practice: A Case Study in Biblical Interpretation* (Cambridge: Grove Books, 2000).

Giles, Kevin, *Trinity and Subordinationism* (Downers Grove, Il.: InterVarsity Press, 2002).

Groothuis, Rebecca M., 'Leading Him Up the Garden Path', *Priscilla Papers* 16(2) (Spring 2002), pp. 10–14.

Grudem, Wayne, and Piper, John (eds), *Recovering Biblical Manhood and Womanhood: A Response to Evangelical Feminism* (Wheaton Il.: Crossway, 1991).

Gundry, Patricia, *Heirs Together* (Grand Rapids: Zondervan, 1980).

Gundry-Volf, Judith M., 'Gender and Creation in 1 Corinthians 11.2–16: A Study of Paul's Theological Method', in *Schriftauslegung–Evangelium–Kirche: Festschrift für Peter Stuhlmacher zum 65. Geburtstag*, ed. Otfried Hofius *et al.* (Göttingen: Vandenhoeck & Ruprecht, 1997).

Haas, Guenther, 'Patriarchy as an Evil that God Tolerated: Analysis and Implications for the Authority of Scripture', *Journal of the Evangelical Theological Society* 38 (September 1995), pp. 321–36.

Hancock, Maxine (ed.), *Christian Perspectives on Gender, Sexuality and Community* (Regent College, 2003).

Hays, Richard, 'Ecclesiology and Ethics and 1 Corinthians', *Ex Auditu* 10 (1994), pp. 31–43.

Hayter, Mary, *The New Eve in Christ: The Use and Abuse of the Bible in the Debate about Women in the Church* (London: SPCK, 1987).

Hooker, Morna D., 'Authority on Her Head: An Examination of I Cor. X1.10', *New Testament Studies* (1964), pp. 410–16.

Hull, Gretchen G., *Equal to Serve: Women and Men in the Church and Home* (Old Tappan, NJ: Fleming Revell, 1987).

Hurley, James B., *Man and Woman in Biblical Perspective* (Grand Rapids: Zondervan, 1981).

Jewett, Paul K., *Man as Male and Female* (Grand Rapids: Eerdmans, 1975).

Jewett, Robert, 'The Sexual Liberation of the Apostle Paul', *Journal of the American Academy of Religion* 47, supp 1. (1979), pp. 55–87.

Johnston, Robert K., 'Biblical Authority and Interpretation', in Mickelsen (ed.), *Women, Authority and the Bible.*

Keener, Craig S., *Paul, Women and Wives: Marriage in Women's Ministry in the Letters of Paul* (Peabody, Mass.: Hendrickson Publishers, 1992).

Klein, William, Blomberg, Craig and Hubbard, Robert, *Introduction to Biblical Interpretation* (Dallas: Word Books, 1993).

Knight, George W., *The New Testament Teaching on the Role Relationship of Men and Women* (Grand Rapids: Baker Books, 1977).

Kroeger, Catherine, and Beck, James (eds), *Women Abuse and the Bible: How Scripture Can Be Used to Hurt or to Heal* (Grand Rapids: Baker Book House, 1996).

—— Evans, Mary and Storkey, Elizabeth (eds), *The Women's Study New Testament* (New York: HarperCollins, 1995).

Kroeger, Richard and Kroeger, Catherine Clark, *I Suffer not a Woman: Rethinking 1 Tim 2.11 in Light of Ancient Evidence* (Grand Rapids: Baker Book House, 1991).

Liefeld, Walter, 'Women, Submission and Ministry in 1 Corinthians', in Mickelsen (ed.), *Women, Authority and the Bible.*

Longenecker, Richard, 'Authority, Hierarchy and Leadership Patterns in the Bible', in Mickelsen (ed.), *Women, Authority and the Bible.*

Lowe, Stephen D., 'Rethinking the Female Status/Function Question: The Jew/Gentile Relationship as Paradigm', *Journal of the Evangelical Theological Society* 34(1) (March 1991), pp. 59–75.

Meeks, Wayne A., 'Image of the Androgyne: Some Uses of a Symbol in Earliest Christianity', *History of Religions* 13 (1973/4), pp. 165–208.

Mickelsen, Alvera (ed.), *Women, Authority and the Bible* (Leicester: InterVarsity Press, 1986).

Moo, Douglas, 'What Does It Mean Not to Teach or Have Authority Over Men? 1 Timothy 2.11–15' in Grudem and Piper (eds), *Recovering Biblical Manhood and Womanhood.*

Motyer, Stephen, 'The Relationship between Paul's Gospel of "All One in Christ Jesus" (Galatians 3.28) and the "Household Codes"', *Vox Evangelica* 19 (1989), pp. 33–48.

Moules, N., 'Jesus the Peacemaker', in *Decide for Peace: Evangelicals and the Bomb*, ed. Dana Mills-Powell (Basingstoke: Marshall Pickering, 1986).

Murphy-O'Connor, Jerome, 'The Non-Pauline Character of 1 Cor 11.2–16', in *Journal of Biblical Literature* 95 D (1976), p. 625.

Neuer, Werner, *Man and Woman in Christian Perspective*, trans. Gordon J. Wenham (London: Hodder & Stoughton, 1990).

Nicole, Roger, 'Biblical Authority and Feminist Aspirations', in Mickelsen (ed.) (1986).

Ortlund, Raymond C., 'Male–Female Equality and Male Headship: Genesis 1—3', in Grudem and Piper (eds), *Recovering Biblical Manhood and Womanhood.*

Osbourne, Grant, *The Hermeneutical Spiral* (Leicester: InterVarsity Press, 1991).

Perriman, Andrew, *Speaking of Women* (Leicester: Apollos, 1998).

Powley, M. 'A Woman's Work', unpub. paper, 2002.

Provan, I. W., 'Why Bother with the Old Testament regarding Gender and Sexuality?', in

Hancock (ed.), *Christian Perspectives on Gender, Sexuality and Community.*

Reed, Esther, *The Genesis of Ethics: On the Authority of God as the Origin of Christian Ethics* (London: Darton, Longman and Todd, 2000).

Reuther, Rosemary R., *Sexism and God-talk* (London: SCM Press, 1983).

Sandom, Carrie, 'The Biblical Pattern for Women's Ministry – Limiting or Liberating?', at <http://www.reform.org.uk/tabloid/2000/womens-ministry.html> (accessed 12 August 2004).

Scholer, David M., 'The Evangelical Debate over Biblical "Headship"', in Kroeger and Beck (eds), *Women, Abuse and the Bible.*

—— '1 Timothy 2.9–15 and the Place of Women in the Church's Ministry', in Mickelsen (ed.), *Women, Authority and the Bible.*

Schreiner, Thomas R., 'Head Coverings, Prophecies and the Trinity: 1 Corinthians 11.2–16', in Grudem and Piper (eds), *Recovering Biblical Manhood and Womanhood.*

Snodgrass, Klyne, 'Galatians 3.28: Conundrum or Solution?', in Mickelsen (ed.), *Women, Authority and the Bible .*

Stott, John R. W., *God's New Society: The Message of Ephesians* (Leicester: Inter-Varsity Press, 1979).

Swartley, Willard M., *Slavery, Sabbath, War and Women: Case Issues in Biblical Interpretation.* (Waterloo, Ont.: Herald Press, 1983).

Thiselton, Anthony C., *The First Epistle to the Corinthians* (Carlisle: Paternoster Press, 2000).

Trible, Phyllis, *God and the Rhetoric of Sexuality* (Philadelphia: Fortress Press, 1978).

Van Leeuwen, Mary S., *Fathers and Sons: A Search for a New Masculinity* (Leicester: Inter-Varsity Press, 2002).

—— *Gender and Grace: Women and Men in a Changing World* (Leicester: InterVarsity Press, 1990).

Volf, Miroslav, *Exclusion and Embrace* (Nashville: Abingdon Press, 1996).

—— 'Soft Difference: Theological Reflections on the Relation Between Church and Culture in 1 Peter', *Ex Auditu* 10 (1994), pp. 15–30.

Vos, Clarence J., *Women in Old Testament Worship (*Delft: Judles & Brinkman, 1968).

Webb, William J., *Slaves, Women and Homosexuals* Downers Grove, Ill.: InterVarsity Press, 2001).

Witherington, Ben, 'Rites and Rights for Women – Galatians 3.28', *New Testament Studies* 27 (1981), pp. 593–604.

12 Authority

Penny Jamieson

The theology of authority

There are two different emphases concerning the nature of authority. Those at the upper levels of the hierarchy tend to see their authority as coming primarily from the first person of the Trinity, as a given. The 1988 Lambeth Report, while acknowledging that 'In any human society, of whatever sort, authority has its basis in the shared life of the community',[1] says 'In the case of the Christian community and fellowship, the life which its members share does not derive from itself but is rooted in that of the crucified and risen Christ and is conferred by God through the working of the Holy Spirit.'[2] The primary emphasis within the trinitarian spectrum is on the originating work of God, so the Creator comes into focus, hence the shift towards the first person of the Trinity.

Elaine Pagels in her study of the Gnostic gospels suggests that the association between monotheism and the power of the bishop originates from the second-century struggle that Irenaeus had with the Gnostics. It was a time when the need to establish doctrinal orthodoxy went together with the need to establish the authority of the Church – hence the association of 'one God, one bishop'.[3] There is thus an early and a clear association between the authority attributed to God the Creator, and the exercise of authority within the Church. By contrast, the theological emphasis within the lower levels of the embedded hierarchy tends to be on the incarnation of Christ and on the work of the Holy Spirit. It sees God as the God of the gathering, of the community, God in our midst; and the Holy Spirit as the creative and relational force within the community. God is therefore embedded within the life of the community, and is certainly not identifiable with one person. This perspective takes seriously the biblical account of the gift of the Spirit to the Church at Pentecost.

It is an oversimplification to see these perspectives as two distinct approaches; they are certainly not opposed to each other, for both find their being within the life of the Trinity. And both see authority within the

Christian community as bestowed by God. Rather it is a question of emphasis; of where, within the life of the Trinity, we locate God. And the answer is, clearly, everywhere. But the simplifying processes of Christian theological thought tend to separate out the persons of the Trinity, and to identify with the different characteristics.

It is not surprising that the ministry of women finds a theological place within both the Incarnation and the life of the Holy Spirit. A woman has a central role in the Incarnation; and the concept of Immanuel, 'God with us', has always related to women's concern with the intimate details of human living. Also, the ministry of women as priests and bishops is still new within the life of the Church; little wonder that the creative and renewing powers of the Spirit are particularly appreciated in that context.

The recognition of authority

With the general decline in respect for institutions, the granting and the holding of institutional authority does not necessarily ensure either that leadership will be effective or that it will be honoured. Two other factors are necessary: the leader must adequately represent the sacred, and he or she must have the ordinary worldly competence to handle the 'nuts and bolts' of the job.

For Christian leaders the authority of the sacred is largely assumed. In episcopal churches the gift of the Holy Spirit at ordination is regarded as both sealing and institutionalizing faith: sealing it, because the laying on of hands follows the ordinand's declaration of faith; and institutionalizing it because his or her public and to an extent private practice of faith is thereafter deemed secure by virtue of the ordination.

Priests and bishops generally operate sacramentally in ways that are both accepted and anticipated. They are 'ordered', as the term 'ordination' suggests. And while nothing can take away their Orders, and traditional sacramental theology affirms that the validity of the sacrament is not negated by the unworthiness of the ordained person, if priests and bishops fail to act within that order then people begin to question the validity of their ordination. For their authority as priests or bishops to be honoured, people need to be sure of their willingness to be bearers of the sacred in public liturgical functioning.

The relationship between a priest's public, liturgical function and the practice and growth in personal faith is an elusive one. This is an age that increasingly recognizes that God can be found without the Church, and there are large numbers of spiritually attuned people who do not need the Church to enable them to identify the presence of God. This can present real questions for clergy for whom the anchor point of their job is the liturgy of the Church. And they are not helped, I believe, by much of what is currently on offer as spiritual direction, which tends to focus on the relationship of the individual to God, disconnected from community. There are some significant spiritual questions here which I shall take up later.

Priestly ministry is not all show, in any case. If public liturgical functioning is not backed up with the practice of a real and genuine private faith and piety, then it becomes hollow. I believe that this is in fact the dilemma that a number of clergy find themselves in. The significance of private piety has grown in recent years, both with the decline of institutional respect and with the rise of individualism. A personal and authentic piety is essential to the practice of Christian ministry. It is cruel to ordain without it; I have seen lives deeply hurt.

The existence of a strong personal piety is not always evident, indeed it is necessarily a personal and private matter, but there is a sense in which its presence reassures the Christian community in which priesthood is practised. Whether intentionally or unintentionally, some clergy cultivate a mystique of distance, which is well aided by the established custom of putting clergy on a pedestal. This distancing operates particularly effectively for bishops. Before I was ordained to the episcopate, a wise old priest suggested that bishops should find ways of sharing their faith authentically, deeply and personally, without ostentation and without intrusion.

Another divide between the institutional and the private is the need for clergy to be effective in their ministry if their authority for leadership is to be validated. They may have the experience and the qualifications, but if they do not have the demonstrated competence in, for example, preaching, liturgy, pastoral care and a personally disciplined approach to these and other tasks, that validation will not be forthcoming.

In practice, effective ministry is a combination of all these factors, held in a flowing balance. If we have authority as clergy, it is because the laity perceive us to be reliable interpreters of the power and purposes of God in the context of contemporary society. And this involves both spirituality and expertise, not one without the other.

The challenge to institutional piety has also come from the many movements around the world for the ordination of women, for the claim of women to be ordained has largely rested on the claim to personal piety, on the call that God makes to women apart from and despite the institutional Church.

The ordination of women has also raised the question of cultural acceptance, acceptance that depends neither upon call nor upon competence, but which acquires some validity, not, I would contend, from the requirement that the conscience of each member of the community be respected, but from the identification of the community as the locus for the legitimation of authority. The work of the Eames Commission on Women in the Episcopate has stressed that the ordination of women as both priests and bishops is subject to a process of 'reception' within the Church, and that the result of that process cannot be presumed upon.[4]

In my experience, both as a priest and a bishop, women are not unaware of the necessity for them to be accepted by the people whom they would serve in God's name. It is not uncommon for women, as they present themselves as candidates for ordination, to stress how well they have been 'accepted' by people who have begun to see the signs of vocation within their lives. This is associated with the general tendency that women have to emphasize the relationships they have with others, the support they have received from other people and the regard in which they are held.

The reasons for this can be found within the wider structures of society, and the place of women relative to men. History, tradition and current practice give women little reason to believe that institutional acceptance will be as readily forthcoming for them as it is for men. There is no ready-made job slot for them to fit into, and women are not the ready and familiar carriers of the symbols of power that men are. So they tend to be insecure, and this social insecurity also reflects the general sense of personal insecurity and lack of self-worth that is often characteristic of women. This has been reinforced by the wide use of the key word 'acceptance' by people who are on the outside of a community in which the ministry of women is in place and who seek to make enquiries. This usage seems likely to continue for some time yet in New Zealand.

But the concept of 'acceptance' can be distorting. I see a danger in this, in that too great an emphasis on acceptance could lead women – or men for that matter, but women are more vulnerable to this – to shape their ministry according to the practices that they believe will earn that acceptance. Where the emphasis on acceptance is too strong, the significance of the call of Christ is lessened, and so is any prophetic thrust. While few women would identify with the imagery in the words of our Lord, 'I am come not to bring peace but a sword' (Matthew 10.34), the underlying truth is that the function of the gospel is not to confirm our prejudices and limitations, but to bring us to the foot of the cross. Gospel values are not those of secular society, and a clearly claimed Christian identity is, for me, an essential mark of call. I would not like to see the ministry of women hamstrung by an over-dependence on acceptance, at the expense of clarity about the Christ they serve.

Where women, or men, anticipate a negative reception, they will generally place more emphasis on their sense of the sacred, on their personal piety and the strength of their relationship with God; it has been so throughout Christian experience in women as widely different as Teresa of Avila and Rebecca Jackson, the black American evangelist of the nineteenth century. Closer to home, for me, is the Methodist lay preacher Mrs Joan Scott, who came to live in New Zealand in 1863. She was a very effective preacher, but not authorized by the Methodist Church in any way. It was said of her, 'Though not allowed the honour of being Conference Evangelist, she certainly is God's evangelist.'[5] The women in the Anglican Church in New Zealand who were earliest in line for ordination, especially those who were deacons for a good many years, have this mark about them very clearly. God is a powerful ally when you are daring to challenge the Church to break with the pattern of centuries.

When I hear women, or men, who come to tell me of the first stirrings of vocation within them speaking of the 'acceptance' that they have received from others, I hear them beginning to claim the authority of God within them. I have seen them, as the authority is recognized and given space to move, growing in confidence and in their ability to talk convincingly about God. Sometimes this becomes for them a powerful symbol of personal liberation, and they are free to move beyond acceptance and into a more challenging and prophetic relationship with the Church, and also with society. It can be an isolated and lonely position, for such people and such messages are not always welcome, but it can truly be said of some that I have known, as it was said of Mrs Joan Scott in relation to the Methodist church, that they are certainly God's evangelists.

Relational authority

Authority is not only given to Christians by God through due process of the structures of the Church, it is also received. But the process of receiving this authority, the route by which it becomes both authentic for the individual concerned and able to function in mutuality with the community that has called, can be quite long and tortuous. Celia Hahn[6] categorized four types of authority that we can experience as we move through our lives, which for some can be usefully regarded as stages of the journey; that is from 'received' authority, through 'autonomous' and 'assertive' authority to 'integrated' authority. For Jesus, the route was much shorter.

When Jesus was baptized he received authority from God; that baptism marked the beginning of his ministry. It was not too long before he began to speak as one with authority of his own: 'But *I* say to you . . .' (Matthew 5.29). The authority of God had become, as it were, internalized, owned and able to be expressed with conviction; it had moved towards integration.

The Church uses many symbolic ways of liturgically enabling those on whom authority is bestowed to demonstrate their acceptance of that authority. The service of ordination for a bishop allows for the giving of a number of gifts. The only one that is mandatory is the giving of the scriptures with the injunction 'Here are the Holy Scriptures; learn from them, teach them, live by them, and proclaim Christ, the living Word.' The new bishop's acceptance of the scriptures is a clear indication of his or her acceptance of episcopal authority.

After this, other gifts are given, and in recent years their number appears to be growing. All are symbols of office and all are given by different communities and sub-communities that either are or will be in relationship with the new bishop. The acceptance of these gifts is a visible and strong symbol of the new bishop's acceptance of the authority that has been bestowed on him or her through the laying on of hands; and of her, or his, willingness to enter into this episcopal relationship. Some of these communities are sub-groups of that community for whom she, or he, will be a bishop. Some are communities with whom he, or she, will enter into a relationship of collegiality.

The impact of the ordination service is so tremendous and so strong that its initial impression is of divinely bestowed authority firmly anchored within the community of the Church. It is given, it is received, but it is yet to be owned.

Hahn calls the first perception of authority as given by the community 'received authority'. It is there when authority is very raw, very new, and it is characterized by a noticeable dependence on and respect for the authority structures of the community. At this stage in my life as a bishop, I well remember spending hours trying to master the Canons and Statutes of our Church so that I would exercise the kind of authority the Church had made very clear that it expected its bishops to exercise. When a person is operating out of received authority, they are clearly aware that the source of their authority is beyond themselves, most frequently seen as being located within the institution. Received authority is in some ways very safe – until, that is, one discovers that a pedantic adherence to the rules and regulations can frequently violate both common sense and one's personal conscience.

The step to a fully owned authority is not quite straightforward, for there are two possibilities en route – autonomous authority and assertive authority – which, depending on personality and gender, people may pass through, pass by or get stuck in. In practice, most people holding any kind of authority tend to move between them according to the demands of circumstances.

Autonomous authority is characterized by a move from dependence on the authority of others to confidence in our own internal authority. For my own part I found myself pushed very quickly into this mode, and I would have to say it was almost a defensive reaction. In the early days of my ordination as a bishop I found myself piled high with the expectations of others, all of which contained images of how I should use my authority. All this was strongly interwoven with the powerful sense of the sacred which had been so public and apparent at the time of my ordination that it seemed as if I was being iconized. The rule books were quickly found to be inadequate and I pulled a ring around myself, metaphorically speaking, turned the icon face to the wall, and began to explore and to exploit my own authority. I began effectively to define my own reality instead of letting other people do it for me. By placing boundaries around myself I began to see myself as I thought I was, and not according to the multiple images that were being projected upon me. But it was a very lonely time, and I was undoubtedly unbearable to live with and to work with.

At this time, and clearly overlapping, I was exercising what Hahn would describe as assertive authority. This was a sense of taking responsibility, and while I was ready enough to do so, there was a certain randomness and unreliability, for both myself and others, about the way I did it. I, as yet, had little security in where I was placed in my relationships with others. Because I was so isolated at that time I was very vulnerable and I experienced any questioning of anything that I did as profoundly and personally threatening. It was an extraordinarily painful time.

But it was not long before I began to seek allies and to draw other people into the confused conversations that were going on in my head. In the process of doing this I began to be aware much more solidly of the bonds that held me with the people who had put me in that position, and mutuality began to grow in our relationships. I had begun to experience what Hahn called 'integrated' authority. While I now – as Hahn would predict and any perceptive human wisdom would assume – still move from one experience of authority to another, I am most certainly much more at ease with it than when I began.

Gender differences

Feminist analyses of authority structures and the way that they are worked out in the lives and modes of functioning of individuals who hold authority very strongly contrast the more confident and dominating style that men are perceived as having with the more diffident and inclusive style that women tend to have.

The basis for such an analysis rests on the structural difference between the roles that men and women customarily play within our society. And there is clear evidence from my own experience, both of myself and of other women, that there does tend to be a diffidence and even anxiety within many women about assuming authority. Women presenting themselves as candidates for ordination will repeatedly stress that they seek this in order to serve, that they do not seek power. Yet it is also clear to me that one of the reasons why more women are seeking ordination is that they feel the need for authorization, the 'received' authority that the institution can bestow, in order to function effectively. It is frequently hard for women to move from their gratitude at being granted authority by the institution, to a clearer sense of who they are, and to the authority that comes from being who they are. When this point is reached there is a real and genuine personal awakening. It has concerned me that within the Church, ordination, for women, has frequently served as a jumping-off point into more owned experiences of authority. I would like to see more lay women claiming that authority without benefit of ordination.

Men, in general, tend not to need or to seek this authorization. Their expectations fit them more appropriately for taking on leadership positions; it is expected of them and they expect it of themselves. However, their assumption of authority is not without its difficulties. As women find it difficult to move into an owned 'autonomous' authority, men can struggle to move out of an owned and 'assertive' experience of authority and into a style that is more mutual and more relational. But when the switch happens, for both men and women, the result is truly effective leadership.

I believe that it is because men assume leadership roles more naturally and more readily that we are seeing fewer men seeking ordination. They simply do not need the authorization of the Church to exercise leadership; some built-in antennae tell them that they are always welcome, as they are. The contemporary challenge to both men and women is to develop patterns of mutuality in leadership that will strengthen the whole Christian community.

Men are, by established social convention, accustomed to a measure of authority in relationships. Frequently this manifests itself as a bias towards independence, to seeking some control in a relationship. I notice this in small ways; for example, if I am driving around a parish, the vicar (male) will almost always express a preference for driving me in his car. It worries me not, but a friend pointed out to me that the action was, whether intentionally or unintentionally, a way of establishing his male authority and that in a small way it diminished mine. For my part, I was more easy about any pattern of behaviour that established relationships that could move away from the formalities and become real; I was interested in establishing connections.[7] This observation, and many others that support this analysis, are a sharp reminder to me that when it comes to questions of authority and relationships it is not uncommon for men and women to view the world in and from 'different frames'.[8] It clearly is an issue when attempting to establish mutuality in relationships with those over whom I held formal authority.

Mutuality in the use of authority

Clearly authority gives the person the power to control who is consulted and who not; as bishop I have a very strong say in who participates in the formal structures of the Church, and consequently who is excluded. I have access to the flow of information within the diocese and to the resources that enable my ministry of oversight to function, and I have the responsibility for licensing the clergy, or not. These are resources given to me by the community that has asked me to serve them in that role.

The process of developing a pattern of 'integrated' mutual ministry involves learning to be more relaxed about who might offer to serve on a committee, to become less hands-on about access to the flow of information and also more generous with the use of resources. It is all part of learning to forgo the need to control, and of sharing the responsibility with others. It is a very important part of community building. When I first became bishop I found there was a very high expectation that all these means of control would stay in my hands. 'After all,' I was told by one of the senior clergy in the diocese, 'we elected *you* to be bishop and not the Archdeacons.' There was a lot of the Church's need for security invested in my keeping the reins tightly in my own hands. It took a while for enough trust to build up for people to trust me when I trusted others. Other people had some learning to do too. But I have discovered how empowering it is to relinquish control – and not only for others, for I too have gained.

Leadership

Any institution needs an authority structure that enables it to achieve the purposes for which it exists, which keeps it faithful to its core beliefs, and which initiates trouble-shooting when necessary. The Church is no exception. However, the core beliefs and values which bind the Church together must be articulated and interpreted in constantly changing circumstances. At the same time, authority rests in a person as much as in a structure, and people cannot be neatly divided into functional parts. There are many images attached to Christian leadership: servant, lord, father, priest, watchman, shepherd, president; and some that invite the imagination to consider the possibilities that are opened up by women's leadership: mother, midwife, nurturer, and so on. However, there are three particular functions of authority within the Church that I want to address. These are to shape the future, to deal with conflict, and to maintain boundaries. This is leadership.

Leadership, like power, gets a bad press these days, but because it seems to be perennially necessary it is as well to consider carefully what it is there for. For leaders too can overstep boundaries. Hans Küng has pointed out that many of the functions we ascribe to leaders are not exclusive to them. But if leaders do not in practice concern themselves with these functions, either directly or indirectly, then nothing will happen. No one else has been given the gift or the commission to make sure that things get done.[9]

However, Jim Cotter has pointed out that leadership, like any other ministry, is a *gift*, a *charism*, always to be exercised as a service, a *diakonia*. All such gifts are given for the purpose of building up the whole body, for *koinonia*, for fellowship, community, communion.[10] The functions of authority that I am considering here must, if it is to constitute authentic leadership, serve these purposes. In short, leadership is sacrament.

Women and leadership

Women often find questions of leadership particularly difficult to deal with, undoubtedly because these are so readily associated with power. Women tend to stress the servant role of leadership, feeling more at ease with a serving use of their authority than with one of power. I think that this is a form of denial of the power that they do have, but it is also, more insidiously, a way of making the power that they hold acceptable to men, for the Christian tradition, essentially paternalistic, has always honoured the serving role of women, and this honour is now generally seen as an ill-disguised but effective way of keeping them in their place.

But 'service' is also sometimes more acceptable to women for the wrong reasons: it is all too often a soft cover for feelings of worthlessness. Women, whose self-image is shaped by their mothering role and who are hungry for the care and affirmation that they are not receiving elsewhere in their lives, will seek, through no fault of their own, to fill the void by taking care of others. Much good has been done through such actions, but if need is not acknowledged, there is no real choice involved and little sense of responding freely to a call. Anyone, man or woman, needs to be able to say 'No' before her 'Yes' is truly free. It is only after a woman has both claimed and rejoiced in all she is meant to have and to be, that she is free to 'give' herself appropriately and to serve the needs of others and not her own needs badly disguised, and to form relationships that are strong and free with those whom she serves. Then such a service has a good chance of being both liberating and empowering.

Leadership as sacrament

The gift of leadership I am here trying to define depends critically on the quality of the relationships that the leader has with the community. He, or she, must be able to listen very carefully to God and to the people, to find where the deepest, often unarticulated longings of the community are placed, where its members have hurt and where they are afraid to move for fear of hurting themselves or others again. It is out of this closeness that true leadership is born. For it then knows, from the particular situation in which it is placed, how to respond to people's yearnings to make sense of their lives, how to attend to the tasks that the community exists to perform and how to interpret the symbols of the tradition that overarch them all. Leadership is the outward and visible sign of the inward and spiritual grace of the Christian community. It is sacrament.

To claim that leadership is sacrament is to relate our practice of leadership to the sacrament of ordination. Ordination is always a public sacrament; the ordinand is questioned, and replies in the presence of the whole Church – bishops, clergy and laity. The public nature of ordination reflects the fact that the character and gifts of each of the three orders of ministry are each present in the body of Christ, but that some members of the body are called to be both sign and agent of these gifts. So *diakonia*, service, is there, very noticeably, for Christian communities are full of good, and loving people; deacons, vocational deacons, highlight this. The fact that we have so few (none in this diocese) is a sorry sign of how little we regard this gift. Priesthood, too, is there in the Christian community which gives flesh and reality to God's redeeming presence in this world and forms the body of Christ. And priests act *alter christus,* as the signs and agents of God's action in Christ, giving human shape to the connection between God and God's people. So also oversight is present within the Christian community. I know, only too well, the deep care that all members of the body of Christ have for the welfare of the whole body, and I know too that God always shows me those people who will, very practically, share that care with me on specific issues. The bishop is simply the sign and the agent of that care. This is the theological context in which it can be claimed that leadership is sacrament.

Styles of leadership

There are a number of ready-made styles of leadership on offer these days. At one extreme, there is the strong charismatic leader who offers an awesome view of the power and the majesty of God; and there is the leader from the more Catholic end of the spectrum whose style of leadership suggests the overwhelming authority of God. Both can operate well within a context of good relationships, but the powerful and prevailing images of these styles mean that they frequently do not. It is all too easy for leaders, both men and women, operating within these images to lose touch with the people they serve, and they do not even know that it is happening.

I have found that some women are particularly skilled at exercising a relational style of leadership. I have observed women, through the quality of these relationships, giving a church a strong sense of its worth and a strong affirmation of its being. In so doing they impart a vision of a community that is generous-hearted, because the God they know and love, and whom they know loves them, is so generous hearted. They are inclusive and open in their relations and find it a privilege to welcome people who are misfits elsewhere in society. These leaders are skilled at recognizing and affirming the gifts that God has given and they encourage their use, knowing the point at which delegation is possible. They co-ordinate the community, ensuring that all are working together and that the efforts of each person contribute effectively to the whole. At its best, such leadership is an enormously satisfying calling. It is a style that is not and need not be confined to women; it is a model for all of us.

This model of leadership works well in parish life; I have found it more difficult to put into practice as a bishop. The primary reason for this is the fact that the community I lead is in fact a community of communities, and as such is very diffuse. The Diocese of Dunedin is large geographically, the largest in New Zealand; and the church communities that make it up are very scattered and often very small. For each of them, their primary community is, quite naturally, their local one.

I have also found that the nature of a bishop's ministry is that I am spread very thin. I visit the parishes regularly, once a year or more, but find that this is insufficient to get to know people well and in depth. But I do my best. There are some, whom I work with more frequently, whom I have become quite close to.

This 'thin spread' has led me to explore different ways of exercising leadership; there is no single community with which I can function in every aspect of my ministry. So I find that I have had to develop a number of different ways of working, in particular a number of different groups with whom I work on particular issues. It can be time consuming, both for me and for them, and I need to be alert and responsive to when people are moving into overload. But it is worthwhile. It is possible, with a group of people, to both explore and capture a vision of the way we are going, and through them to begin to communicate this to the wider group.

Primarily, the style of leadership that I am exploring and suggesting relies on modelling for the communication of its essence. It self-destructs with an excessively authoritative style, and it often depends on hints and humour for its effectiveness. It is essentially about the nature of the Christian community, about its culture; and it relies on a measure of personal closeness.

Managing conflict

Conflict within a community always hurts, and the hurt within a Christian community is particularly marked. Christian churches are supposed to be places of peace and harmony where people come together to worship God, to pursue the cause of God's justice and to be the Body of Christ in the world. Conflict tears that body, re-crucifies Christ.

There are many techniques and processes available for assisting communities caught in conflict. I have found that it is essential that I am prepared to initiate such a process; it is usually impossible for those concerned to do so by themselves. I have also found that it is an essential part of my role to offer reassurance, prayer and hope, while a parish is going through the painful process of working through their difficulties. Optimism, the optimism of God, is one of the best gifts that I can bring.

There is, then, a clear association between the holding of authority and the willingness to engage in the resolution of conflict. In fact, it is in times of conflict that appeals to authority are most often made. At such times it can feel like a very raw need. The report of the last Lambeth Conference saw very clearly the connection between conflict and authority:

> The operation of authority in the Church involves conflict and disagreement. Indeed it would probably be true to say that authority in the Church works primarily *through* rather than in spite of disagreement. Its primary function is not, then, to provide ahead of time answers to all possible questions, but to assure that when disagreement occurs it is settled in accord with the principles according to which Christians normally discern the mind of Christ for them: that the solution is rooted in Scripture, consonant with the mind of the Church, and 'reasonable' in the sense that it speaks a language the world can understand – that it makes 'good sense' even if the

> sense it makes is unexpected. At this level, authority in the Church refers not so much to an absolute right to decide, vested in some particular individual or group, as it does to a right to orchestrate argument and consultation with a view to guaranteeing that what emerges from disagreement will be an understanding that grows out of the authentic sources of the Church's life.[11]

It is most humiliating, but also salutary, to acknowledge that our human inability to resolve conflict is one of the most pragmatic reasons why we have authority structures.

Notes

1 *The Truth Shall Make You Free*, The Lambeth Conference 1988 (London: Anglican Consultative Council) #70, p. 99.
2 Ibid. #71, p. 99.
3 Elaine Pagels, *The Gnostic Gospels* (Harmondsworth: Penguin Books, 1982), pp. 59ff.
4 *The Eames Commission: The Official Reports* (Toronto: Anglican Consultative Council, 1994), p. 83.
5 Ruth Fry, 'Prim Preachers to Ordained Ministers', in Ruth Fry, *Out of the Silence: Methodist Women of Aotearoa 1822–1985* (Christchurch, NZ: Methodist Publishing, 1987), p. 210.
6 Celia Allison Hahn, *Growing in Authority, Relinquishing Control: A New Approach to Faithful Leadership* (Bethesda, Md.: Alban Institute, 1994).
7 See Deborah Tannen, *You Just Don't Understand: Women and Men in Conversation.* (London: Virago, 1991), p. 36.
8 Ibid. p. 33.
9 Hans Küng, *Why Priests?* (London: Collins, 1972, quoted in Jim Cotter, *Yes, Minister? Patterns of Christian Service* (Sheffield: Cairns Publications, 1992), p. 58.
10 Cotter, *Yes, Minister?*, p. 63.
11 *The Truth Shall Make You Free*, pp. 104–5.

Bibliography

Cotter, Jim, *Yes, Minister? Patterns of Christian Service* (Sheffield: Cairns Publications, 1992).
The Eames Commission: The Official Reports (Toronto: Anglican Consultative Council, 1994).
Fry, Ruth, 'Prim Preachers to Ordained Ministers', in Ruth Fry, *Out of the Silence: Methodist Women of Aotearoa 1822–1985* (Christchurch, NZ: Methodist Publishing, 1987).
Hahn, Celia Allison, *Growing in Authority, Relinquishing Control: A New Approach to Faithful Leadership* (Bethesda, Md.: Alban Institute, 1994).
Küng, Hans, *Why Priests?*, trans. John Cumming (London: Collins, 1972).
Pagels, Elaine, *The Gnostic Gospels* (Harmondsworth: Penguin Books, 1982).
Tannen, Deborah, *You Just Don't Understand: Women and Men in Conversation* (London: Virago, 1991).
The Truth Shall Make You Free, The Lambeth Conference 1988 (London: Anglican Consultative Council).

13 Women in Leadership: A British Baptist Perspective

Myra Blyth

Notions of leadership

In the Baptist tradition the power of decision-making resides within the collective life of gathered believers, meeting at local congregational, regional association and national assembly levels. The mind of Christ is the authority under which the assembled company meets, to discern God's will and to make decisions for the life and witness of the Church and for the well-being of its members.

This language may feel slightly odd or pietistic but it accurately reflects the position of British Baptists. The 2,000 congregations and 140,000 members within the Baptist Union of Great Britain have recently attempted to express this self-understanding in more contemporary ways, identifying five values which sum up what Baptists in essence believe to be the nature and calling of the Church. We are a gospel people called in Christ to be a prophetic, sacrificial, missionary, inclusive, worshipping community.[1]

What has not changed in the 300 years of Baptist life and witness is the essentially voluntarist nature of Baptist ecclesiology and polity. Those in leadership carry authority less by dint of the office they hold than because of the charisms they exercise. The relationships they enjoy with the constituency they seek to lead are essentially open, trusting and mutual. Historically, the non-hierarchical understanding of leadership among Baptists, coupled with the contemporary disliking for central structures of co-ordination reinforce one another and result in a robust egalitarianism. At its best this system nurtures the values it espouses, but in the real and messy world which we know, it is open to abuse. Like any system, it can be used to perpetuate excluding and exclusive practices towards those in life who are often marginalized and written off, on account of their gender, status and other circumstances.

Experiencing limitations

The Baptist story is one that has allowed space for women in leadership from its earliest times, and there are great early examples of the recognition of women preaching, teaching, evangelizing and having oversight over groups of churches. This of course became part of the criticism of separatists – that women took part and even preached. Early Baptist records of the seventeenth century tell stories of women such as Mrs Attaway of the General Baptist church in Bell Alley, London. She started preaching to groups of women, but men soon joined – young men, apprentices and less 'respectable' people. The meetings were a great success, marked by much laughter and hilarity. This right to preach was sometimes challenged from within, as well as from outside. This is clear from the church in Fenstanton where Sister Annie Harriman threatened to withdraw her membership because 'Brother Naudin has said that he would not walk with such as gave liberty to women to speak in church, whilst she, for her part, would not walk where she had not this right.'[2]

As the organization of congregations and the training and recognition of ministers was developed, however, the early practice was not honoured. Doctrinal conservatism and scriptural literalism in the eighteenth and nineteenth centuries meant that women were increasingly silenced. This has been gradually corrected with the re-emergence of women leaders in the structures of the Church, first through foreign mission, then in diaconal orders and most recently, since 1918, in the full and equal accrediting of women into the ministry of word and sacrament.

During my time as the Deputy General Secretary of the Baptist Union of Great Britain, I came to appreciate the strengths and weaknesses inherent in our particular story. As a local minister and as a minister working in the wider ecumenical scene, I had enormous freedom to act and speak according to my conscience. As a national leader I was much more limited in what I could do or say. I quickly found that I was expected to toe a line. This is, of course, the common experience of all those who enter into institutional office – it is a feature of organizational life both sacred and secular. But the inevitability of this does not make it acceptable. Limiting institutional environments need to be analysed and evaluated alongside the principles and polity that motivate and shape a particular ecclesiology.

In my experience, the 'limitation factor' I felt while in the leadership of the Baptist Union was due to several interlocking influences. First, Baptists locally feel very ambivalent about those in leadership speaking on their behalf. They tolerate it, especially if they think what is being said is appropriate, but become very annoyed when they feel it is contrary to their views and therefore misrepresents them.

Second, current Baptist life is not fully comfortable with diversity. In our minds, we know it is healthy to have a diversity of views, but in practice we still behave as if difference and disagreement represent a threat to our unity and a weakness in our thinking. Early Baptist leaders were sometimes more radical and more discerning about where consensus is crucial and where disagreement need not preoccupy or divide. A striking, though untypical, example of this can be seen in the covenant that was made between the believers who founded the church at New Road in Oxford in the seventeenth century. The covenant respects the rights and consciences of its members to practise either infant or believers' baptism. What was more important to them than achieving purity of practice in the question of baptism was to establish significant places of worship in Oxford where freedom of conscience and extempore prayer would be able to thrive.

Third, the culture, ethos and style of the Baptist Union as an organizing/co-ordinating body was experienced by some (including myself) as overbearing. Great efforts were made to correct this, and to balance different styles and approaches, but in the end this is not just a balancing act: it is a question of essence. Who and how are we called to be, as Christ's Church?

Fourth, female leaders in the decision-making structures of the Baptist Union are still simply too few to be able to bring an alternative influence to bear on the ways of working and relating.

Current feminist critique on authority, leadership and organizational culture has yet to make a significant impact on the Baptist scene, but this is not the huge or impossible journey some might imagine. I remain convinced that much in Baptist history, thinking and practice is deeply sympathetic to views expressed by feminists about equality and egalitarianism. But more of that later. The story of women's re-emergence into leadership within the Union during the twentieth century needs to be particularly noted in the context of this book because it is both a remarkable and a cautionary tale.

A lack of debate

Baptists have included women in leadership and have ordained women longer and more consistently than any other mainstream historic tradition in England. However, the numbers of women in ordained ministry and of women (lay and ordained) in leadership today does not match this glorious fact. The poor rate of growth of women entering the ordained ministry in recent times is peculiar, in the circumstances, but let me try and explain it. First, the local autonomy of congregations is relevant: to be ordained, a person must be called by a congregation. Therefore, women may be trained for ordination at one of the several Baptist theological colleges in the country, but if no church calls them, they will not be ordained. Second, and most importantly (in part because it explains the first reason), the relative absence of debate historically among Baptists about gender and authority, and the inadequacy of debate still today, must be a vital contributing factor. Scholars have noted the incredulous fact that at the historic point when the Baptist Union Council approved the resolution to ordain women in 1918, no significant theological debate took place. The Council minutes simply record that, there being no reasons theological or practical to reject women, the resolution was approved.

So what are the reasons for this incredible non-debate? One explanation is that the diverse views held at the time were not honestly aired and that as a consequence churches and colleges against women's leadership simply continued and intensified their practice of discouraging women from exploring any sense of calling to the ministry of word and sacrament. In 1922 the first woman was accepted for training in a Baptist college. Violet Hedger first applied to Spurgeon's but was turned down since the college did not accept women. Instead, she was accepted by Regent's Park College, by the then principal Dr Gould. Unfortunately, by the time she arrived there was a new principal, Dr Wheeler Robinson, who did not approve of her presence and made the point by trying to ignore her. It was the custom of this time that the principal paid the examination fees for the student – but Dr Wheeler Robinson would not do this for Violet Hedger because she was a woman.[3]

An alternative and perfectly plausible explanation for the non-debate about women in leadership within the Baptist Union in the early twentieth century is that Baptist polity has always been inherently, though unconsciously, sympathetic to many of the values and views often espoused by women with respect to leadership and authority in the Church. The notion of leadership in Baptist discourse is inclusive, prophetic and missionary in its character. It is inclusive because wide consultation and collective discernment is the way to reach decisions. It is prophetic because it is about speaking out (without counting the cost) in the name of truth and justice. It is missionary because it is driven by a spirituality that nurtures openness, generosity and vulnerability. At its best, Baptist ecclesiology and polity view leadership and authority in a manner akin to New Testament and early Church experiences of charismatic and apostolic leadership: transitional, experimental and free-thinking.

A third and perhaps most likely reason for the non-debate about ordained women in Baptist life, past and present, is that Baptists have always approached the question of women in leadership in an essentially androgynous way. By glossing over gender difference and diversity, with the notion that all are one in Christ, Baptists conclude that faith takes us beyond gender and beyond difference. This well-meaning approach is surely ill conceived. The Church in all its ecclesial manifestations will be stronger, wiser and more authentically itself when gender difference and diversity are recognized and affirmed in the calling of people (men and women) into leadership.

It has been demonstrated by a number of scholars, and Rebecca Lyman makes reference to it in her contribution to this book, that women's leadership in the early Church was diminished and marginalized the more charismatic leadership within the early Christian movement was contained and controlled by institutionalizing church leadership. It behoves the churches today to recover those aspects of leadership which were lost with the exclusion of women from the public realm. It should do so not simply by appointing women to leadership, but by honouring the diversity of styles and approaches which women may bring to the office of leader/bishop/overseer. Women who currently reach the 'highest' offices in the Church are under particular pressure to conform to existing patterns. They rarely have the permission or colleague-power to make the differences they could. Only by substantial representation of women in the leadership of the Church will the context be set for significant changes to take place in the style and organizational ethos of the churches.

The debate about women priests and bishops in the Church of England, and in the Anglican Communion as a whole, has been, in stark contrast to the Baptist story, long, heated, very public and intensely uncomfortable. The irony of this, however, is that the tortuous Anglican route may prove to be the more profound journey in the long run. Ordination statistics at least would tend to point in this direction. When the day comes that the Church of England appoints women bishops, this well-travelled road may leave the Church better prepared to let women exercise leadership in a way which is authentic to their personhood and charisms.

Notes

1 *Five Core Values for a Gospel People* (Didcot, Oxon: Baptist Union of Great Britain, 1999).

2 Ruth Gouldbourne, *Re-inventing the Wheel: Women and the Ministry in English Baptist Life*, the Whitley Lecture 1997–8 (Oxford: Whitley Publications, 1998), p. 14.

3 Ibid., pp. 27–8.

Bibliography

Baptist Union of Great Britain, *Five Core Values for a Gospel People* (Didcot, Oxon: Baptist Union of Great Britain, 1999).

Gouldbourne, Ruth, *Re-inventing the Wheel: Women and Ministry in English Baptist Life*, the Whitley Lecture 1997–8 (Oxford: Whitley Publications, 1997).

14 Humanity Fully Represented Before God: A Liturgical Approach

Bridget Nichols

THE WAY WE PRAY illuminates what we believe: *lex orandi, lex credendi.*[1] So our liturgical action affects our theology, including our understanding of the Church, its sacraments, its ministry, and crucially for our purposes, its episcopal leadership. For, in the experience of most people – clergy, lay people who are regular churchgoers, others who come to church at Christmas and attend the occasional confirmation – the bishop is a figure who is seen pre-eminently in church. It is as the leading figure in ceremonial that the bishop is most accessible and most understandable, and it is through this medium that most people come to perceive the nature of episcopacy.

As the Church of England anticipates the first ordinations of women to serve as bishops, people will speculate about change. A number of projected changes may prove wide of the mark. Why, for example, should female bishops bring greater pastoral experience than their male counterparts, except that society still has high expectations of women as nurturers?

Presuppositions and cultural idiosyncrasies abound and it is all too easy to be distracted by stereotyped assumptions about the differences in stature, quality of voice, visibility in procession, style of wearing vestments, and administrative method that will characterize women bishops. This is the stuff of which fears and misgivings about disconcerting differences and the rupture of order are manufactured, and mere theorizing about women as bishops in the Church of England will not seriously displace them.

On the other hand, matters which are taken for granted – especially the words of the Church's common prayer – may be unexpectedly illuminated when a woman presides. It is therefore appropriate that the liturgy itself, both liturgy about bishops (the Ordinal) and liturgical forms in which the bishop might preside, should determine a distinctive approach to the appointment of women bishops. This chapter considers these two areas, beginning with a discussion of the Ordinal which sets the terms for a general reflection on episcopal ministry, its demands, and the expectations placed on those who are called to be bishops. The discussion then moves to the specifics of the bishop's participation in worship, in each case asking what it might mean for a woman to preside. What emerges is a view of the bishop as representative person, a question which the chapter takes up in its closing assessment of the contribution that the episcopal ministry of women will bring to a Church that is still in the process of becoming fully representative of humanity, and fully represented before God.

The Ordinal

The rite for the ordination or consecration of bishops brings together two important questions: 'What is to be understood from the ritual procedure for making a bishop?' and 'What is a bishop expected to do in church?' Once we turn to the Ordinal in current use,[2] it is immediately clear that, were the Church of England to ordain women to its episcopate tomorrow, there would be no need to alter more than the pronouns relating to the bishop-elect, in order to make it usable. Nor would things be very different were any of the earlier Anglican Ordinals to be chosen instead. While their Prefaces restrict eligibility for appointment to men, the texts themselves would stand with only slight adjustment of pronouns and the substitution of 'sister' for 'brother'. The Epistle (1 Timothy 3 'A bishop therefore must be . . . the husband of one wife') may appear to present a contradiction, but it would not have been much less contradictory in the case of unmarried Tudor bishops. It is a forceful reminder that the Church's understanding of *episkope* is a complex one, developed over many centuries, and informed by an ongoing dialogue between scripture and tradition. Contemporary ordination rites have acknowledged this richness and complexity by proposing a wide choice of biblical passages.

When it comes to the activities prescribed for the bishop in recent Ordinals (ordaining, baptizing, confirming, teaching, exercising authority), the earlier Ordinals are silent. The first Anglican Ordinal (1550) made no reference at all to the liturgical duties of those to be ordained bishop, and it was only in 1662, a century and a half after this first Reformed English Ordinal had appeared, that the absence even began to be addressed. The Ordinal of the 1662 Prayer Book tersely asks candidates, 'Will you be faithful in ordaining, sending, or laying hands upon others?' It is a question of political as much as liturgical significance, reminding bishops and later readers that, after the ban on the use of the Prayer Book during the Interregnum, the pressure to defend the practice of episcopal ordination in the Restoration Church was great.

Since then, there has been a marked shift in the consciousness of bishops' liturgical responsibilities in rites for their ordination. As David Holeton has shown, the revisions which emerged across the Anglican Communion from the 1970s onwards have dramatically changed the 1662 Book of Common Prayer's emphasis on maintaining firm control over the authorization of priestly and episcopal ministry. Holeton shows that 'the prayers of consecration used for bishops now make particular reference to the liturgical ministry of bishops'.[3] He sees in this addition a radical change in the understanding of the bishop's role in the Church, so that 'a ministry which normatively was assumed to be juridical and exercised from a distance is now expected to be pastoral and proximate'.[4] This has powerful implications for practice. As Holeton explains:

> The liturgical texts assume that bishops will be a regular part of parochial life and, when present, will not be relegated to the 'bishop's chair' and merely be 'allowed' to confirm, but that they will preach the gospel, baptize, and preside at the eucharist, showing clearly whose ministry it is, and that the incumbent exercises these ministries on an ongoing basis not as an inherent right but, rather, in the bishop's stead and as the bishop's personal delegate.[5]

None of these functions depends upon gender, and the role of chief pastor, responsible for the Church's teaching ministry, the care of the clergy, concern for the lost and needy, and the exercise of authority and discipline with mercy and humility, could be fulfilled as well by suitably gifted women as by suitably gifted men. Yet fundamental acknowledgements based on ordination rites and bishops' characteristic duties are more complex in real life, and there is a powerful presupposition of masculinity attached to episcopacy and episcopally led worship. One bishop has commented on the inherent maleness of what he calls 'sacristy culture'. This achieves an extreme form before large cathedral-style services, where the vestry can begin to resemble a religious locker room. Women robing with their male colleagues can expect comments on the 'fetching' appearance of vestments which ordinarily never attract comment, and occasional remarks like, 'I love women in clerical dress'. They may find themselves being physically moved round the robing area by the shoulders with a tactile freedom normally absent from vestries.

Until the gap between theory and practice is closed by women exercising episcopal leadership, the Church will not come to a proper understanding of their ministry. Yet lest that should suggest a great hiatus between present and future, there are two important pointers to continuity. First, the Church of England is a member of a Communion, parts of which have already received the episcopal ministry of women.

Second, it is able to draw on its knowledge of women in senior cathedral and diocesan posts within its own territorial boundaries, and to hear those women's accounts of occupying prominent roles. Their ministries do not, and indeed should not, offer previews of women in the episcopate, but the nature of their work enables them to speak directly of matters that will concern women who are appointed to the office of bishop, notably ceremonial, authority, and the way in which a role is modelled.

Context, role and gender

One view is that variation in the style of leading liturgical action on a large scale will depend more on occasion than on gender: that the size of the building, the length of the processional route, the visual aspects of vesture and ceremonial, all carry greater impact than individuals involved in the action in very visible roles. A Christmas midnight Eucharist with the bishop presiding, attended by some local people as well as many visitors and infrequent churchgoers, is likely to create a solemn, stately dignity around the bishop quite different from the intimacy of a Maundy Thursday Blessing of Oils and Renewal of Vows. Asked about the ways in which women who have come relatively recently to prominent roles in the Church have modelled their liturgical style, the Dean of Leicester observed that 'most of [her] generation of women have simply adopted many of the ways men had of leading liturgy'.[6]

A different view comes from a woman who is an Archdeacon as well as a residentiary canon of a cathedral. She is emphatic in saying that she has not 'modelled [her] liturgical style on that of male colleagues'. Instead, she has striven in her diocesan and cathedral roles to 'facilitate worship in a way which is authentic to who [she is]'. She has encountered a range of responses from worshippers. 'Some have been explicit in affirming the enrichment brought by a woman's contribution to the liturgy, both in presiding and preaching. Others remark on such things as tone of voice, manner of communication, body language, a personal and reflective dimension.'[7] She notes that there are 'still so few women in senior positions that [they] don't often experience each other's liturgical ministry in context'.

Yet another assessment comes from a woman who is a bishop in the Episcopal Church of the United States of America. She comments that gender does not play an overt role in the way in which she leads worship. 'I am simply who I am, and my presidential style is the result of my physical and spiritual presence.' Prior to ordination, she had spent her whole adult life 'as a woman in traditionally male-dominated occupations, so the experience of being a bishop has not been particularly different'. At the same time, she acknowledges that she was the ninth woman to be ordained bishop in the United States, and the fifth to become a diocesan bishop, so that she assumed a role for which there was already an established precedent.[8]

These three views do not negate one another. The first gives an overview of a whole action, where coherence and orderly progression depend upon timing, a correct sequence of actions, and the ability of those in ministerial roles to be in the right positions at the right moment without signs of conferring or uncertainty. Individuals, in this evaluation, are always subordinate to the rite. The second draws attention to the sense of personal relationship that comes to exist between the person in the presidential role and the worshippers, even on large occasions where greater formality might be observed. Here, gender difference seems to have sharpened the consciousness of a personal liturgical style in a positive way which promotes trust and confidence. The third account continues the theme of the liturgical president as individual, but emphasizes personhood over gender. It also points usefully to a pre-ordination career as the setting in which confidence about working in a male-dominated profession has developed, although it is clear that this witness has found it easier to be a bishop in a Church where several women had already been appointed bishops.

The insights of these women give the broad outline of their roles as leaders of public worship without engaging with the detail of the liturgical text. Instead of working exhaustively through various rites, however, imagining hypothetical women as their episcopal presidents, I have concentrated on two areas where consciousness is likely to be significantly raised. These are, respectively, the governing images which the Church has traditionally applied to its understanding of episcopacy, and the relationship of the bishop to the words that are used in worship.

Governing images

The familiar image of the bishop, 'father in God', occurs in literature *about* episcopacy, but only appears in an Anglican Ordinal as an address to the ordaining archbishop.[9] Within the Ordinals, the role of the bishop has been figured pre-eminently as that of 'chief pastor'. The Book of Common Prayer adds to the description of the bishop as one of the Pastors of the Church, that he should be a 'wise and faithful servant', and a 'shepherd not a wolf'. The Alternative Service Book begins with the notion of 'servant'. It takes up the 'chief pastor' image, relating it to unity, mission and proclamation, following the 'example of the Apostles'. It also offers metaphors for the Church (other than the flock of Christ), referring to the

Petrine vision of 'a holy people, . . . a royal priesthood'. The bishop should be a 'true shepherd', a 'wise teacher', 'steadfast as a guardian of [the Church's] faith and sacraments', a 'ruler over [God's] household' (another ecclesiastical figure), and an 'ambassador for Christ'. These images recur in the modern Ordinals used across the Anglican Communion.

There will be some who ask whether distinctive metaphors will need to be sought to characterize the episcopal role of women. The reply to that question must begin by recognizing that the existing descriptive repertoire offers rich and scripturally resonant images, many of them alluding to Christ himself, or to the ministry of the apostles. They may be daunting, but as the closing words of the Archbishop's Charge to the Bishop-elect in the rite for the Ordination and Consecration of a Bishop of the Church of the Province of Southern Africa reminds us, 'No one is sufficient for these things'.[10] Women and men alike who respond to the call to be bishops will find ample inspiration and the challenge to constant self-examination in these ungendered types of pastoral care and oversight.

What the emergence of women in the leadership of the Church asks, is that rather than inventing new images, the Church should refresh and deepen its grasp of existing images. And if it is agreed that these images will adequately illuminate aspects of the ministry of female bishops, the way in which they operate will require deeper understanding. Archbishop Rowan Williams demonstrates the kind of reflection that might take place in an address on pastoral ministry delivered to an international gathering of prison chaplains:

> When Jesus in the fourth gospel describes himself as shepherd of his people, the primary image is certainly about nurture, feeding; but there are two aspects of the language here that do not easily reduce to unquestioning care and support. One is the clear insistence on the risks the shepherd runs, risk to the shepherd's own life or identity; the other is the repeated concern with mutual knowledge. The shepherd knows and is known: shepherd and sheep are in some way transparent to each other.[11]

The qualities of reckless self-giving, honesty, consistency and recognizability that this meditation evokes are also the qualities most to be desired in the Church's chief pastors, women and men, but we have to be patient with the metaphor in order to reach that insight.

Another image worth developing is that of the apostle, who is the type of faithfulness, courage, persistence, and costly determination to proclaim the gospel. Additionally, it provides an opportunity for the Church's ordained women to make a real and practical claim on the honoured place given to Mary Magdalene as 'the apostle to the apostles' – a model instance of the continuity between the tradition taught through the Calendar and through the Church's ministry.

The bishop and the liturgical text

Every image prescribes a certain way of seeing the bishop, and the illustrations we have been contemplating indicate that there are many ways of characterizing the role. They show, too, that images call for the kind of critical engagement that saves them from being turned into idols by dangerous sentimentality, or mystification, or co-option into a particular set of gender characteristics. For at their strongest, these figures can encourage deeper reflection about the bishop's task, and sometimes, though not always, they will shape an encounter. It should be remembered, of course, that they are drawn from a variety of Anglican Ordinals and consequently exist in a setting where a good deal of energy is focused on teaching about the nature of episcopacy and episcopal ministry.

A much more overt and unstable relationship is to be found at other liturgical occasions between the words which are used and those who speak them, read them and hear them, and there are many ecclesiastical anecdotes involving inapposite texts and their comic or shocking effects. There was the bishop who found that the Gospel reading appointed for his enthronement was taken from the eleventh chapter of Matthew. He was alarmed, when it came to verse 3, to hear the question, 'Are you the one who is to come, or are we to look for another?' Slightly built bishops who have processed into churches to the accompaniment of *Ecce sacerdos magnus* must have paused for thought. For women, however, the convergence of word and person has the potential to be more forceful than these stories suggest. Imagine a woman bishop or priest presiding at the Eucharist and using Prayer G of the Common Worship set of eucharistic prayers:

> How wonderful the work of your hands, O Lord.
> As a mother tenderly gathers her children,
> you embraced a people as your own.
> When they turned away and rebelled
> your love remained steadfast.
>
> From them you raised up Jesus our Saviour, born of Mary,
> to be the living bread,
> in whom all our hungers are satisfied.

'Mother' is likely to be animated in this prayer in a new way when a woman presides, if only because of obvious biological and cultural factors. Yet this is a transitional moment in liturgy, whose force is to carry the whole worshipping body beyond human motherhood, and to offer it the picture of Jesus, longing to gather Jerusalem as a hen gathers her brood under her wings (Luke 13.34; Matthew 23.37). Christopher Cocksworth and Rosalind Brown have said of priesthood that 'we must be very cautious about images of priestly ministry that might appear to treat the priest as a cloth to be wrung out by others. Yet the energy of motherhood and the willingness of mothers to risk their lives in the giving of life are strong and powerful pictures of the calling of a priest.'[12] The same analysis applies to bishops. Take, for instance, the moment of laying on of hands at Confirmation. As the candidate kneels in front of the bishop, these words are said: 'God has called you by name, and made you his own.' They come almost unchanged from Isaiah (43.1), where they signal the unique choice of a nation created and redeemed by God. But in this setting, they carry an intimate and almost parental gentleness, and the association created when a woman pronounced them would be different from the effect produced by a male confirming bishop.

Other convergences of text and person carry destructive rather than constructive potential. Consider the case of a woman archdeacon invited to lead a session on the significance of the Bible at a Diocesan Clergy Conference immediately after the reading of 1 Timothy 2.12 ('I do not permit women to teach or dictate to the men; they should keep quiet'); or of a woman installed as an honorary canon of a cathedral during choral Evensong who took her oath after Judges 14 (Samson's vengeance against his Philistine wife's relations) was read as the First Lesson.[13]

These sorts of convergences raise serious questions about the authority of scripture in every aspect of the Church's life, but in the setting of worship it requires a particular kind of response. It will not be good enough to persist in a situation where some readings, 'though [they] make the unskilful laugh, cannot but make the judicious grieve'.[14] Nor should such difficult texts be discarded in an energetically political reconstruction of the biblical canon. But that places an obligation on the Church to discover a new and profoundly thoughtful way of living with them. Liturgical worship has a unique responsibility for modelling a faithful, attentive and critical engagement with biblical texts in the context of prayer and reflection. What now strikes worshippers as horrifying legalistic injustice – the stoning of old men for gathering sticks on the Sabbath, for example – can be heard against a vision of the Law through the lens of love in the New Testament. The visual and dramatic dimensions of worship speak more eloquently than words when a text seems to challenge the role of a particular individual in leading the assembly. Paul's anxiety about women speaking in gatherings of Christians makes this point well. As a gathering of many different people, worship is able to show that painful and rebarbative passages may not be restricted in their effect, but have an impact on the whole body. The death of Jephthah's daughter reflects the practices of a whole society, not just the pointless death of one young woman.

All of these issues would play a part in recovering a reinvigorated hermeneutic, which took account of the multiple 'horizons'[15] of the text, the worshippers, the leaders of worship and contemporary society. A fully inclusive ministry finds the Church actively needing to be a biblical Church: confronting difficult texts, wrestling with the apparent incommensurability between their teaching and other developments in the Church's life, and engaging in a lively and serious way with those who hear them in the contemporary context.[16]

For female bishops, there will be a particular need to realize this potential in a courageous and thoughtful ministry of preaching and teaching, matched by a quality of pastoral care that truly expresses the gospel. It is here, rather than in ceremonial action, that awareness that the bishop is a woman will be most powerful.

The bishop as representative person

Hard words in the language of the liturgy are always hard words, but as we have seen, it takes the fact of a woman leading the worshipping assembly to raise consciousness, and to make explicit the obstacles and opportunities that lie within the life of the Church at prayer. At one level, this may be very simply explained as the comparative unfamiliarity of a woman in a prominent role. At another level, however, it is a reminder that symbol and practice lie very close together in worship, and the practical question, 'Who is leading the assembly?' is inseparable from the symbolic question, 'What does he or she represent?'

In a consideration of the theology of choosing diocesan bishops in the Church of England, Bishop Michael Nazir-Ali sums up the representative nature of the episcopal role:

> a bishop's ministry is 'representative' in *several different senses*. A bishop represents the local church to the wider, but also the other way round. Bishops represent Christ to the people, but also bring the people and their prayers to God. Finally, they often represent God and his Church in the world at large. We have seen that this ministry is shared with other ministers, and also that the whole Church has a representative ministry. The ordained ministry, and especially episcopal ministry, has, nevertheless, a specific role in representation.[17]

One reading of this scrupulously gender-neutral account might see in it a tacit declaration that the inclusion of women in the episcopate will make no theological or functional difference to the Church's existence. While that is a desirable interpretation, it easily overlooks other significant differences which will emerge with women bishops, and which can be drawn out of a more rigorous reflection on each point.

The representation of the local church to the wider Church, and vice versa, is complex. Not only does it speak of the relationship of diocese to territorial church, and territorial church to Communion; it also reaches out to the whole Church Catholic. Women in the Church of England's episcopate will bring continuity between the membership of the three orders of ministry in their own church and that of other Anglican Churches. They will also alter the Church of England's relationship to Anglican Churches which do not admit women to the episcopate.

The arrival of women as bishops in the Church of England will be the completion of conditions for full ecumenical agreements with a number of other Churches. Already, the Porvoo Agreement of 1995 links the Anglican Churches of England, Scotland, Wales and Ireland with the Lutheran Churches of Estonia, Lithuania, Finland, Sweden, Iceland and Norway, with interchange of ministries, while the Meissen Agreement of 1988 created a relationship between the Church of England, the Evangelical Churches in Germany, and the Federation of the Evangelical Churches in the German Democratic Republic. The Anglican–Methodist Covenant should advance towards completion rapidly, once women are represented in all three Orders of Ministry in the Church of England.

At the same time, it is equally likely that closer ecumenical relationships with the Roman Catholic and Orthodox Churches will be at least temporarily stalled. An Anglican Bishop from southern Africa who serves on an international ecumenical commission believes that the essential quality in this situation is honesty.

> The point is that the Anglican Church does have women bishops and any ecumenical discussions have to take this into account. We can only negotiate with any credibility if we are true to who we are and not what others might want us to be. And we have to be true to the journey we are on as a Communion.[18]

Women entrusted as priests with representing Christ to the people have already brought a fuller sense of the divine nature to many, and an earlier section of this chapter has already suggested how traditional images of the Christlike model of episcopacy will be freshly understood when they are interpreted by the ministry of women. On the other hand, those who ascribe an iconic value to the priestly representation of Christ, and insist that the representative person is male, will be equally or more resistant to women bishops.[19] These misgivings need to be carefully and sensitively probed, for their roots often extend into the deepest ground of their holders' belief. They can only be displaced by radically reversing the poles of representation, by turning away from maleness defining Christ, and towards Christ embodying the humanity of men and women in the great representative act of salvation. When women exercise the ministry of priests and bishops, the incomplete representation of the people to God by an exclusively male priesthood and episcopate is redressed.

Representation is not impersonation. Even the exalted form of impersonation that might be implied by the claims of male clergy to be presiding *in persona Christi* surely speaks of a limited Christology that restricts the full benefits of Christ's life, death and resurrection to particular groups. On the other hand, representation has a strong element of the *imitatio Christi*, but in the sense that the aspiration to the likeness of Christ is an aspiration for the whole Church. Already, the ministry of women as priests and deacons has brought a visible representation of all humanity into the sacramental life of the Church of England. But having found themselves represented in the Church's priesthood, men and women cannot be complacent. The likeness of Christ is something constantly in formation, and the prayer (in some way or another) at every eucharistic gathering is: 'form us into the likeness of Christ'; 'that we may grow into his likeness'.[20] It is the role of the Church's leaders to make this aspiration possible. How will women bishops contribute?

Growing into the likeness of Christ

In all liturgical activity, we are not so much reaching for the extraordinary, as reimagining ordinary things – the bread and wine of the Eucharist; the water of baptism; the oil of anointing; light and darkness; the proximity of other human beings. It is a list which could be much further expanded.

What the liturgy teaches the Church about bishops is that they are centrally concerned with the quality of its relationship with sacred ordinariness. The Church asks of its bishops that they teach, govern and exercise discipline. Symbol and practice therefore exist in very close proximity. As normative president of the Eucharist and Baptism and, in Anglicanism, the only minister of Confirmation, the bishop enacts the responsibilities of feeding, admitting new Christians, and teaching. At the institution of a parish priest, the bishop gives the new incumbent a share in 'the cure of souls which is both yours and mine'. At the annual Chrism Eucharist, where oils for the anointing of baptismal and confirmation candidates, the sick, and the dying are blessed, and ministerial vows are renewed, the bishop is the focus of unity,[21] the figure around whom others gather.[22]

The women who become bishops will bring new insights and emphases to all these aspects of ministry, to the great benefit of the Church. But as the Lutheran liturgist Gordon Lathrop conveys in his vision of the worship of a post-denominational Christianity, the novel perceptions that may reach the worshipping body through the symbolic order will ultimately be less important than the faithful and confident exercise of episcopal leadership which is the expectation placed on all the Church's bishops:

> A woman presider may 'bring the power of women' or, in many places still, the power of surprise that the leader is a woman, to her tasks in the meeting. She may bring the explosive force of the new social awareness of gender equality. She may be powerfully capable at empathy, community-building and shared leadership . . . But these powers as well as any symbolic powers are not enough. She must turn whatever power she brings to serving the assembly in the ordo. After the Scripture is read and in critical responsibility to it, she will preach. In dialogue with the assembly, according to the discipline of *eucharistia*, she will give thanks. Together with others, she will see to it that there is a collection for the poor. She will receive the newly baptized and assist in reconciling the alienated. Nothing else.[23]

Here are both the novelty of women as church leaders and the rhythmic ordinariness of the role they undertake. The novelty will wear off rapidly, but it is only by doing 'nothing else' than the duties of the chief pastor, that female bishops will bring something more to the ongoing formation of the Church, for this is how the Church lives out what it prays, continually recalling women and men to their vocation pattern their lives on Christ, and to 'grow into his likeness'.[24] That longing has been part of the Church's prayers from a very early point in its history. It is no better expressed than in the Collect for the First Sunday of Christmas, drawn originally from the sixth-century Leonine Sacramentary:

> Almighty God,
> who wonderfully created us in your own image
> and yet more wonderfully restored us
> through your Son Jesus Christ:
> grant that, as he came to share in our humanity,
> so we may share the life of his divinity.

Notes

1 An epithet attributed originally to the fifth-century lay monk Prosper of Aquitaine. For a full discussion of its appropriation in the Anglican tradition, see W. Taylor Stevenson, 'Lex Orandi – Lex Credendi', in Stephen Sykes and John Booty (eds), *The Study of Anglicanism* (London: SPCK, 1988), pp. 174–88.

2 The first Anglican Ordinal appeared in 1550, a year after the First Prayer Book of Edward VI was published. It reappeared with few changes in the Second Prayer Book of Edward VI in 1552, but was more extensively revised and expanded for the Book of Common Prayer of 1662. The Church of England continued to use the 1662 rite until 1980, when the Alternative Service Book brought a modern-language Ordinal with different emphases. This rite is still in force, with slight revisions made in 2000. A new Ordinal is currently in preparation.

3 David Holeton, 'The Bishop Leading his Diocese', in *The Bishop in Liturgy*, ed. Colin Buchanan (Bramcote, England: Grove Books, 1988), pp.25–33, esp. pp. 25–7.

4 Ibid., pp. 26–7.

5 Ibid., p. 27.

6 The Very Revd Vivienne Faull (personal correspondence). These women began their career in ministry as deaconesses. They were ordained deacons as soon as legislation to admit women to the diaconate was passed, and likewise priested as soon as this was possible (1994).

7 The Ven. Dr Joy Tetley, Archdeacon of Worcester (personal correspondence).

8 Katharine Jefferts Schori, Bishop of Nevada (personal correspondence).

9 See, for example, Colin Buchanan, 'The Bishop in Action', in Buchanan (ed.), *The Bishop in Liturgy*, p. 51. See also the opening paragraph of the Church Commissioners for England report *Called to be a Bishop* (B&C)(99)1 (London: Church Commissioners, 1999), which gives an overview of the roles and activities in the Church of England. Legal documents addressed to a bishop in the Church of England, e.g. Letters Patent, begin 'Right Reverend Father in God'.

10 2 Corinthians 2.16. These words were inscribed on the inside of Lancelot Andrewes' episcopal ring.

11 Rowan Williams, 'Ministry in Prison: Theological Reflections', *Justice Reflections* 2 (2003), p. 2.

12 Christopher Cocksworth and Rosalind Brown, *Being a Priest Today* (Norwich: Canterbury Press, 2002), p. 34.

13 See Zoë Bennett-Moore, 'Male and Female in the Image of God?', *The Bible in Transmission*, Summer 2003, pp. 12–13.

14 William Shakespeare, *Hamlet*, III.ii.25–6.

15 The term developed in the hermeneutical theory of Hans-Georg Gadamer to describe the situations or perspectives from which different interpreters approach each other. See *Truth and Method*, 2nd revd edn, trans. and ed. Joel Weinsheimer and Donald G. Marshall (London: Sheed & Ward, 1989). This concept is treated in depth by Anthony C. Thiselton in *The Two Horizons: New Testament Hermeneutics and Philosophical Description with Special Reference to Heidegger, Bultmann, Gadamer and Wittgenstein* (Exeter: Paternoster Press, 1980) and *New Horizons in Hermeneutics* (London: HarperCollins, 1992).

16 I am grateful to the Rt Revd David Beetge, Bishop of the Highveld, for discussing this point, drawing on his experience as a church leader in contemporary South Africa.

17 Michael Nazir-Ali, 'Towards a Theology of Choosing Diocesan Bishops', in Archbishops' Council, *Working with the Spirit: Choosing Diocesan Bishops*, GS 1405 (London: Church House Publishing, 2001), p. 107.

18 The Rt Revd David Beetge (personal correspondence).

19 An excellent analysis of Methodist, Roman Catholic and Church of England approaches to priesthood and gender is given by Jacqueline Field-Bibb in *Women Towards Priesthood* (Cambridge: Cambridge University Press, 1991).

20 I am indebted for this insight into 'formational language' to the Revd Christopher Irvine. His current research on issues of liturgical formation will be published as *The Art of God: The Formation of Christians in the Likeness of Christ* (London: SPCK).

21 David Stancliffe, 'The Bishop in his Cathedral', in Buchanan (ed.), *The Bishop in Liturgy*, pp. 32–9.

22 Increasingly, dioceses are making provision in their orders of service for this occasion for licensed readers and other laypeople to make a renewed commitment to ministry, alongside the clergy.

23 Gordon Lathrop, 'Christian Leadership and Liturgical Community', *Worship* 66 (1992), p. 121.

24 Ibid.

Bibliography

Bennett-Moore, Zoë, 'Male and Female in the Image of God?', *The Bible in Transmission*, Summer 2003, pp. 12–13.

Buchanan, Colin, 'The Bishop in Action', in Buchanan (ed.), *The Bishop in Liturgy*.

—— (ed.), *The Bishop in Liturgy: An Anglican Symposium on the Role and Task of the Bishop in the Field of Liturgy* (Bramcote, England: Grove Books, 1988).

Church Commissioners for England, *Called to be a Bishop* report B&C (99)1 (London: 1999).

Cocksworth, Christopher J., *Being a Priest Today* (Norwich: Canterbury Press, 2002).

Field-Bibb, Jacqueline, *Women Towards Priesthood: Ministerial Politics and Feminist Praxis* (Cambridge: Cambridge University Press, 1991).

Gadamer, Hans-George, *Truth and Method*, 2nd revd edn, trans. and ed. Joel Weinsheimer and Donald G. Marshall (London: Sheed & Ward, 1989).

Holeton, David, 'The Bishop Leading his Diocese', in Buchanan (ed.), *The Bishop in Liturgy*.

Irvine, Christopher, *The Art of God: The Formation of Christians in the Likeness of Christ* (London: SPCK, forthcoming).

Lathrop, Gordon, 'Christian Leadership and Liturgical Community', *Worship* 66 (1992), pp. 98–125.

Nazir-Ali, Michael, 'Towards a Theology of Choosing Diocesan Bishops', in Archbishops' Council, *Working with the Spirit: Choosing Diocesan Bishops*, GS 1405 (London: Church House Publishing, 2001).

Stancliffe, David, 'The Bishop in his Cathedral', in Buchanan (ed.), *The Bishop in Liturgy*.

Stevenson, W. Taylor, 'Lex Orandi – Lex Credendi', in Stephen Sykes and John Booty (eds), *The Study of Anglicanism* (London: SPCK, 1988).

Thiselton, Anthony C., *New Horizons in Hermeneutics* (London: HarperCollins, 1992).

—— *The Two Horizons: New Testament Hermeneutics and Philosophical Description with Special Reference to Heidegger, Bultmann, Gadamer and Wittgenstein* (Exeter: Paternoster Press, 1980).

Williams, Rowan, 'Ministry in Prison: Theological Reflections', *Justice Reflections* 2 (2003), pp. 1–15.

15 The Vocation of Anglicanism: An Orthodox–Catholic Suggestion

Robin Gibbons

IN MY EXPERIENCE it would be fairly true to say that when faced with the new, we either move forward with some degree of expectation or hold back with some measure of trepidation. This seems to be the case when talking with colleagues and friends about the ordination of women to the episcopacy in the Church of England. However, in discussion, I am faced with a dilemma. What happens within the ecclesial setting of the Anglican Communion is, in one sense, outside of my own pastoral and theological setting. I come from a very different tradition, which does not ordain women at all. I was baptized, confirmed, professed and ordained in the Roman (Latin) Catholic tradition, but moved into the Eastern, Melkite Greek-Catholic Church, which follows Byzantine tradition and is strongly linked to the Greek Orthodox Patriarchate of Antioch. Our church is mainly Arab and in England comprises of one mission with a centralized parish in London. Its custom and law is linked to Eastern Orthodoxy; in doctrine the theological tradition of the East holds firm except for our being in communion with Rome. Hence from both a Catholic and an Orthodox viewpoint, in this church the issue of women bishops has not occurred. However, I come from a family that is partly Anglican, my theological work is in an ecumenical setting and, pastorally, I minister to people in a wider context that includes contact and connection with female ministers and priests.

The dilemma is simple. As a priest of my own tradition the issue of women deacons, let alone priests or bishops, is an item not on the 'official agenda'.[1] However, on the Roman Catholic side, despite papal teaching and the *Responsum* of the Congregation for the Doctrine for the Faith (October 1995), the matter of women's ordination is not an *ex cathedra*, infallible statement. Indeed the Board of the Catholic Theological Society of America produced a report in which it reminded theologians that 'Canon Law makes it clear that no doctrine is to be understood as infallibly defined unless this is manifestly established' (Canon 749.3).[2]

The report goes on to emphasize that this is manifestly not the case. Far more importantly for my consideration as an Eastern Catholic is that even if, in the Orthodox East, tradition has not allowed the ordination of women, the selfsame tradition will prove to be invaluable in any discussion of women's diaconal ministry. In fact the living tradition of the Church often throws up some remarkable shifts and changes in its 2,000-year-long pilgrimage. One of my great devotions is that of Haghia Sophia, Holy Wisdom, who in iconography has sometimes been portrayed as an angelic, sometimes feminine figure dressed in bishop's vesture, a reminder of the unity of both male and female in the Divine One.

What of my own reaction to the prospect of women bishops in the Church of England? First, it is one of ecclesiology. In my work with Anglicans I recognize part of the Church of Christ that has come from a different tradition than my own but which shares many common things, not least the baptismal call to holiness and living the gospel life in Christ through the Holy Spirit. It is also a Church that through history has attempted to weave a *via media* between continental Protestantism and Roman Catholicism. The Anglican Communion recognizes the plurality of experience within the Spirit in a way that is of value to us all, and which presents a task that lies before all Christians: discernment of the Spirit today and in the future.

From my point of view, the Church of England, within its own ecclesiology of a 'Protestant and Catholic matrix', having already ordained women as deacons and priests, cannot theologically deny the next step which is to ordain them as bishops, especially as the Anglican Communion has already ordained women as bishops in several Provinces.

My second reaction is that of a liturgical and sacramental theologian. From this viewpoint Anglican ordination (of men and, much later, women) was, from an historical and reformed perspective, not understood as a sacrament in the 'Catholic' and 'Orthodox' sense. The theology and practice of the ordained ministry has been successively reworked within that tradition, which indicates that the strictures of the historical Catholic and Orthodox viewpoint have already been changed.

I would tentatively suggest that the vocation of Anglicanism is not to emulate the tradition of Roman Catholicism or Orthodoxy but to discern the Spirit's work for their community in the first instance. In that way, new ways of experience become part of ecumenical and liturgical praxis, moments of dialogue and sacraments of 'new encounters'. Robert Bellah sums up my own thoughts:

> The communities of memory that tie us to the past also turn us to the future as communities of hope. They carry a context for meaning

> that can allow us to connect our aspirations for ourselves and those closest to us with the aspirations of a larger whole and see our efforts as being, in part, contributions to a common good.[3]

Within this context it would seem that the ordination of women to the episcopacy within the tradition of Cranmer, Hooker, Donne, Seddon, Nightingale and other visionaries can only be part of that renewal of hope.

Notes

1 See Pope John Paul II, *Ordinatio Sacerdotalis*. 9 June 1994, pp. 50–2.
2 *Tradition and the Ordination of Women*, report submitted to CTSA, Minneapolis 1997.
3 Robert N. Bellah *et al.*, *Habits of the Heart: Individualism and Commitment in American Life* (Berkeley, Calif.: University of California Press, 1984), p. 153.

Bibliography

Bellah, Robert N., *et al.*, *Habits of the Heart: Individualism and Commitment in American Life* (Berkeley, Calif.: University of California Press, 1984).

John Paul II, *Ordinatio Sacerdotalis* (1994).

Tradition and the Ordination of Women (Minneapolis, Minn.: CTSA, 1997).

16 Living the Experience: Holding the Reins of Authority

Geralyn Wolf

HIS FACE REDDENED as he strode down the aisle with a large black Bible tucked under his left arm. Raising his right arm and striking the air with his index finger, he announced in a large voice, 'Women can't be bishops!' Then, taking the Bible in his hand and lifting it up for all to see, he said with anger and conviction, 'It's all in the book, it's right here!'

The ushers were caught off guard and the man was almost at the front of the nave when they started down the aisle. I was on the top of the altar steps, about to give the offertory sentence, when the self-proclaimed prophet stopped in front of me and stated his desire to address the congregation. The cathedral community was stunned into silence, taken aback by the swift and deliberate action of this unexpected visitor.

A similar experience when I was the vicar of a small mission prepared me for this unusual occasion. I decided not to challenge the man. Instead, I acknowledged that he had something very important to say, and invited him to address the congregation for a few minutes (always a risk, of course). He proceeded up the steps, turned around to face the congregation, opened the Bible and quoted from 1 Timothy 2.12, 'I permit no woman to teach or to have authority over a man; she is to keep silent.' He thanked me and promptly walked out. At the time, I was the Dean of Christ Church Cathedral, Louisville, Kentucky, and the announcement of my election as Bishop of Rhode Island had just appeared in the newspaper.

As dramatic as this experience may have been, it was observed by many people and relatively easy to respond to with hospitality and grace. During almost 30 years of ordained ministry, I have learned that it is the subtleties that are far more difficult to deal with. Subtle glances and manipulations, outward approval and interior loathing are signs of difficulties that are hard to identify, no less address. While the Church revels in its preoccupation with things sexual, I find gossip and innuendo to be far greater sins.

The cynicism and constant natter that I observe in the Church today transcend gender, and are an outgrowth of an increasing distrust of authority coupled with a strong individualism, in Western societies. Women, in positions of leadership, must both contend with the changing times, and with the culturally conditioned responses that remain strong in our relationships between men and women.

During the first three months of my episcopate, I visited at least 20 of our parishes and missions, and each person in the diocese was given the opportunity to worship with me and to share in a reception following. The worst experience was when the host priest stood close to me during the entire Eucharist, announcing hymns, page numbers, directing 'traffic', and showing me the proper page when he thought I didn't know my place. In a word of complaint he told members of the parish council that I was controlling! I was told that two of the women set him straight.

Women are an intricate part of the cultural changes that have occurred in the Western nations since World War II, and most dramatically since the 1960s. The well-defined borders that once shaped the identity of our secular and church life, and the roles of its peoples, are changing with swiftness and unpredictability. Women wearing mitres and holding croziers are strong outward and visible symbols of the reality of this change. For some, it speaks of a painful discontinuity with Catholic and Orthodox faith, for others it has been and remains too slow in coming, and for many in our culture, it does not matter.

My grandparents entered an arranged marriage in the early part of the twentieth century. He was in love with her, but she had wanted to marry another man. It seemed incredible to me, at the age of 20. I remember asking my grandmother how she ever managed to live with him for such a long time. 'It was so different in those days,' she said, 'we knew our roles and our responsibilities. He went to work and provided for the family, and I provided for the upbringing of the children and the keeping of the house.' With a smile on her lips, she added, 'We learned to love each other.'

There are many good things to be said for the world of my grandparents, but my grandmother lived long enough to praise the choices and freedoms that we have today.

As ordained women we have had some excellent role models from faithful and generous male colleagues. However, our voices hold a different timbre, we were raised with a different set of expectations, and we face dissimilar and distinct projections from others. In truth, ordained women of our time are a generation formed without experienced women mentors. We are the wedges in the soil, softening the ground for the rich seeds of Christian witness that we have been given to plant. While we have seen a harvest in our own time, the yields will increase long after we have passed away. We share with Mary in her 'Yes' to a spoken yet unseen promise.

It is a great honour to be a woman in this time in the life of the Church. To be the plough, to prepare the way, to cry in a desert that will some day be in full flower. We live in hope. We have placed our dreams in the hope of God's kingdom, and though we wander around in a changing desert, we share a sense of adventure and joy that will never be taken away. We have placed our whole heart and soul and mind in Christ, and we have not been disappointed in our faith.

The Paschal Mystery best describes the spiritual experiences that have given definition to my episcopate. The sermons I preach, the many decisions that I must make, the columns and articles that I write, are always open to judgement. Some people offer grateful praise and others find reason for complaint. It is critical that I find my identity and rightness not in the responses, but in the intersection of what I do and who Christ is calling me to be. As a very public figure, even food shopping and taking a walk give opportunity for personal encounter. By the vegetable counter I was asked, 'How does the bishop cook her asparagus?' In a local coffee shop, a woman came to my table, sat down and proceeded to explain why she 'hated' the Peace. I could give many, many examples. It is a ministry that is in the Church, and in the marketplace, and by my presence it is one ministry and one place. The bishop sits in that place where the cross intersects, with arms laden by rejection and misinterpretation and a heart filled with the profound and exciting experience of new life.

The subtleties of which I spoke earlier are outgrowths of people wrestling with anger, envy, pride, abandonment, rejection, and all the other sins that distort our wholeness in Christ. Every priest and bishop has been the host and target of these sins. However, with women, they are complicated by gender identification and expectations that are in themselves in a state of change. Being the object of gossip remains painful for both men and women. False accusations are always frustrating and wearisome. Projection is a constant reality. Even the slightest glance is open for scrutiny. However, without previous experience with a woman bishop (or priest), the responses people make to similar behaviour in men and women is often different. For example, a male head of committee said that when strong men show a level of vulnerability, the group responds positively, suggesting that when women of vulnerability show strength the response will be the same. Many people do not know what to do when a woman's response is outside their level of comfort. The common perception that men are strong and women are aggressive has a strong ring of truth.

The joy of the episcopate is that no two days are ever the same. I tend to be a highly creative person, and I like the challenge of responding to and initiating a variety of experiences. I find myself energized by the complexity of issues, and able to meet the physical and emotional demands of the vocation. God has placed me in the midst of situations that call forth a broad range of personal gifts. They demand clarity and flexibility, an ability to admit wrong and the strength to move on. These become spiritual opportunities as Jesus becomes more deeply the way, the truth, and the life for me. The Word reveals itself in new and compelling ways. The Christ of the Passion, and the Christ who defies death by becoming Life, are the theological arms of the episcopate. In the midst of personal and corporate brokenness, of the heartache of suffering, and the profound pain of loss, a light of hope burns within. It is the source of strength for the daily task.

Some day, the Church of England, will ordain and consecrate women as bishops. The first woman will live under many demands. Some of her colleagues will wonder why she was chosen, instead of someone else (maybe them). If the woman was not a forceful member of MOW (Movement for the Ordination of Women) or WATCH (Women and the Church), others may condemn her for 'not paying her dues'. Should she be a priest with whom you have never gotten along, her every action will be judged.

To my sisters and brothers in our Mother Church, please remember that we are all human, full of weaknesses, and words we wish we had never uttered. If we are not a people of forgiveness, our sense of Jesus' love for us will wane, and we shall be lost and our moorings loosened. Many will expect 'the woman bishop' to carry their concerns into the House of Bishops, and to bring a new voice to the deliberations. Indeed, she may. However, do not forget that a critical mass is usually needed for critical change. Don't expect too much too soon. Remember, she is the plough woman. She is turning up the soil, loosening the earth that has been trodden upon for centuries. She is being called both to uproot and to plant, to rend and to mend. She, and those who follow her in the early days of such profound change, will need the forgiving support of others. The seeds of their faith and imagination will grow because the community of faith is willing to labour with them.

The women bishops in other parts of the world await your presence. You continue to be for us the church of our spiritual ancestors. In your branch of the Anglican Communion we rediscover our heritage. We give thanks to God for your patient and faithful witness, and for the vision to press on towards the fullness of the Church's ministry.

Let me end with these selected and inspiriting words from Jane Laurie Borthwick's hymn 'Come labour on'. They have always raised my spirits, and lifted me to a noble place.

Who dares stand idle on the harvest plain
While all around us waves the golden grain.

The enemy is watching night and day,
To sow the tares, to snatch the seed away;

Away with gloomy doubts and faithless fear!
No arm so weak but may do service here;

Claim the high calling angels cannot share
To young and old the Gospel gladness bear;

No time for rest, till glows the western sky,
Till the long shadows o'er our pathway lie,

And a glad sound comes with the setting sun,
    Servant well done.

The Church and the World

17 Why Women Bishops are Still on the Waiting List in Africa

Esther Mombo

ASKED ABOUT what was the most remarkable thing he saw at Lambeth 1998, a Kenyan bishop replied, 'I was surprised to see women bishops.' Another bishop, when asked about women bishops, retorted, 'I do not want to see one in my lifetime.' Another one said, 'If a woman bishop is nominated, we shall call an extraordinary meeting of the synod to decide on the matter.' Although the Church in Africa has not said 'No' to the consecration of women bishops (for example, the Episcopal Church in Sudan sees no official reason for not consecrating women as bishops, having voted that women can be ordained), it has not yet consecrated one woman as bishop. In the African Church the issue of women bishops is riddled with too many questions and too many objections. These questions and objections are more socio-cultural than theological. Look, for instance at the following case study:

> When the diocese of x fell vacant after the death of a bishop, some members of the electoral college decided to nominate a woman who was a member of the diocese but was on study leave. She had served as a priest and some of the members felt that she had the ability to manage the diocese. Academically she had done a Diploma in Theology, a Master of Divinity and was studying for a Master of Sacred Theology in New Testament. Some members of the electoral college felt that she had both the academic and theological qualification and the international exposure that a bishop would require in this particular diocese. After consultation, these members went ahead and nominated her. They followed the laid-down rules, so that her papers were signed by the right kind of people and in accordance with the constitution. A number of the young clergy supported the nomination of this woman because they saw in her the type of leader they wished to have. As soon as the nomination was made public there was an uproar in the diocese, especially among some members of the electoral college. Men were seen wagging their heads and asking:

> 'Are you going to become her chaplain when she becomes bishop?'
>
> 'What will happen to the diocese when she goes on maternity leave?'
>
> 'Time has not come for a woman bishop in Africa.'
>
> 'Are you sure the Province will accept her candidature?'
>
> 'There will have to be a provincial synod to decide on whether a woman bishop is acceptable.'
>
> 'If she becomes bishop, it is her father who will be running the Diocese.'
>
> After the nomination this woman was expected to appear before a search committee. But that was not to be. She was duly compelled to withdraw her nomination.

While most Anglican dioceses in Africa today ordain women to the priesthood, there is little openness actually to putting women bishops in place. In the situation where women constitute the majority in the churches, and in some parts they literally run the churches, why is there surprise at the idea of women bishops? Why is there a sense of shock and dismay at women bishops? Why is there strong opposition and pessimism about women bishops?

There are several reasons for this. These include the structure of the Anglican Church as it manifests itself in Africa; the patriarchal nature of African leadership; the colonial legacy of the Anglican Church in Africa; and African cultural attitudes towards women. No convincing theological reason has been put forward by the leadership of the Anglican Church in Africa refuting the idea of women bishops.

The questions raised concerning having women bishops in Africa are more socio-cultural than theological. In his article about episcopacy in Africa, Bishop Leslie Brown observed that an important factor affecting the style of episcopacy in Africa is that:

> the bishop is seen not only as the ultimate authority in the Church, but as a man in relationship to the church members. It is a family relationship and the Church is analogous to an extended family. The universal way of addressing the bishops is, 'Our father in God.' This implies a relationship of mutual trust and interdependence.[1]

Add to this the tribal factor: in some places the bishop is expected to be a member of the right tribe and clan. This breeds the wrangles of episcopal elections that manifest themselves in most dioceses. If a bishop happens to be chosen from a different tribe from that of the dominant tribe of his diocese, it may lead to the division of the diocese to create a home for each of the tribes represented. This affects women, because women are generally viewed as outsiders in the tribe in which they are born and strangers in the tribe into which they are married. In this case the social and ethnic expectations of episcopacy make it hard for a woman to be nominated to that post.

The social and ethnic expectations of a bishop in most groups in Africa include the socially constructed roles for both men and women. Offering hospitality is a case in point. A bishop is expected to give hospitality to members of his immediate family and also to the church members who come to his house, often unannounced. This places a great burden on a bishop's wife because she is viewed as one who is there to entertain. Because of the gender-constructed roles, it makes it difficult for people to envisage a woman bishop.

Although Africa is not one homogeneous group of people but a continent of different tribal groups, leadership has been largely patriarchal. Yes, there were places in Africa where female leadership was well accepted. But with the coming of patriarchal Christianity, the focus of leadership shifted from women to men.[2] The Church justifies this patriarchy by using a selective appropriation of biblical texts. For instance, 1 Timothy 3.1–7 is used to argue against women bishops. Such texts are read out of context, with no more objective analysis than demanding literal application. Such texts are used to reinforce the gender-constructed roles, and thus lend blind support to the patriarchal nature of leadership. Although most Anglican Provinces in Africa will claim to be Bible-believing churches, when it comes to leadership it appears that it is the local patriarchal cultures – and not the Bible – which determine what kind of leaders the Church needs.

There is also the issue of the colonial legacy of the Anglican Church in Africa. The Anglican Church in Africa is a colonial church, founded by mission agencies from England in its colonies. The well-known missions to Africa include the Church Mission Society, the Society for the Propagation of the Gospel, and the United Missions to Central Africa. Apart from ministering to the English colonies far from home, these missionary societies evangelized the local people. The nature of episcopacy set up reflected the colonial legacy of leadership. A bishop, like his administrative counterpart the District Commissioner or Governor of the colony, was a man who was feared. His word was final and a lot of authority was vested in him.

When the African bishops took over, they combined both the colonial power and the tribal powers into their formidable office. This kind of leadership has no place for women, as it is rule by the rod. Women are not seen to wield that kind of power. Hence there is a fear of nominating women for the bishopric, but how far this fear extends depends on one's notion of power. Looking at the Anglican Church in Africa, one notes that women are more than one-half of the membership in the churches. Their contribution to the Church is immense. Consequently, they constitute a huge and vital resource to the community of faith. Both bishops and priests will acknowledge the fact that if one Sunday all the women stayed away from the churches, then many churches would be left with only a handful of men ministering to themselves. However, when it comes to choosing women as bishops, the idea is not welcome. Women are regarded as good enough only to supply flower arrangements on the altar and provide catering to the Parish Council meetings. Such biased attitudes only serve to deprive the church of the more substantial and vital contribution that women could make.

In an ordination service in one of the dioceses I attended, mention was made of affirmative action in the church as had been proposed for parliamentary elections. A bishop remarked that he supported affirmative action for the government but not in the Church. If women are marginalized in the Church like this, how can the Church criticize secular society? Can the world listen to a Church that proclaims justice, human dignity and human rights, while being riddled with sexism and tribalism itself?

The church constitutions are very important in the election of Bishops. I have consulted a cross-section of Anglican Constitutions of the Provinces of Eastern Africa, and have discovered no written code preventing women from becoming bishops. Perhaps most dioceses, like that of Sudan, agree theologically that if women are ordained as deacons and priests, there are no obstacles to ordaining women as bishops. But socially or culturally, they still seem unable to make this move.

I began by pointing out that, while on the one hand the Church in Africa has not said 'No' to the consecration of women to the episcopate, on the other hand it has failed to produce a single woman bishop. The predominantly male leadership continues to use socio-cultural justification for keeping women at bay, and the women continue to groan: 'How long, O Lord . . .' (Revelation 6.10).

Notes

1 Brown, Leslie, 'Episcopacy in Africa', in *Bishops – But What Kind?*, ed. Peter Moore (London: SPCK, 1982), p. 141.

2 Mercy Amba Oduyoye, *Daughters of Anowa: African Women and Patriarchy* (Maryknoll, NY: Orbis Books, 1995). See also Isabel Phiri, *Women, Presbyterianism, and Patriarchy: Religious Experience of Chewa Women in Central Malawi* (Blantyre, Malawi: CLAIM, 1997).

Bibliography

Brown, Leslie, 'Episcopacy in Africa', in *Bishops – But What Kind?*, ed. Peter Moore (London: SPCK, 1982).

Oduyoye, Mercy Amba, *Daughters of Anowa: African Women and Patriarchy* (Maryknoll, NY: Orbis Books, 1995).

Phiri, Isabel, *Women, Presbyterianism, and Patriarchy: Religious Experience of Chewa Women in Central Malawi* (Blantyre, Malawi: CLAIM, 1997).

18 Identifying the Needs of the Twenty-first-century Church

Carolyn Tanner Irish

MY OWN EXPERIENCE of nearly eight years in the Diocese of Utah is almost entirely positive. This context is of course very different from that of other dioceses, given the overwhelming presence and power of the Church of Jesus Christ of Latter Day Saints (Mormons). However, being a tiny minority church scattered about in America's most conservative state is a wonderfully liberating challenge. It draws us closely together, yet our doors are open to all. Our people were pleased with the 'statement' they made in my election, particularly since women have no ordained leadership role in about 98 per cent of other church memberships in the state (Mormon and Roman Catholic). For the most part, our members have stood by me at every turn, representing as we do a progressive voice in the national Church and certainly in Utah. Even with some dissenting voices within, I feel entirely free (as many bishops in the Protestant Episcopal Church in the United States of America, PECUSA, do not) to speak out on public issues, such as the war in Iraq, carrying concealed weapons, an English-only law in state government offices, nuclear waste disposal in Utah, capital punishment, and so on. Moreover, our diocese has openly welcomed gay and lesbian members and leaders for many years.

A woman bearing religious authority – sometimes perceived (and sometimes exercised) as mere power – may generate some distinctive tensions, however. Theologically of course the Church is not based on human power: 'It shall not be so among you', and 'My Kingdom is not of this world', Jesus said. Nothing could illustrate the difference between authority and power more graphically than his cross. People do confuse them though; on my very first working day, a priest cheerfully called me 'boss' – which she meant well, but it was hardly the way I thought of myself. Power is often a lesser form of authority's exercise, and again one that is directly refused in scripture – in the story of Jesus' temptations in the wilderness, for example. Yet it is true that bishops must sometimes use the historic authority of their episcopal role in an exercise of straightforward power, particularly in the context of conflict.

Authority or power may be oddly fearsome when the bishop is a woman, and I say oddly because until recently there have been very, very few women in 'top roles'. The fear, often covered by expressions of extraordinary courtesy, probably reflects a complex mix of subconscious forces – psychological, cultural and religious. As someone recently said to me, 'Everybody had a mother', which is to say, in part at least, that everyone has known vulnerability. Still, this particular fear may not continue as that, or in ignorance, unfamiliarity, jealousy, or prejudice, but rather in a kind of subterranean misogyny, which is found as clearly among women as men.

As undercurrent, misogyny is difficult to bring to the surface or deal with rationally. Literally, it means a hatred of women, but I believe hatred is more symptom than cause. Like contempt or anger toward women, its deepest root is fear – which of course few will own up to. Historically, women have taken a lot of trouble to rescue others from it, because they stood to lose everything otherwise. In male–female relationships, women have tried in a variety of ways to assure men of their superiority, and in general to stroke insecure egos, male and female. But whatever we may say of that in other institutions, it is unhealthy, indeed patronizing behaviour, and it should not be any part of faithful Christian leadership.

Generally speaking, misogyny seeps into relationships when there is conflict over power, and it can become particularly virulent when any sign of weakness, vulnerability, or even humility appears in a woman; that is what abuse, rape and stoning are all about. These manifestations may not be part of the experience of women who are bishops, but as undercurrent or vestige, something of it seems to remain.

An old southern saying goes, 'Don't want 'em weak and don't want 'em strong either!' Yet quite apart from the gifts women bring, or the essential requirements of the office, or even the origins of fear and conflict, misogyny can show itself in particularly ugly, demeaning and personal ways, and women often react with feelings of shame. Though its expressions may be cloaked for reasons of political correctness, thoughts and comments about a woman's body, what she looks like, and what her behavior 'really' signifies are not uncommon. Misogyny is often dressed as a 'joke' among insiders – and insiders there usually are, since it doesn't survive well outside of a small-group dynamic that assures its members of their superiority. Sometimes, too, the image of 'man-hater' attaches to the woman who is the object of such scorn – such a projection one would think it totally embarrassing to express, even within the select group.

Why we need women in the episcopacy

In this nearly inevitable dynamic, the question might be asked, 'Why would a woman *want* to be a bishop?' as well as 'Why do we *need* women bishops?' First, as we become less notable simply as women, *disruptive* misogyny is less frequent and can be ignored in time, or others are willing to challenge misogyny more openly. Any number of times, I have heard someone ask, 'Would you say that if the bishop were a man?' Or, 'That is so sexist I can't believe you said it!'

Second, Christ's work of healing is an essential dimension of our personal and common life – indeed, it is part of the very meaning of 'salvation'. If we do not all mature and grow into the dignity of 'the full stature of Christ' then both we ourselves and our relationships are impaired. The whole community suffers this. So, the hope of having women as well as men serving in positions of ecclesiastical authority is that fewer and fewer people will be willing to tolerate, still less support the indignities that this particularly odious, childish, destructive undercurrent of misogyny brings to the life of the Church.

Third, there are several aspects of the Church's wider mission for which the participation of women in the episcopacy is essential. To think otherwise seems to suggest that the original diversity of male and female described in the very first chapters of the Bible is somehow insignificant – an accident or a mistake! It suggests as well, that women have not already been involved in ministry throughout the historical origins and development of the Church. At the present time, and in the context of theological reflection, decision-making, and religious leadership, the mix of male and female participation makes for health and vitality in the life and mission of the twenty-first-century Church. Of course women want to be full partners in that! Being denied the opportunity to discover this by continuing the present restrictions on the episcopate will deprive the Church of much wisdom, as well as many gifts, voices, energies and alliances – all much needed today. Especially because bishops represent the unity of the whole Church, a 'Men only' sign on that particular door is outright hypocrisy.

The mission of the Church

I turn now to the matter of the Church's mission because the criteria and selection of leaders must be informed by that most of all. First, though, a word about 'need' – as in 'needing' women bishops. Need is always contingent, which is to say that it becomes most apparent in the logic of a hypothetical statement: 'If life is to continue, then oxygen is necessary.' 'If a democracy is to work, then social education for it is needed.' 'If equality is to mean anything, then the gap between rich and poor must be reduced.' 'If peace is to be lasting, then justice must be done.' Such statements about our biological, socio-political and moral life are generally too obvious to require hypothetical statement, and of course people may state these or others differently. I offer them, however, simply to illustrate my premise, which is that the needs of the modern Christian Church are in some way contingent on how we understand and live out the Church's mission.

I believe it makes little sense to think that the needs of today's Church derive only from the past or the *status quo*. Abiding and uncontingent are the central *beliefs* which the Christian community by its very definition assumes: that God's hand is at work in creation; that Jesus Christ is God's most fulsome self-expression in this world, as the scriptures give witness; and that the presence of the Holy Spirit continues to illumine, strengthen and guide God's people. Yet evolving are the *practices* of Christian community – broadening the inclusivity and participation of its members, worshipping in the languages of its people, discovering more and more depth in the sacraments of baptism and communion. Changes in practice come about because we recognize the greater needs, deeper understandings and broader visions the gospel presents to our experience of the faith.

Anglicans could argue that if we are to continue in apostolic and catholic tradition, then we need bishops *per se*, and that if there are enough men who are willing and competent to serve as bishops, then women are not needed in any statistical sense. It strikes many people, however, that such an argument has a very narrow, defensive and unresponsive basis.

If we consider the needs of the Church from the wider perspective of mission – which is always present and future as well as past – then many new possibilities present themselves. Such possibilities exist in both continuity and discontinuity with our faith traditions – as indeed Christianity does with Judaism, Methodism does with Anglicanism, and the American Episcopal Church does with the Church of England. Needs are not just abstract eternals, unrelated to time and place; they *evolve*. We live in a time of changing historical perspectives and truly global awareness, and our discernment of needs must be undertaken in the context of the world we are called to serve.

Consider the Church's call as reconciler in a world of injustice, conflict, and violence; as healer and steward of creation in cultures that continue to exploit and ravage it; as guardian of the moral and spiritual teaching of Christ; in communities that are all about entertainment and consumption. If we are to be responsive to such calls, then our leadership must draw on the gifts of all God's people, exploring new ways to proclaim and encourage kingdom life. And our leadership also must reflect the great variety of people among whom we live and serve – if in differing races, ethnic origins, languages and cultures, then why not in gender?

Having women in the episcopacy will not meet all of these or other challenges of course, but I believe it does open up new ways of addressing them. Such a change is not little: it is not a matter of 'letting them in', or breaking social barriers, or attending to a special interest group. Nor does this shift alter the deeper meaning of 'apostolicity'. But we need the insights and gifts of this half of the human race in a whole and unified Church, and in all its leadership, lay and ordained, if we are to rise to the challenges of our times. Specifically we need the 'feminine' capacities for relationship, collaboration, nurture, community, commitment, creativity and non-violent alternatives to conflict. It is not that men don't also have such capacities, but they are not well or fully exercised when their voices are the only ones the Church takes seriously, or their experience is the only one called upon. Moreover, there is a painful way in which the *status quo* restrictions on women unwittingly support, and certainly do not stand against, the nearly universal demeaning of women, which is one essential step towards the abuse of women.

In any case it does not seem reasonable to me that past practice rather than evident need should set the boundaries of leadership in the Church. We deprive ourselves and the world we serve by front-end exclusions of whole categories of persons from service in the episcopate. I have never thought the world 'sets the agenda' for the Church; God's mission in the world does that. Still, we do live, move and have our being *in* the world, and it is *this* world – not just yesterday's world – for which Christ died.

19 Doing Things Differently

Bill Ind

I WAS, FOR ABOUT 14 YEARS, a priest in the Diocese of Winchester, and for ten of those years, 1975–85, John Taylor was the Bishop. He was a profound influence on me and many others in all sorts of ways, and perhaps above all in the way that he helped us to think about the nature and purpose of God and of the ministry to which we were called.

These, of course, were the years when the debate about the ordination of women as at its height and, as always, John Taylor took thinking about it on to a different plane. He made it clear that what we were thinking and talking about was the mysterious business of priesthood, and in an address to the General Synod on 3 July 1975, he said:

> Both the difference and the complementarity of male and female lie far deeper than function. It is not a matter of the division of labour carried on, one from the pulpit and the other from the kitchen stove, men and women are different to the tiniest particles of their being. They are different even when they sit side by side at a concert, or when together they try to comfort a friend. The contribution of both, the complementary elements of human nature is in all functions, just as both male and female each in its distinctness must contribute to that holiest of all functions, the procreation of life. The responsibility for the life of this world cannot safely be left in purely male hands because they are too authoritarian, too manipulative and too ready to turn our God-given dominion into raw domination.

Now, more than a quarter of a century later, I am still struck by those words and especially in my work as a bishop; work which women are still not permitted to perform. There are about 40 women priests in this diocese and as I share in their ministry and reflect upon it, I realize increasingly the significance of difference and complementarity. The difference was revealed to me by an experienced male churchwarden who admitted that his new female parish priest worked in a completely different way from all the previous incumbents that he had known. I asked him what he meant. He explained that he had unconsciously developed techniques and ways of dealing and working with former incumbents. He knew where they were coming from. His new priest was different. She did things in a different way. She introduced things differently and the churchwarden admitted with a smile that he had to adopt new ways of working and, indeed, of thinking.

On the other hand, it has been a common experience to hear people say that in all sorts of pastoral situations what has come to the fore has been skill, sympathy, intuition and understanding. As a result, the gender of the particular priest has been irrelevant.

Of course, there are outstanding female priests as there are outstanding male priests, but the point I want to make is that priesthood is enriched and strengthened by what women have brought to it simply by being women rather than honorary men. I talked about this to Paul Wignall, the Director of Training in this diocese, and in a note he says:

> I have for many years been very taken by Schleiermacher's delightful dialogue, *Christmas Eve*. In it he makes a clear distinction between the response of men and women to the Christmas Eve service. The men, he says, come home and sit down to discuss the sermon; the women and children, however, go to the tree and sing carols. Schleiermacher does not imply any hierarchy in these different responses. He simply notes that they are different, equally valid, and that a fullness of faith requires the presence of both. In an Episcopal church, does not the absence of women from all layers of ministry and leadership simply impoverish the language and so also the experiences of the church, tilting the balances of (often hidden) power inappropriately?

And all that leads me straight back again to John Taylor, and his passionate insistence that the vocation of human beings is to be the priests of all creation. There are truths about the mystery of God that can be uncovered only by women as they reflect on their experience of being human and their relationship to all that is.

Of course, in a very important sense women already do this as they fulfil their baptismal vocation. But this experience needs to be made available in the episcopate, and sooner rather than later, in order that their experience of the episcopate can be reflected upon by women who are living out the role of bishop. It may be that the Church, like the male churchwarden, has to adopt new ways of working and thinking, but the more we delay, the more we hinder our own wholeness.

20 We Wish You Were Here: Some Views from the Pews

Carrie Pemberton

ON PALM SUNDAY 2004, I was sitting with my family during Morning Prayer. There was a baptism that day as well. I began to think about the sort of Church the baby girl was being baptized into. Our church, set in West Cambridgeshire, is part of *The Archers* heartlands of conservative Anglicanism – the small-village agonies and ecstasies of the long-running BBC Radio 4 programme well reflect life here. We recognize the existence of the urban in our life, but we are solidly clunch and rubble, with an English Heritage grant for our south aisle roof securely in our pocket and preparations for the summer fête already being talked about during coffee and juice after the service. With a mixed congregation, evenly distributed across age sets and with a gentle bias of female representation, regular churchgoers this Sunday shared their normally half-empty church with family and friends of the baby. I put to them the question: 'Should women be made bishops in the Church of England forthwith?'

The congregational members aged between seven and 70 scribbled furiously on the back of postcards during the calm between Blessing and Dismissal. With their comments, the anonymous respondents added their age set (30s, 40s etc.), gender and whether they were regular or occasional worshippers. Their view was overwhelmingly one-sided – 100 per cent of the 70 per cent response rate said, 'Yes, and immediately.' Not one contradictory voice was raised.

This was an impromptu piece of market research, and cannot bear the pressure of sample and range which evidence-based research demands. However, I was interested to see not only the overall result, but also the reasons offered. Here are some examples:

> Excluding women from positions of authority in the Church increases the anachronistic nature of the institution. To survive in an increasingly secular world the Church of England needs to reflect the world at large.
>
> Male 40–50, not regular attender

> Women would make good Bishops because in the modern world women are recognized as equals, and bring compassion and understanding in a woman's unique way. They bring the necessary diversity to the community of the Lord.
>
> Female 50–60, regular church attender

> Strongly in favour – it will make the Church seem less odd – the positive inclusion of the values seen to be carried by women, care, insight, efficient, committed and not self-serving – this is really important.
>
> Male 60–70, not regular attender

These contributions reflect a sense of displacement, of the Church being out of kilter with the society it serves. The Church without women bishops is called 'anachronistic' and 'odd'. It fails to reflect positive values in society. In civil law women carry the right to equality of opportunity, inheritance, pay, educational access and political and economic power – although in practice we know that in some cases women are still paid less than men for doing the same jobs, and are seriously under-represented in the Cabinet, around boardroom tables, as silks, as members of the British Academy or the Royal Society, in university professorial posts, civil engineering, and even in the wealthiest persons list. But churches and religious bodies have been granted special exemption from the impact of equality legislation since 1975.[1]

Doing theology in context

We are called to express a theology and practice that demonstrates the dynamics of the gospel in a conversation with the values held by the communities in which the Church is set. Expressions from the pews of feeling out of kilter with the surrounding community are important for our theology. Life and doctrine is of a piece, and we are invited to seek out where God is working in our traditions and in the real conditions of our contexts.

In his essay, 'Richard Hooker and the Ordination of Women to the Priesthood', Stephen Sykes uncovers a contextualizing theology at the very roots of Anglicanism. He argues that Hooker's theology took with utmost seriousness his contemporary intellectual consensus on the scientific, biological and legal status of women. It was this which legitimized the way in which the Church kept priesthood male and confirmed the subaltern position of women.[2] The three types of law that Hooker uses are those of reason, the divine law of the scriptures and human law. Church constitutions are all situated within human law, but are subject to the interplay of reason and the divine law. Hooker's method opens up a way to handle change in the way that we understand the world in which we are situated, and indeed the radical impact of modernity, which has transformed our understanding of almost everything.

We were once Aristotelian in our scientific outlook. Aristotle based his biology on the premise that heat is the fundamental principle of perfection in animals, and believed that a lack of heat in women led to all sorts of defects in comparison to a man, including inferior brain size and proneness to despondency and to lying. Basing his work on the heat production construed to generate semen over against the inferior blood discharge of women's menstrual discharge, Aristotle placed an architecture of biological, ethical and political differentiation on the processes of reproduction which the church fathers of both East and West found difficult to resist. Woman was a departure from the norm – the archetype being the male.[3] And so down the ages woman's place in the scientific imagination was still viewed as essentially subordinate to the male.[4] For example, for Freud, women's psychological inability to emerge from the Oedipal stage of her life meant that in a complex world the 'work of civilization has become increasingly the business of men – which compels them to carry our instinctual sublimations of which women are little capable'.[5]

The discipleship of equals

Radical equality in Christ, proclaimed in the baptismal announcement of Galations 3.28 – where there is neither Jew nor Greek, slave nor free, male nor female – tore through Jewish and Gentile communities of the first century. As Elizabeth Schüssler Fiorenza puts it, 'the baptismal declaration (of Galatians 3.28) offered a new religious vision to women and slaves, it denied all male religious prerogatives in the Christian community based on gender roles . . . conversion to the Christian movement for men meant relinquishing their religious prerogatives – which included the abolition of social privileges as well'.[6] But the radical equality was modified in the first century itself. The equality quickly became one that was interpreted spiritually, not to be lived here on earth. So what has changed to make the landscape more clement to an understanding of the discipleship of equals and its direct implications as to the role of women within the Church? What has happened to provoke a regular male church attender in his 40s to protest on a Palm Sunday morning in 2004 that 'excluding women to become bishops is a clear injustice which the Church should not be seen to condone'?

What has happened is that there has been a substantial shift in our scientific understanding of what it means to be human, and this shift informs the juridical, philosophical and political goals of our society. Where science has threatened humanity we have acted to reassert, in sometimes new forms, the significance of human being, regardless of and in defiance of any hierarchies. Indeed, it is significant that Henri Dunant's original Geneva Convention of 1864 was prompted by the inhumane technologies on display at the battle of Solferino. Recent decades, particularly following the Nazi holocaust, have produced a sequence of conventions: the fourth Geneva Convention, the Human Rights Convention, the Convention on the Eradication of Discrimination Against Women and the Beijing Platform.

Any call to see women made bishops in the Church of England is made in this new cultural world, which seeks to hold diversity and equality together. It can be seen as a theological and ecclesial reawakening to the scriptural mandates in Galatians 3.28 and Genesis 1.26. Hooker's three-dimensional process handles the vicissitudes and variety of human history through the interplay of reason, the divine law of the scriptures and human law. This method provides Anglicans with a means of managing with integrity a theological and constitutional *volte-face* in its own internal organization.

The mission of the Church

Church membership is still shrinking. Women make up a majority of church members and lead in children's ministry. The impact of falling female membership will be felt in the impact of reduced children's affiliation to the Church. In the Scottish Church Census of 2002 two-thirds of people leaving the churches in Scotland between 1994 and 2002 were female, and half of those were aged 20 to 45. It is not surprising that this is the case. Let the Church of England take note! If our Church continues to stand against the cultural tide of equality of opportunity we should hardly be surprised that women and indeed men find the established Church an organization whose internal mission statement and employment practices lack credibility. The following comment carries a sense that the Church of England is in serious decline and that the gendered hierarchalism of the organization is aggravating the damage which the Church is currently experiencing:

> If women are not accepted as bishops, this will hasten the certain death of the Church of England.
>
> Female 40–50, regular church attender

A male participant of our postcard made a range of points:

> I think the Church of England should have women bishops now because
>
> 1 It makes no sense to have women priests and exclude women bishops.
> 2 Excluding women bishops is a clear injustice which the Church should not be seen to condone.
> 3 Women bishops would bring new skills to church leadership which are desperately needed.
> 4 It would reflect, in a more balanced way, the motherhood of God.
>
> Male 30–40, regular church attender

To place women alongside men in episcopal authority is a missiological issue, which can be seen to be grounded in theological precepts of baptism and the demands of our contemporary society to hear the Church speaking in an organizational language it can understand.

The successful missionary impact of the Church in Africa and in Asia brought the language and form of the Church into an engagement with the accepted modes of the surrounding culture. It had to be aligned sufficiently so that the voice of the Church could be heard, but not so as to undermine the essential lineaments of the gospel.[7] The tragedy at present is that the Anglican Church in England and some other parts of the world is unable to make her full social contribution because she is perceived as institutionally sexist and not in harmony with the key goals of the wider national and international communities. This strikes at the heart of the effective mission of the Church.

Archbishop Rowan Williams made the connection between baptism and the ordination of women to the priesthood public in his Epilogue to the WATCH decade commemorative publication *Voices of this Calling*. He states that:

> If women cannot be ordained then baptised women relate differently to Jesus from baptised men – not a doctrine easily reconciled with the New Testament . . . What we should be looking for and praying for is the revived commitment to what the identity in Christ of the baptised is all about; only then can the ordained effectively do their distinctive job of telling and showing the Church what it is.[8]

Williams goes on to cite William Stringfellow and his central quality of discipleship: 'advocacy' which speaks to God and to God's world 'on behalf of those who are isolated from God by suffering or humiliation, self hatred and sin'.[9] The demonstration of solidarity in baptism streams through every aspect of the Church's life. Episcopacy is one aspect that requires the renewing waters of baptism to flow through it and renew its life and potability for a thirsty world.

Postcards away from home

The 1993 World Conference on Human Rights (WCHR) in Vienna challenged humanity to eliminate all forms of discrimination against women and to develop a radical critique of contemporary civilization in its use of violence and intimidation as a leading motif in the organization of international and interpersonal relationships. The world is all too full of cruel, horrifying, disturbing examples of the impact of women's subordination and exploitation. Sometimes in the most brutal forms – the systematic rapes by militias in Congo; sometimes in the manipulations of the world economic structures which men control. The recognition of the priority of women's empowerment, representation and legal protection at every level of society is in every key United Nations document since the 1980s. In the face of this cultural tidal wave promoting women's empowerment, the Church of England has responded with the priesting of women – but has built into its protocols legislation which prevents ordained women's participation in many areas of the Church's life.

Most importantly, this includes the Act of Synod of 1993 with its provision for churches to 'opt out' of accepting women priests, and its generous provisions for clergy who conscientiously could not stay in a women-ordaining church. If there are still church councils and members who simply cannot agree with the presence of women priests and women bishops there are other denominations which operate different theological methods than those articulated by Hooker, which will offer them a location for their divine worship in a sanitized environment. When a leading church paper can report as follows, we are back to blaming Eve:

> **Final cost of women priests revealed**
> . . . the cost of conscience over women's ordination for a cash-strapped Church of England will run up to £26 million.[10]

The cost to the Church was not caused by the long overdue ordination of women, but by inappropriate legislation through Synod which enabled compensation to be paid out to those who would no longer work in a church alongside women as colleagues, as brothers and sisters together in the priestly commission of Christ (and which also enabled priests who left and took the conscience money, subsequently to return to the Church of England without refunding any of that money). This culture of compensation for men has not yet run its course. The work of the group studying women in the episcopate headed by the Bishop of Rochester is due to report soon. There are rumours of up to 300 male clergy leaving who cannot accept women bishops – and the consequent compensation cost is causing no little anxiety in Church House.

At no stage in these discussions, since the days of Cranmer, has the exclusion of women from the priesthood in the Church of England been an issue of compensation or restitution. Many women have wrestled with the sense of a vocation to the priesthood. Nor has there been any proper analysis of the impoverishment of the new wave of ordained mothers caring for children or elderly parents, or wives of ordained men. They have, under some pressure, taken non-stipendiary appointments to fulfil their vocations, since suitably flexible stipendiary appointments have not been made available. They have thereby lost hundreds of thousands of pounds in income and pensions earnings because of an institution structured around a male priesthood, traditional male work culture and male episcopal leadership.

Not just a private affair

Research by the Change Partnership, a leading City mentoring consultancy, *The Changing Culture of Leadership: Women Leaders' Voices*, indicated that not only has the Church of England a serious issue with exclusion, but so have businesses in the FTSE 100.[11] Of 1,178 directors in 1999, only 69 of those appointments were held by women – and only eight women were executive directors. Across all of Britain's publicly listed companies, only 3.32 per cent of non-executive directors and 2.67 per cent of executive directors were women. 'The upper echelons of organizational life', the report writers concluded, 'is mono-dimensional, [with its consequent] detrimental impact upon the ability to formulate rounded strategies to meet the needs of its customer base. Recruiting and retaining high-performing executive women has an impact, for the better, upon the performance of the organization.' The report goes on to describe the actual leadership style and expressed values of the top women who were executive directors of medium to multi-million-pound companies as those of:

- open styles of leadership with their personal values transparent to the organization;
- encouragement of creativity as a vital part of leadership;
- visionary and future orientated;

- setting high standards for the quality of care across their organizations and the appropriate development of their teams;
- a lifelong commitment to excellence;
- working towards value-driven responsible networking structures rather than status-laden hierarchical structures;
- being aware that their presence in itself signalled a paradigm shift in cultures – signalling a new role model for leadership and the organizations which they figured as chief executives or directors in the post-2000 world;
- desiring to be seen as women in their own right, and not as substitute men.

The report is a welcome breath of graciousness in its insistence on the requirements of diversity in the organizations of 2000 and beyond. The world beyond the west door of our churches is changing rapidly. The Church desperately needs, and the communities outside our doors require, the skills of women in all their diversity.

Wish you were here

The time has come for the Church of England to respond to the theological call for equal discipleship and leadership. Legislation for equality of opportunity for women in work, home, school and recreation is enshrined in law. There is an urgent need for the situation of gender inequality in our society to be addressed by the Church. The Church with its gospel of the discipleship of equals should have been leading the way, rather than finding itself left behind.

The church is called to be a beacon, a lamp placed upon a lampstand showing its truth and living its mission. Whether we think that women bring particular gifts to the world, as some of the postcards from the pews suggest – 'compassion and nurturance', 'practical care and lack of concern for status', 'the emotional language of motherhood and the feminine attributes of loving attention', 'long-term commitment and pastoral insight' – or whether we hold simply that since women alongside men are created in the image of God and make up the reality of human being, this needs to be reflected in the episcopacy. The time has now come to put away the shibboleth of women's irrationality, Eve's sin, men's God-given right to dominate and guard the Church against all forms of female error and uncleanness. The appropriate Anglican, mature, contextualized theological response is to recognize that bishops, priests, deacons and congregations are all called, male and female, child and crone, black and white, whatever our physical abilities, into rank equality in the death and resurrection of Christ through the waters of baptism. The Church of England should not delay in responding to this clear call of grace because of fear of political and economic machinations of those who would resist this paradigm shift in our understanding. The call from pew and pavement is clear – 'We wish you were here' – bring on women bishops.

Notes

1 The Sex Discrimination Act 1975 was amended in 2001 with a significant shift in the burden of proof in cases involving alleged sexual discrimination, intimidation and harassment from supplicant (employee) to the defence (employer).
2 Stephen Sykes, 'Richard Hooker and the Ordination of Women to the Priesthood', in *Unashamed Anglicanism* (London: Darton, Longman and Todd, 1995).
3 Aristotle, *Generation of Animals*, 775a14–21. Cf. Nancy Tuana, *The Less Noble Sex: Scientific, Religious, and Philosophical Conceptions of Woman's Nature* (Bloomington, Ind.: Indiana University Press, 1993), pp. 20–1.
4 See e.g. Immanuel Kant, *Anthropology from a Pragmatic Point of View*, trans. Mary J. Gregor (The Hague: Martinus Nijhoff, 1974), p. 75. Charles Darwin, *The Descent of Man, and Selection in Relation to Sex* (London: James Murray, 1901), p. 778.
5 Sigmund Freud, 'Civilisation and its Discontents', in *The Freud Reader*, ed. Peter Gay (London: Vintage, 1995), p. 745.
6 Elizabeth Schüssler Fiorenza, *In Memory of Her* (London: SCM Press, 1983), p. 218.
7 Anthony F. Walls, 'The Missionary Movement in Christian History', in *Studies in the Transmission of Faith* (Edinburgh: T&T Clark, 1996).
8 Rowan Williams, 'Epilogue', in Christina Rees (ed.), *Voices of This Calling* (Norwich: Canterbury Press, 2002), pp. 213–14.
9 Ibid.
10 *Church of England Newspaper*, No. 5704 (19 February 2004, available at <http://www.churchnewspaper.com/?go=news&read=on&number_key=5704&title=Final%20cost%20of%20women%20priests%20revealed>) (accessed 18 July 2004).
11 Elizabeth Coffey, *The Changing Culture of Leadership: Women Leaders' Voices* (London: Change Partnership Ltd, 1999).
12 Ibid., p. 8.

Bibliography

Coffey, Elizabeth, *The Changing Culture of Leadership: Women Leaders' Voices* (London: Change Partnership Ltd, 1999).
Darwin, Charles, *The Descent of Man, and Selection in Relation to Sex* (London: John Murray, 1901).
Fiorenza, Elizabeth Schüssler, *In Memory of Her* (London: SCM Press, 1983).
Freud, Sigmund, 'Civilisation and its Discontents', in *The Freud Reader*, ed. Peter Gay (London: Vintage, 1995).
Kant, Immanuel, *Anthropology from a Pragmatic Point of View*, trans. Mary J. Gregor (The Hague: Martinus Nijhoff, 1974).
Rees, Christina (ed.), *Voices of This Calling* (Norwich: Canterbury Press, 2002).
Sykes, Stephen, 'Richard Hooker and the Ordination of Women to the Priesthood', in *Unashamed Anglicanism* (London: Darton, Longman and Todd, 1995).
Tuana, Nancy, *The Less Noble Sex: Scientific, Religious, and Philosophical Conceptions of Woman's Nature* (Bloomington, Ind.: Indiana University Press, 1993).
Walls, Anthony F., *The Missionary Movement in Christian History: Studies in the Transmission of Faith* (Edinburgh: T&T Clark, 1996).
Williams, Rowan, 'Epilogue', in Rees (ed.), *Voices of This Calling*.

21 Reflections from the Anglican Church of Australia

Peter Carnley

AUSTRALIAN ANGLICANS learned a good deal from the strained and difficult journey that led to the ordination of women to the priesthood in 1992. Prior to that time there had been much legal confusion as to whether a canon of the Australian General Synod was even necessary; some legal opinion held that it was already within the power of at least some of the Australian diocesan synods to proceed in a piecemeal way. One of the curiosities of the Australian Church is the variety of ways in which dioceses were constituted in the colonial era, some by consensual compact and others by Act of Parliament. The legal quandary about the extent of resulting constitutional powers was only resolved when diocesan legislation was tested in the civil courts. These at the end of the day refused to uphold injunctions against the first ordinations. This is not a train of events to be repeated as the Church begins to address the question of the admission of women to the episcopate.

At its 1998 sitting in Adelaide, the General Synod therefore set up a Working Group on Women in the Episcopate. The aim was to chart a way forward which would avoid the difficulties that had been encountered during the saga leading to the ordination of women as priests. The Report of this Working Group came before the next General Synod which met in Brisbane in July 2001.

The Working Group was very representative of the spectrum of opinion in the Church on the subject. It included ardent opponents as well as passionate proponents of the admission of women to the episcopate. Its work involved a huge amount of consultation in the Church at large in order to find a way forward. Eventually the members of the Working Party provided a paradigm for working consensually to resolve the conflict of ideas. Their co-operative work together on this process was universally applauded.

The result of their work was to produce, as the preferred option, General Synod draft legislation in the form of a clarification canon, which would have made it clear that those dioceses which wished to elect a woman bishop certainly had power to do so, while not requiring those of a contrary mind to vote positively on such a measure at General Synod level. The proposed legislation was designed to end any possibility of continuing legal argument, which might end up in the civil courts, as to the question of whether a General Synod canon was necessary or whether a diocesan canon alone would be sufficient. Also, if passed, it would have ensured that all dioceses, and not just a sub-set with congenial constitutional provisions, would have been given a green light to pass diocesan legislation to allow for the appointment and consecration of a woman bishop should they wish to do so. At the same time, the desire was to develop creative ways of providing pastoral care for those unable to accept the ministry of a woman diocesan bishop in a particular diocese.

When the matter came before the General Synod in 2001, however, it soon became clear that protocols for providing pastoral care to those unable to accept the ministry of a woman bishop were a sticking point. The measure to approve the admission of women to the episcopate was approved in principle by the General Synod by 135 votes to 95. But the Synod was clearly divided over the protocols which would have given metropolitans the responsibility of providing alternative pastoral care within the diocese of a woman bishop should a particular parish seek to avail itself of that alternative. For one thing, many were concerned that the woman bishop's authority would be compromised and the integrity of the diocese within which she ministered would be fractured at least in some degree. Others were clearly unimpressed by the idea that metropolitans would be given a power to interfere directly in a diocese other than their own.

The utter impossibility of redrafting the protocols on the floor of the Brisbane Synod resulted in a decision to refer the matter back to the Standing Committee for further work to be done before bringing the matter back to the next General Synod. A Working Group was therefore established to bring draft proposals to the next General Synod, which will meet in Fremantle in October 2004.

There are a number of things to be said about the present situation in the Anglican Church of Australia on this issue. First, insofar as no concrete action was taken with regard to the proposed clarification canon which came before the General Synod at Brisbane in 2001, the Church is in a sense between a rock and a hard place. This Bill for a Canon sought to find a way of dealing with this matter from within the Church so as to head off any possibility of future recourse to civil courts. There are still those who are of the view that a General Synod canon is not really necessary at all. It seems likely that if dioceses were to enact local legislation today and that legislation were also to be challenged in civil courts, the outcome would be the same as in the case of the ordination of women to ministerial priesthood. In other words, it is unlikely that civil courts would act to prevent a diocese from proceeding to appoint and consecrate a woman bishop. The failure of General Synod to act in 2001 has thus left a gaping legal void. This was in fact pointed out from the floor of the General Synod in Brisbane by Mr Justice David Bleby, a Judge of the Supreme Court of South Australia. There are clearly those who are of the view that General Synod legislation is not really necessary anyway. By not acting in 2001 the prospect of independent diocesan action remains theoretically possible.

It is also surely unfortunate and undesirable for the Church to find itself facing a future situation in which some dioceses, differently constituted from others in the colonial period, might today be legally able to proceed, should they wish to do so, while others almost certainly do not have the same constitutional powers. There is an added complication, given that the Australian Church's highest legal body, the Appellate Tribunal, has already ruled that women ordained to the diaconate, priesthood or episcopate overseas in a Church in communion with this Church, may be invited to minister in this Church. Theoretically an Australian Diocese could opt to translate a woman bishop from overseas!

But even worse, the General Synod's failure to act in 2001 has left the Church in a situation in which there is no agreed provision for the pastoral care of those unable to accept the ministry of a woman bishop. The Church is therefore in the uncomfortable position of having to exist for the present in a legal void in which all these matters are entirely unresolved. In this situation the responsibility has fallen on the bishops to act collegially and in a way that will serve the best interests of the unity of the Church. Their best counsel to date has been to encourage patience. As Isaiah says: 'Whoever believes will not be in haste.' But protracted indecision will be equally undesirable. It will therefore be very important that this matter be resolved in 2004.

Then there is the question of the protocols, and whether or not a decision will ultimately be taken to require dioceses to make adequate provisions for ministering to those who cannot accept the ministry of a woman bishop. This might be provided, for example, by a male bishop from a neighbouring diocese being invited by a woman diocesan bishop to minister to dissenting parishes within her own diocese. This would at least be the case in a diocese which might at some time choose to elect a woman to the episcopate as diocesan, though it does not seem that there is so much of a problem in the case where a woman is appointed to be an assistant bishop. Where there are two bishops in a diocese, one male and one female, it is pastorally uncomplicated to ensure that a male bishop makes visitations to parishes preferring maleness.

The originally proposed protocols would have required a diocese to put in place provisions of this kind for the pastoral care of dissenting minorities before the diocese would be permitted to proceed to the election of a woman bishop. It is also clear that there have been some very negative reactions to the very idea of these previously proposed protocols for providing pastoral care by a form of alternative or extended episcopal oversight for those in a particular diocese unable to accept the pastoral ministry of a woman diocesan bishop. It can be acknowledged that there is some anomaly in this kind of proposal insofar as a woman bishop would be subject to restraints to which male bishops are not subject. There are certainly those in the Church who are uncomfortable with the protocols on these grounds. Nevertheless, the Church inevitably faces a new and pastorally demanding set of circumstances. In this set of circumstances it may have to accept a degree of anomaly, at least as a temporary measure in a period of reception while the Church as a whole comes to a common mind. A compromise in the form of an outcome that may be thought by some to be less than absolutely satisfactory may be unavoidable. But the reality is that there may be no way ahead right now in relation to resolving the question of women in the episcopate other than with alternative or extended episcopal oversight of some kind. It may be a matter of having women bishops who minister under the restraint of some kind of protocol, or of not having women bishops at all.

We can take the point that any requirement that might compromise the integrity of a diocesan bishop's ministry and authority by requiring some kind of extended episcopal oversight of parishes unable to accept the ministry of a woman bishop would be unusual, if not anomalous. However, in some situations anomalies have to be tolerated while new developments are processed and managed. Given that it will take time for some people to come to terms with and be able to accept the ministry of a woman bishop, some way quite simply must be found to meet their needs.

There are already many examples of arrangements which are designed to provide episcopal ministry to meet specific needs that even a male diocesan bishop may not himself be able to meet. For example, the bishops of the Anglican Church of Australia already work quite effectively with agreed protocols that govern the ministry of visiting indigenous bishops. Both the Aboriginal and the Torres Strait Islander bishops minister under agreed protocols to indigenous communities within dioceses other than their home diocese of North Queensland.

The last Lambeth Conference may provide us with a paradigm for our handling of this. In relation to ecumenical dialogue, the Lambeth Conference of 1998 in the report of *Section IV: 'Called to be One'*, Chapter 4 on 'Consistency and Coherence', began to speak of the need to live with anomalies of some kind in periods of transition. What was in mind was the possible need to live with an anomaly in relation to the practical reception of ecumenical agreements. For example, the Church of South India lived with an anomalous situation in which, for an interim period of 30 years, it was accepted that, while all new ordinations were to be episcopal from 1948 onwards, there would be some ordained clergy who had come from non-episcopal traditions and who would continue to minister in that Church without episcopal ordination. The same Lambeth Report of 1998 notes that similar anomalous situations are countenanced by both the Porvoo Declaration and the Concordat for intercommunion between the Lutheran Church and the Episcopal Church in the United States of America. In the Roman Catholic Church, following Vatican II, and the switch to vernacular liturgies, some congregations have been permitted to continue to use the Tridentine Latin Mass. Overlapping Latin Rite and Eastern Rite administrative structures and parallel liturgical traditions within a single geographical diocese are also not unknown in the Roman Catholic Communion. A principle of economy dictates that uncompromising purist positions sometimes have to be accommodated to what will be of most pastoral benefit to people, particularly as they process and come to terms with new developments in relation to matters of church discipline.

This suggests that those who support the possibility of the consecration of a woman bishop, particularly a diocesan bishop in a diocese where there are no assistant bishops who are male, may have to consider living with a form of extended episcopal oversight, even if this, to a purist way of thinking about a bishop's jurisdiction, may be perceived to contain an element of anomaly. Such anomalous situations should, of course, be kept to a bare minimum to serve practical pastoral necessity. But in a diocese where there is a difference of opinion, careful attention, as a matter of pastoral principle, should be paid to the needs of minorities. The Church should do all in its power to ensure that those in this situation will be appropriately ministered to in the most satisfactory way that can command agreement. In the interests of responding to the overarching need to provide adequate and acceptable pastoral care, a jurisdictional anomaly may therefore have to be countenanced.

Whether the Church at large is currently ready for the ministry of a woman bishop, and whether the protocols need to be enshrined in a schedule to legislation, or simply in conventionally agreed-upon guidelines of the House of Bishops, are things which will have to be addressed at General Synod in October 2004. But it seems that some form of arrangement by protocol may certainly be needed if a provision to allow for the possible consecration of women to the episcopate is to succeed at all.

22 The Road to Women Bishops: The Scottish Experience

Ruth B. Edwards

ON 12 JUNE 2003, the General Synod of the Scottish Episcopal Church, meeting in Edinburgh, voted by more than two-thirds majorities in each of its three 'Houses' in favour of an amendment to Canon 57 to read, 'Words in both the Canons and Ordinals importing the masculine gender shall include the equivalent words importing the feminine gender.' This seemingly minor clarification will enable a woman to be canonically elected as a bishop, should a diocese so choose, when a vacancy occurs.

This decision was the culmination of a long process by which our Church has recognized that God can call women to every form of ministry within the threefold order. After various unsuccessful attempts to open the ordained ministry to women, the first major step came in 1986 when our General Synod confirmed by the requisite two-thirds majorities, a canonical change, given its first reading the previous year, permitting women to become deacons. Ordinations followed the same year, including those of many women who previously felt called to ministry many years previously and had hitherto served as deaconesses, lay readers, or as lay pastoral assistants.

The presence of women unambiguously in 'Holy Orders' was a decisive step in the path that has led to their eligibility for the episcopate. It gave ordinary church members the opportunity to experience women's ministry in new ways. Women were preaching, conducting services, ministering pastorally, sometimes even running congregations. There was a growing conviction that to bar them from presiding at the Eucharist was illogical and unjust. By 1993 it was felt that the time had come to test whether our Church was ready to open the presbyterate to women. With the support of the then Primus, Richard Holloway, a first reading of a motion effecting this canonical change was passed in all three 'Houses' of the General Synod.

At this time there was concern about how the integrity of those who could not in conscience accept the change might be protected if a second reading confirmed it. There was little support for the idea that financial compensation might be paid to priests who felt they had, in conscience, to leave the Episcopal Church (in fact, very few left). Nor did the bishops wish to pursue the appointment of 'Episcopal Visitors' ('Flying Bishops') of the type approved by the Church of England in its 1993 Act of Synod. Instead they committed themselves to a pastoral approach. They also agreed that, if the canonical legislation was approved, a period of six months should elapse before implementation to allow time for reflection and discernment on both sides.

After consultation in the dioceses, the legislation in favour of women priests was passed at its second reading in June 1994. At the request of the Chair, the decision was received in silence. Those in favour were reluctant to express their own happiness, because they knew that the decision would cause pain to others. A resolution was passed affirming that in making this decision the Synod 'desires and intends no break with the tradition of the One Holy Catholic and Apostolic Church . . .'; those who cannot in conscience agree with the decision would 'continue for all time to come to have a valued and respected place within the Scottish Episcopal Church'. It also acknowledged with deep sadness that the Synod had felt called to act without a consensus in 'all branches of the One Holy Catholic and Apostolic Church' and expressed penitence for any further divisions caused by that day's action. It recognized the fallibility of all the Church's councils and prayed for the Holy Spirit's guidance that we may all 'grow together in faith into the one Body of Christ'.

The passing of this resolution, with the overwhelming support of the Synod, was a sign of the solidarity between those opposing and those favouring women's ordination and our Synod's determination not to let its decision divide the Church. The first women were ordained priests in December 1994, in five of the seven dioceses where there were women prepared and waiting, to the joy of those concerned.

Logically the opening of the episcopate to women belongs with that of the presbyterate. It had not been proposed earlier because it was felt that the Church was not yet ready for it. In the year 2000, following an initiative from the Diocese of St Andrews, a working party was appointed to prepare a Green Paper setting out the issues and indicating what canonical changes would be necessary should it be decided to open the episcopate to women. The Green Paper was received by the 2001 General Synod and demitted to the dioceses for consideration. While some felt (particularly in my own Diocese of Aberdeen and Orkney) that more time was needed for discussion, it was clear that diocesan opinion was strongly in favour of canonical legislation being brought forward. The brief amendment to Canon 57 detailed at the start of this chapter was accepted at both its first (2002) and second reading (2003). The debate was calm and courteous, with time being given to everyone who wished to speak. The decision in favour, by 124 votes to 24 (with a two-thirds majority in each 'House' voting separately) was received with dignified silence.

Again, no formal legislation was prepared for those who could not in conscience accept the development. Instead the bishops issued a 'Statement of Intent', acknowledging that differences of opinion existed and seeking to provide a context in which pastoral issues could be addressed, rather than trying to provide for every eventuality. This Statement recognized unreservedly that a woman called to the office of Diocesan Bishop would hold jurisdiction and authority within her diocese. It was envisaged that, if problems arose over pastoral and sacramental care, members of the College of Bishops might make themselves available to each other and provide mutual assistance. Candidates for election as Scottish bishops would be made aware of this *Statement of Intent* and have the opportunity to respond to it. It was suggested that the College of Bishops might, after a time, review the *Statement* in the light of experience. The June 2004 Synod also accepted without dissent a motion virtually identical with that passed in 1994, when the priesthood was opened to women, affirming that no break was intended with the One Holy Catholic and Apostolic Church.

The change in canon law accepted in June 2003 means that members of any diocese are free to nominate a woman as candidate for the episcopate. There is currently (summer 2004) a vacancy in the Diocese of St Andrews and another due soon in the Diocese of Brechin. (No woman candidate was shortlisted for Argyll and the Isles earlier in 2004.) Whether or not a woman is nominated or elected, the important point is that this is canonically possible. The bar against women exercising their gifts in episcopal ministry has been lifted in this small part of the Christian Church.

Are there any lessons for the Church of England from the Scottish experience? The most obvious one is that the threefold order of ministry may peacefully be opened to women without formal legislation to cater for those who cannot in conscience accept the change. This is only possible through good will among all concerned, and much patience and forbearance on the part of both the ordained women (and their supporters) and those who believe that a wrong decision has been made.

At the same time one has to recognize that the Scottish Episcopal Church is extremely small compared with the Church of England: it is unrestricted by parliamentary authority and bishops are elected by their dioceses. There is no possibility of a woman bishop being imposed on any diocese against its wishes. When a woman bishop is elected in Scotland it will cause problems for some, though much joy on the part of others. I have confidence that our Church will cope with this situation, as it has with women priests. There are still inequalities in our ministry, but those in England who long for the full recognition of women's calling in the Church should be encouraged by the Scottish experience.

23 Afterword

Marilyn McCord Adams

THIS BOOK CONTAINS contributions full of nuance and detail, on which I – as a professor of historical and philosophical theology – normally place a high value. This time, however, the issue strikes me as extraordinarily simple. Carolyn Tanner Irish names it; many other pieces allude and testify to it. In my judgement, it is the heart of the matter, and bears repeating in starkest form.

Misogyny is a sin. If not the original sin, it is ancient and honoured. Whether or not psychoanalytically rooted in infantile dependence on and vulnerability to mothers, misogyny is persistent and pervasive in human societies in which it replicates and reinvents itself in manifold forms. The cultures of the Bible participate in it. The Church has always participated in it. Reform and liberation movements notwithstanding, contemporary cultures are rife with it. From Afghanis who were denied education, to New York and London executives bumping up against the glass ceiling, women have countless and wide-ranging stories to show that it is so.

In asserting the prevalence of misogyny, I am not accusing all men of self-consciously hating some or all of the women in their lives. Some do; but equally, some women hate them back! Usually, misogyny (like racism) is a sub-conscious conviction and an unspoken cultural presupposition. As such, it is all the more insidious because of its power to shape us without our noticing how. Misogyny rests on the premise that men cannot be as big as they need to be unless women are made to seem smaller than they really are. Misogyny compensates by fostering an inflated sense of male entitlement, which, at its worst, spawns social systems that put women entirely at men's disposal, available to be used and abused at male whim. Women as well as men are co-opted by it, whenever they shrink themselves in order to puff up male egos. We don't have to think about it or consciously believe in misogyny in order to be stained by it. We are all complicit in it to the extent that we play a role and have a stake in social systems that are riddled with it. From the gospel point of view, misogyny enforces a lie that patronizes both men and women, and prevents either from rising up to their full stature in Christ. As heralds of the Reign of God, the Church and its leaders are called to name it, repent of it, and work against it by cutting off opportunities for its institutional expression.

Human societies embody many falsehoods. Some are superficial, but others run deep. Misogyny (like racism) is a deep-structure deception, and so – like the snake in the garden – lies ready to twist and trick our reasoning and practice even when we try to base ourselves on solid ground. Put otherwise, our ways of seeing and valuing the world, our senses of what is meet and right or ghastly and revolting, are deeply shaped by our families of origin, by the wider societies and cultures in which we participate. In our appeals to scripture and tradition, we have a duty to second-guess ourselves, and to examine whether we are not using the systemic sins of the fathers to justify our continued participation in the same. Recent historians of the American Civil War have targeted religious defences of slavery from scripture, and observed how the abolitionists got the worse of the exegetical argument. Happily, God is willing to work with sinners whose social arrangements are riddled with systemic evils (after Eden, there weren't any others of the human kind). Biblical narratives show that, in trafficking with humans, God is slow to anger and does not problematize everything at once. What this means, however, is that we cannot take the human authors' claims to divine authorization (e.g. of the genocides of Joshua and Judges and the holiness code of Leviticus) at face value. The gospel proclaims the Reign of God, that utopia that human beings have always longed for in which the flourishing of each is integrated into the common good under God. The Reign of God stands in judgement over all human social arrangements, including those in which the Bible characters lived!

In our current controversy over women in the episcopate, some stress that any change in gender eligibility for offices of oversight would have to be 'received' by the Church in which it was proposed that women officers might lead. Several authors in this book point out how diocesan election (as opposed to top-down appointment) of bishops serves to test and prepare the way for the acceptance of the new leader, and note how women bishops have in fact been as well accepted in their dioceses as many of their male colleagues have. Some opponents of ordaining women to the episcopate seem to have something stronger in mind, however. They seem to imply that the Church should not move to make women bishops legal unless and until some sort of Quaker consensus in favour of it is reached, whether within the Church of England, within the Anglican Communion at large, or across all Christian bodies (especially including the Roman Catholic and the Eastern Orthodox Churches). They seem to give

Christian unity a priority, and to assign great presumptive weight against doing anything that might (further?) shatter the unity of the Church.

Yet, misogyny is a sin. It is part of the deep structure of the human societies in which the Church participates. Continued hesitations and reservations about making women bishops legal, epicyclical accommodations of those who cannot accept women in office, rumoured wishes to turn back the clock to a time when women couldn't legally be ordained at all – all send the message that the Church is still vice-gripped by misogyny, that it still respects rather than contradicts the underlying feeling that men cannot be as big as they need to be unless women are made to seem smaller than they really are! In European and North American societies, where gender norms are shifting, this contributes to making the Church look ridiculous precisely because the Church was supposed to be a vanguard of the Reign of God.

Deep-structure changes shake the foundations, and certainly bring an end to many cherished forms of life. They bring up to consciousness implicit sinful presuppositions, to be contradicted and corrected. It is unrealistic to think that such challenges would meet with Quaker consensus in advance. On the contrary, the Bible predicts vehement, even violent resistance that crucifies the messenger.

One instructive non-biblical example is the mid-twentieth-century civil rights movement in the United States. Martin Luther King and other African-American leaders named racism as a sin before God and a betrayal of the American dream. They organized non-violent protests against the segregation of public facilities. Demonstrators were attacked with police dogs, arrested and jailed. White civic and church leaders urged King not to make things worse by upsetting the *status quo.* Vigilantes murdered civil rights workers and bombed African-American churches. Nevertheless, the federal government imposed school desegregation, equal access to public facilities and the ballot box by force of law and sometimes by the National Guard. In this case, institutional structures were legally changed, even while many citizens were vehemently opposed. As African-Americans have moved into new roles in society, people's expectations have shifted. They are no longer surprised to have an African-American postmaster or mayor, professor or secretary of state; fewer and fewer Americans experience this as a remarkable incongruity. Racism is not dead, but some progress toward the Promised Land has been made.

Many women and men are not comfortable with female clergy. This is not surprising, because – in many and various ways – our societies have taught us that this should not be so. More remarkable is the fact that the last ten years in England (the last 30 in the United States) have seen a shift in people's expectations. People have not quite got used to an all-female cast of clergy (as can now happen), but some find themselves altogether inspired. The Church of England has already conceded that there are no theological barriers to women bishops. The time to take its next significant step against the sin of misogyny is now!

The Society for Promoting Christian Knowledge (SPCK) was founded in 1698. Its mission statement is:

To promote Christian knowledge by

- **Communicating the Christian faith in its rich diversity;**
- **Helping people to understand the Christian faith and to develop their personal faith; and**
- **Equipping Christians for mission and ministry.**

SPCK Worldwide serves the Church through Christian literature and communication projects in over 100 countries, and provides books for those training for ministry in many parts of the developing world. This worldwide service depends upon the generosity of others and all gifts are spent wholly on ministry programmes, without deductions.

SPCK Bookshops support the life of the Christian community by making available a full range of Christian literature and other resources, providing support for those training for ministry, and assisting bookstalls and book agents throughout the UK.

SPCK Publishing produces Christian books and resources, covering a wide range of inspirational, pastoral, practical and academic subjects. Authors are drawn from many different Christian traditions, and publications aim to meet the needs of a wide variety of readers in the UK and throughout the world.

The Society does not necessarily endorse the individual views contained in its publications, but hopes they stimulate readers to think about and further develop their Christian faith.

For further information about the Society, visit our website at *www.spck.org.uk,* or write to:
SPCK, 36 Causton Street,
London SW1P 4AU, United Kingdom.